Research Methodologies for Art Education

Edited by
Sharon D. La Pierre
Independent Scholar
Boulder, Colorado

and

Enid Zimmerman
Professor and Coordinator
Indiana University

1997

National Art Education Association

About NAEA

Founded in 1947, the National Art Education Association is the largest professional art education association in the world. Membership includes elementary and secondary teachers, art administrators, museum educators, arts council staff, and university professors from throughout the United States and 66 foreign countries. NAEA's mission is to advance art education through professional development, service, advancement of knowledge and leadership.

©1997 The National Art Education Association, 1916 Associaiton Drive, Reston, Virginia 20191-1590.

ISBN 0-937652-97-0

TABLE OF CONTENTS

Foreword	Zimmerman
	v
Introduction	La Pierre
	xi
The Second Search: Metaphor, Dimensions of Meaning, and Research Topics in Art Education	Wilson
	1
Qualitative Forms of Research Methods	Stokrocki
	33
Historical Research Methods in Art Education	Stankiewicz
	57
Reading and Interpreting Research Journal Articles	Koroscik and Kowalchuk
	75
Standardized Testing and Authentic Assessment Research in Art Education	Sabol and Zimmerman
	137
Researching Paradigms in Art Education	Carroll
	171
Feminist Research: Themes, Issues, and Applications in Art Education	Collins and Sandell
	193
ACTION RESEARCH	
Part I: "Teachers-as-Researchers"	May
	223
Part II: Action-Oriented Study as Research	Diket
	241

FOREWORD

ENID ZIMMERMAN
NAEA Research Commission, Chair (1993-1997)
Professor and Coordinator
Indiana University

The field of art education is maturing and coming of age. There is a growing interest regionally, nationally, and internationally in developing a research agenda for visual arts education. In 1994, The National Endowment for Arts in Education Program and the U.S. Office of Education Research and Improvement published the *Arts Education Research Agenda for the Future*. In the same year, the National Art Education Association's (NAEA) Commission on Research in Art Education produced a final report, *Art Education: Creating a Visual Arts Research Agenda Toward the 21st Century* and an accompanying booklet, *Blueprint for Implementing a Visual Arts Education Research Agenda*. Concurrently, NAEA Research Commission Task Forces were formed in eight research areas to help plan future initiatives and directions for art education research. *Briefing Papers: Creating a Research Agenda Toward the 21st Century* written by Task Force Chairpersons, will be published and distributed to all NAEA members.

There is also a growing interest internationally toward setting objectives and promoting research in art education that would emphasize a variety of contexts with diverse populations. In 1994, for example, objectives were set forth for the International Society for Education Through Art's (InSEA) newly formed research board. Three years prior to this, the Australian Institute of Art Education established a national research council with a mission to promote research in the field of art education in Australia.

For more than 2½ decades, The Seminar for Research in Art Education (SRAE), a multinational affiliate of NAEA, has been a major influence in promoting research efforts in art education. In recent years, SRAE has published *A Survey of Research Interests Among Art Educators* (Burton, 1991) and two monographs,

Art Education Historical Methodology: An Insider's Guide to Doing and Using (Smith, 1995) and *New Waves of Research in Art Education* (Stokrocki, 1995).

As NAEA Research Commission Chairperson, member of the InSEA Research Board, and Consulting Editor for *New Waves* I have been privileged to collaborate with others on research issues of primary concern in the field of art education. I was pleased when Sharon LaPierre asked me to coedit this book with her. *Research Methods and Methodologies for Art Education* represents an important collaborative effort between NAEA and SRAE. The content of this book originated as a series of instructional workshops on research methodology sponsored by SRAE and conducted during the 1994 NAEA National Convention in Baltimore, Maryland. Eight workshop sessions were held at this convention and nine of the original workshop leaders have contributed chapters to this book. With the help of Karen Carroll, a faculty member at the Maryland Institute College of Art, these workshops took place over two days and were offered for college credit.

David Burton, past SRAE Secretary/Treasurer, and Peter Smith, then President of SRAE, were supporters and contributed to the success of this project. Sharon LaPierre, current President of SRAE, was the guiding light for the workshops, selecting and recruiting presenters and organizing most events. She also promoted, and saw to fruition, having the content of these workshops published as a resource for future research in art education. Authors of chapters in this book include well-established researchers; also others who have written collaboratively with those more senior in the field. Each chapter represents a description and analysis, with personal applications, of research methods and methodologies pertinent to each author's interest and participation in contemporary research in art education.

The intended audience for this book is a whole range of professionals, from classroom art teachers to university level art educators. That includes anyone interested in delving deeper into the myriad issues and problems relevant to teaching and learning in art education and in building a research base that addresses both theoretical and practical concerns. An underlying premise is that research is exciting and challenging for those who become involved in unlocking answers to questions that can help move the field of art education forward in the next century.

There is a timely interest in searching and critically examining theory and practice in art education with an aim toward accepting, revising, or rejecting accepted conclusions based on rigorous, exhaustive inquiry methods and methodologies. The form and content of such searching is as varied as the researchers who are engaged in inquiring into what we do and how we do it. This book represents a diversity of views and means of understanding the universe that comprises art education and how one goes about conducting art education research. Chapters in this book address both *methods* and *methodologies* for conducting contemporary research in art education. In chapter seven, Georgia Collins and Renee Sandell challenge readers to "distinguish between methods as techniques or specific sets of research practices... and methodology as a perspective or very broad theoretically informed framework which may or may not specify its own appropriate research methods or techniques."

A number of visually-oriented researchers in this book have diagrammed concepts and created symbols to explain how components of art education research might be integrated and understood as a comprehensive whole. In the introduction, Sharon LaPierre presents a figure that takes the form of a continuum of educational research methods and possibilities with true experimental research design models at one end and artistic research design models at the other. On the other hand, in chapter one, Brent Wilson's configuration consists of a wheel with a central circle of classifications or dimensions of meaning, a second ring showing major kinds of relationships between various dimensions of meaning and topical classifications, and five outer concentric rings that list major topical classifications to which research might be directed.

In chapter four, Judith Smith Koroscik and Elizabeth Kowalchuk use a grid to describe types of research journal articles with types of articles, descriptions, examples, and purposes or problems as rows and specific article types as columns. In part II of chapter eight, Read M. Diket uses a metaphor of archery to portray different types of research using equipment, associated with the sport of bow shooting, to explain similarities and differences between quantitative and qualitative methods as related to action-oriented research. Not wishing to be left on the art education research sidelines, I offer my own configuration of research methods for art education influenced by my studying, more than two decades ago, with philosophers of education Elizabeth Steiner and George Maccia. Mine is a logical, hierarchical model in which various types of research methods for art education are shown in their relation to larger categories of research inquiry (see Figure 1).

These models and configurations represent personal views of the world of art education research that often guide individual researcher's goals and practices. In chapter two, Mary Stokrocki reminds researchers to use tables, graphs, diagrams, or charts to depict visually their processes of thinking and writing. I imagine all

Research Methods and Methodologies for Art Education

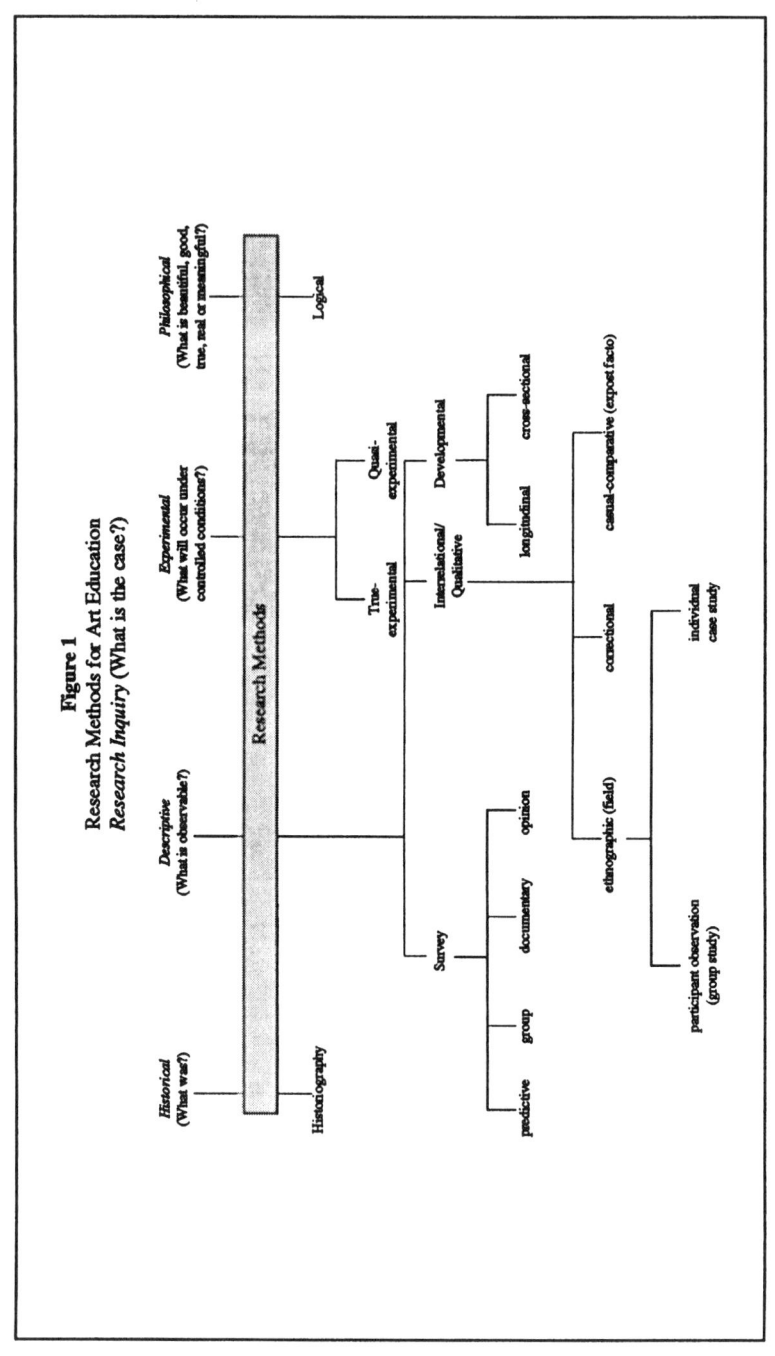

Figure 1
Research Methods for Art Education
Research Inquiry (What is the case?)

would agree with Brent Wilson, however, that "there is no satisfactory structure of primary topics or sub-topics that might be associated with art education researchers." Ways of presenting ideas about research visually open a window to universes of thinking, both theoretically and practically, about topics and concepts that challenge us as art education researchers. New technologies and their capabilities present possibilities heretofore unavailable to researchers for collecting, categorizing, analyzing, and disseminating information to colleagues around the world. We are on the threshold of a whole new era of research possibilities in art education with unlimited resources; it is up to art educators to take the opportunities that are offered to embark on new inquiry voyages into the future.

References

Art Education: Creating a visual arts research agenda toward the 21st century. (1994). Reston, VA: National Art Education Association.

Blueprint for implementing a visual arts education research agenda. (1994). Reston, VA: National Art Education Association.

Briefing papers: Creating a visual arts research agenda toward the 21st century. (1995). Reston, VA: National Art Education Association.

Burton, D. (1991). *A survey of research interests among art education researchers.* Seminar for Research in Art Education.

National Endowment for the Arts and the U.S. Department of Education. (1994). *Arts Education Research Agenda for the Future.* (Pelvin Associates Inc. Contract No. RR 910990). Washington, DC: U. S. Government Printing Office.

Smith, P. (Ed.) (1995). *Art education historical methodology: An insider's guide to doing and using.* Pasadena, CA: Seminar for Research in Art Education/ Open Door Publishers.

Stokrocki, M. (Ed.) (1995). *New waves of research in art education.* Pasadena, CA: Seminar for Research in Art Education/ Open Door Publishers.

INTRODUCTION

SHARON D. LA PIERRE

Seminar for Research in Art Education (SRAE), President (1994-1996)
Independent Scholar
Boulder, Colorado

The *American Heritage Dictionary* defines *inquiry* as a means to put a question forth, to request information, or to make a close examination of some matter in a quest for *information* or *truth* (Morris, 1971). According to Eisner (1991), "inquiry is a broader concept than either research or evaluation. [Whereas,] research and evaluation are examples of inquiry" (p. 6).

For example, if I ask directions to the nearest gas station, I am requesting and making an inquiry for general information. I am not interested in whether this particular gas station is the biggest station with the most pumps and the best service. If I want to know that kind of data, I would count the number of pumps from various stations within a certain radius to see which one has the most. Then, I might take a survey of customers to determine which of these specific gas stations has the best service according to those people polled. As seen in this example, research is specific in nature and, therefore, requires procedures to draw conclusions about the specific nature of gas stations in a certain area.

This book contains research methods that can be used specifically to study aspects of the field of art education. These methods have been proven to contribute to research knowledge within the field. A question might arise as to whether there is a difference between research procedures used in the arts and those used in the sciences, such as the behavioral, life, or physical sciences. Researchers in art education are looking, thinking, and observing from an artistic perspective and creating new parameters that reflect a knowledge base that is directly related to the arts. In a search to identify a research style in the arts, it "is not just a matter of the physical, perceptual characteristics of art; it is also the way, manner, or style in which individuals are asked to make art and respond to art" (Hamblen & Smith, 1994, p. 15). The world of the arts is known for its interpretive, passionate, and sensory characteristics. These characteristics are thought to originate from the unique expressiveness of artists that perform and exhibit them and the artistic experience itself (La Pierre, 1992). Research in the arts focuses on expressive representation and what it means to the field of art education in regard to learning, testing, behavior, and cognitive abilities (La Pierre, 1988). According to Short (1995), "Lack of prescriptive solutions in the visual arts suggests that the development of art understandings may be more demanding than the development of understandings in other fields of study" (p. 155).

To utilize educational research methods for the arts, researchers should seek methods most appropriate to their inquiries. This is always the case in choosing appropriate research methods, but what makes it more important for the arts is the focus on intuitive, spatial, and concrete elements that characterize the cognitive structures of artistic endeavors. The interrelationships of these concepts constitute domain-specific knowledge and choice of research methods that involve decisions among the following issues: (1) characteristics of individual participants (descriptive statistics) versus mean scores of a group of characteristics and subjects within groups (inferential statistics); (2) small samples versus large samples and how each affects reliability or the ability to generalize findings; (3) standardization practices to increase objectivity and consistency versus researcher involvement; (4) adapting research findings from outside the field and what effect this has on the validity of content from within the field; and (5) authentic, practical, or realistic settings versus laboratory-manipulated experimentation.

One of the main issues that sets inquiry conducted in the arts apart from other domains, such as biological or medical research, is the fact that art content deals with cognitive structures such as *disciplined action* or *practice* that make learning experiences automatic and progressive. For example, disciplined action can be observed as a developing force in musical practice rooms, rehearsal halls, as well as painting, pottery, and weaving studios. It is this concentrated effort by individuals to express their personal responses by achieving a level of mastery and perfection that makes this domain unique. A self-imposed condition of both mental and physical preparation for purposes of shaping one's own course of action is specific to the arts. The creator is constantly preparing to reach for and expand to higher and higher levels of personal expression, as well as to call attention to interpretations. Degrees of excellence are stretched and striven for on a daily basis and become the foundation of learning. This kind of cognitive structuring is what Hyman (1965) calls the "prepared mind" in "creative achievement" (p. 7).

The development and understanding of such learning activities spans a lifetime from being a child to being an adult, not only in creating art but in appreciating, observing, interpreting, critiquing, philosophizing about, and recounting or recording creative acts. The expressive acts or conditions for artistic learning become more difficult to quantify as separate from the individuals or settings being studied and the strengths individuals possess in the struggle to perfect and impart personal images. To separate such cognitive structures from the researcher's field of vision makes it difficult to determine what is "real" and what is "not real" in the total picture being observed; part of this reality may have to do with open-ended results and personal perspectives. Therefore, artistic considerations have to be compatible with the researcher's understanding of the role that these kinds of conditions play in the collection and meaning of data. Eisner (1985) says it well when he makes the following comment: "To know a rose by its Latin name and yet to miss its fragrance is to miss much of the rose's meaning. Artistic approaches to research are very much interested in helping people experience the fragrance" (p. 198). Hence, the art education researcher should utilize that which is specific to the arts domain as an integral part of reporting the thoughts, behaviors, or processes embodied and experienced in the arts. A perfect example of a research method that stems from the qualities found in the arts is Elliot Eisner's *connoisseurship and criticism method* (1991). It employs the expertise of an experienced connoisseur to appreciate the qualities being observed and the illuminating appraisal of the critic to disclose what is being experienced and appreciated.

I have developed "A Continuum of Educational Research Methods and Possibilities With Terms Affecting Research Outcomes" which moves from *true-experimental research design models* to *quasi-experimental research design models* to *artistic research design models* (see Figure 1). A researcher can use various aspects of these different research models, depending on the purpose of his/her study, and slide figuratively from side to side on this continuum. Artistic research design models involve settings, conditions, and thinking habits which reflect a domain specific to the arts. On

Research Methods and Methodologies for Art Education

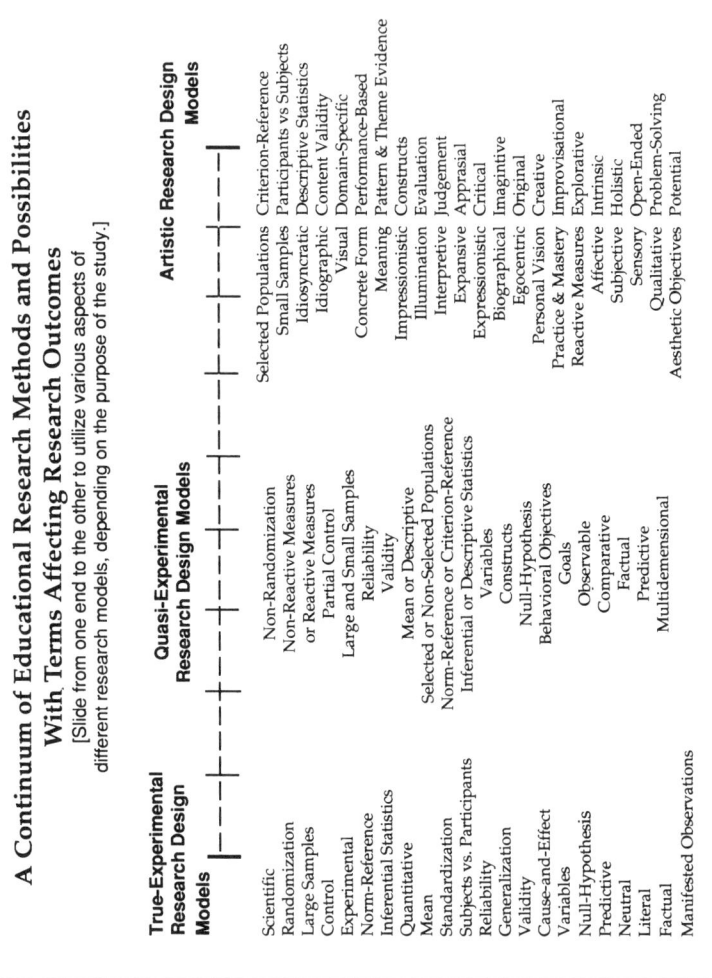

Figure 1

the other hand, true-experimental research design models may better reflect the concerns of medical or biological studies.

The process of thinking through an activity, such as creating with one's hands, the flow of bodily movements, or the compilation of knowledge structured by disciplined action, technique, and experience makes the arts unique. The transformation of "potential" behavior or the unfolding of physical and mental growth into a creative, active force is an endowment of the arts. This ability to be flexible with change or to experience the full potential of something empowers and frees the act of expression and imagination and leads to interpretation. It is, therefore, the intent of the art researcher to not only describe and observe the person sitting in the chair, but to understand how the space around that person sitting in the chair affects the nature of the surrounding space and how that space also plays an important role in understanding the person sitting in the chair.

Jeffers (1993) explains that there exists what she terms *a living relationship between research as art and art as research*. The art researcher must have an understanding of the possibilities in regard to methodology. As investigators become more aware of these possibilities, standards can be set in the field of art education for what might be most appropriate for specific inquiries. New methods should be developed and older methods adapted that enhance our knowledge of art and educational theory and practice.

References

Eisner, E. W. (1985). *The art of educational evaluation: A personal view*. Philadelphia: The Falmer Press.

Eisner, E. W. (1991). *The enlightened eye: Qualitative inquiry and the enhancement of educational practice*. New York: Macmillan.

Hamblen, K., & Smith, S. (1994). Identifying a research art style in art education. *Art and Learning, 11*(1), 14-24.

Hyman, R. (1965). Creativity and the prepared mind (Research Monograph No. 1 Sponsored by the Viktor Lowenfeld Memorial Fund). Reston, VA: National Art Education Association.

Jeffers, C. (1993). Research as art and art as research: A living relationship. *Art Education, 46*(5), 12-17.

La Pierre, S. (1988). Spatial reasoning and its measurement. In R.A. Fellenz (Ed.), *Spatial reasoning and adults* (pp. 1-31). Monographs of the Kellogg Center for Adult Learning Research, Montana State University, Bozeman, MT, 2. [ERIC Reproduction Service, No. ED298 252]

La Pierre, S. (1992). *The professional artist's thinking style: An in-depth study.* Paper. Phoenix, AZ: National Art Education Association Convention, (ERIC Reproduction Service, No. ED349 219].

Morris, W. (Ed.). (1971). *The American heritage dictionary of the English language.* Boston: American Heritage Publishing & Houghton Mifflin.

Short, G. (1995). Understanding domain knowledge for teaching: Higher-order thinking in pre-service art specialists. *Studies in Art Education, 36*(3), 154-169.

Mark Tansey, *The Innocent Eye Test*, 1981. The Metropolitan Museum of Art, New York. Promised gift of Charles Cowels, in honor of William S. Lieberman, 1988. All rights reserved, The Metropolitan Museum of Art.

The Second Search: Metaphor, Dimensions of Meaning, and Research Topics in Art Education

The Meaning and Purpose of Research in Art Education

In art education, what is the biggest, the most important, and the most difficult research problem imaginable? Since I'm only imagining, why settle for anything less? And since the issue of imagination has been raised, are there relationships between generating ideas for a work of art—say a painting like Mark Tansey's *The Innocent Eye Test* (1981, Metropolitan Museum of Art, New York)—and developing ideas for research in art education? Addressing these questions requires a journey through possible art educational research themes, topics, problems, dimensions of meaning, methodologies, and the role of metaphor in inquiry.

I like to think of research as *re-search*, to search again, to take a closer second look.[1] Research implies searching for evidence about the ways things were in the past, how they are presently, and even about how they might be in the future. Research includes the construction of theories, the mounting of philosophical arguments, and the making of critical interpretations and judgments. One of the distinguishing characteristics of educational research is that it relates what *is* with what *might* be and what *ought* to be.

---

[1] I first heard this idea expressed by Elizabeth Steiner Maccia in a course on empirical theory construction offered at The Ohio State University in 1964.

BRENT WILSON
The Pennsylvania State University

The Purposes of Educational Research

Art educational research is about disclosing insights into such things as art content, art learners, art instruction, and instructional setting. More importantly, research can point to ways art enriches individual human lives, society, and civilization. But how does research help us to connect the things we desire for art-learners and society with the means we might employ to achieve desired outcomes?

Too frequently we think, naively, that research will tell us what we art educators ought to do with the students in our classrooms. Unhappily for those who wish for clear-cut directives, research yields no easy solutions to the pedagogical problems that beset us. Nevertheless, good research can help us to think clearly about goals and purposes—to think about things our students should learn in and through art. It can also provide information about where and what students have learned and the most effective and efficient means to get them to learn.

Art education reflects conflicting sets of values that abound in pluralistic societies, in the worlds of art, and the worlds of education. We art educators have obligations to state as clearly as we can why we teach our subject and what benefits will come to our students and to society if the goals we posit are achieved. Indeed, goal making is the starting point for both teaching and research. Before I present an overview of research in art education, I feel an obligation to reveal the values that underlie my thinking about the purposes of art education.

The One Big Goal for Art Education

One could write a fascinating and credible history of art education merely by providing a chronological account of the various reasons given over the last century and a quarter to justify the teaching of art in schools. One of the most recent manifestations of art educational goals, for example, is found in *National Standards for Arts Education* (1995). These goals, stated in the form of standards, reflect much of our current thinking about the content and outcomes of art education. They also suffer from the shortcomings of numerous previous goal statements inasmuch as they fragment the outcomes of art education into discrete bits while failing to distinguish between outcomes of greater and lesser importance. Rather than resorting to a laundry list of objectives, I think that we art educators ought to hold ourselves to the higher standard of making a single coherent global statement of the purposes of art education. If educational outcomes implied by the visual art standards (and the rhetoric that introduces them) were synthesized into one statement, it might be:

The principal goal for art education is students' acquisition of special knowledge, insights, and understandings—of self, of the realities of past and present worlds, of imagined and future realities, and of the norms by which individuals govern their lives—that come from works of art.[2] The goal for art education is for students to connect the idea-filled works of art they create to the artworks of others—artworks from other times and their time, from other places and their place, from other peoples and their people—whose meaning students interpret. The goal for arts education is that students will also connect the artworks they create and interpret to significant works and ideas from other disciplines and realms of experience, and finally write the special art-pervaded knowledge, insights, and understandings they have acquired into the texts of their own lives within and beyond school.[3]

This one big goal for art education is a personal one—one that guides my art teaching, my research, and, curiously, even my art-making. I do not expect that others will necessarily accept it; rather it is presented to show the biases and values that underlie my introduction to research in art education.

The One Big Goal for Art Educational Research
My one big goal for art educational research parallels the one big goal for art education:

The principal goal for art educational research is to provide knowledge about the ways art-learners use special artistic insights to expand their conceptions of themselves, past and present worlds, imagined and future worlds, and the norms by which individuals govern their lives through writing the texts of art into the texts of their lives within and beyond school.

---

[2]This statement owes an enormous debt to Hans and Shulamith Kreitler (1972) who in their book *Psychology of the Arts* show the power of the arts to expand conceptions of the realities of the self, the common, prophetic, and normative realities (pp. 325–354).

[3]The idea of writing the text of an artwork into the text of one's life comes from Roland Barthes. Barthes (1985) tells of watching Nureyev perform, of first thinking the dancer ordinary, and then gradually realizing his genius. This prompted Barthes' second realization, that in grasping Nureyev's incomparable quality, he was reliving a scene from one of Proust's works where a narrator provides an account of coming to a similar awareness while watching Berma act. Barthes writes that he left the theatre "amazed by the genius ...of Proust: we never stop adding to the 'Search' (as Proust kept adding to his manuscripts), we never stop writing it. And no double that is what reading is: rewriting the text of the work within the text of our lives" (p. 101).

Research Methods and Methodologies for Art Education

How Does Research Change Art Education?

Perhaps the more basic question should be, *does research in art education affect the way art is taught in classrooms?* Or stated in a more positive manner: *if, through our research, we were to arrive at some tentative conclusions about the nature of things such as artistic development, effective art teaching, and the ways art education affects individuals' lives beyond schooling, what could and what should we do with this information?* These questions are not easily answered; answering them depends upon our tolerance for ambiguity as we trace patterns of cause and effect.

There is no question that in the past 120 years or so art education has taken a variety of distinct forms; there is a question, however, regarding the extent to which these changing philosophies and practices were affected by research. In the late 19th century, industrial drawing (Smith, 1872) and forms of art education based on the elements and principles of design (Dow, 1899), and the child study movement (Sully, 1896) each began to shape the forms that education would take in the new century. While the elements and principles of design and child study (later transformed into child art and creative expression) continued throughout the 20th century, industrial drawing virtually disappeared from art education. More recently we have experienced the discipline-based art education of the 1980s and 1990s (Clark, Day, & Greer, 1987). What role did research play in the establishment, growth, and refinement of these movements?

Although the initiators and proponents of these movements made claims about the benefits of their particular forms of art education to the individual and society, only one of these movements was accompanied by a substantial body of research. In fact, the large body of research that accompanied the child study movement of the 1870s and 1880s continues to grow. One of the primary reasons for the ongoing research relating to children's drawings is that psychologists, who conduct most of the studies, saw, and still see, drawings as a way to gain understanding of children's cognitive development. On the other hand, little of the research on children's artistic behaviors is directed toward evaluating art educators' assumptions about the benefits to children's "creative and mental growth" that might come through making art.

An examination of research in art education, or the lack of it,[4] shows us that the field is quite capable of evolving new forms and new practices largely without benefit of research—without a rigorous testing of assumptions, theories, practices, and outcomes. It is also obvious that research is merely one of the ways—along with such things as entrepreneurship, conventional wisdom, practical experiences, and common sense—through which ideas are presented. When the field of art

The Second Search

education begins to trade in an old set of ideas for a new set, which eventually becomes a new form of art education, those who use great care to *re-search* it have no special corner on the influence market. Rather, when new values arise in the field, they can be traced to a variety of sources such as contemporary interests, societal needs, changes within the art world, and evolving conceptions of education. Art educational researchers generally don't create the ideas that drive art education practice. They are merely members of a crowd of specialized traders; they create one form of art educational capital and trade it in the open marketplace.

The ideas of researchers do have marketplace advantage that the ideas of practitioners do not have. The researcher must publish the results of her or his *second-searches*. Before reports are published in research journals, there is often a rigorous review and editing process to assure that studies and their findings have merit, that proper research procedures were followed, and that the ideas are accompanied by sufficient evidence to allow opportunities for discounting findings, arguments, and conclusions. This process of review and evaluation, publication, and scrutiny by an informed audience gives research a special value.

At this point, we might ask, *is research really necessary?* but a better question is, *would art education be better served by a more coherent and well organized research effort?* Personally, I think the field would benefit enormously by more and better research. Research expands our conceptions of our field—of things such as art, students, teachers, schools, society, culture, and the past. If we know more about these things, if we conceive of them in more subtle ways, in more complicated ways, in simpler and more elegant ways, in ways different from the usual, and in new ways, then there is a greater likelihood that we will change our ideas about things such as art learning and art teaching. If our ideas about these things change, then there is the accompanying likelihood that we will act differently toward them. When we change our ideas, art education also changes. If new ideas are based on inquiry that yields useful insights, then art education may undergo positive change.

---

[4] I don't wish to imply that art education is bereft of research. *Studies in Art Education* and other research publications reveal a considerable amount of inquiry. Little of this inquiry is cumulative, however, where well-articulated theories of art teaching and learning are evaluated through the efforts of a community of researchers who build on each others' efforts. In the case of children's drawings, literally hundreds of psychologists have pursued both the construction and evaluation of theory.

I would like to explore the various dimensions of a comprehensive art educational research agenda. The place to begin is not with research methodology but rather with the possible content of research.

The Content of Art Educational Research: The Questions We Might Ask

Research often is informed by analogy and metaphor. To establish the content of art educational research, I would like to borrow an analogous structure from the art world.

The painter Mark Tansey is obsessed with ideas and his paintings show it. In one of his best known works, *The Innocent Eye Test*, a cow has been led into a museum gallery where six men—four business-suited curatorial and art historian types, an apparent research technician in a white lab coat with pen and clipboard at the ready, and a custodian-type who wields a mop—look on attentively as Paulus Potter's huge painting, *The Young Bull* (1647, Mauritshuis, The Hague), unframed and leaning against a wall, is unveiled before the cow. *The Innocent Eye Test* has attracted considerable critical attention. Judi Freeman sees it as a "painted metaphor for the perception of art, we are the cow, and the scientists want to know how and what we see" (1993, p 54). Arthur Danto, on the other hand, sees in it "the wit and the art-historical learning that make the painting a test for the *sophisticated* eye, while the painting *in* the painting is wryly the focus of a kind of scientific experiment for testing whether the eye is ever innocent" (1992, p. 16). Danto concludes, "that the quest for pure visual experience, so central to the modern Western conception of painting, has in truth blinded us to the intellectual power of art. In seeking, as scientists, to test for innocence, we display a far greater innocence" (p. 18).

What is the origin of this painting, which is so rich in meaning and in its allusions to the art world, mythology, modernism, critical theory, and art education? Of more interest to the topic at hand, *are there things that art educators could learn about research from* The Innocent Eye Test *and from how it came into being?*

The painting provides insights into the act of inquiry itself. Freeman (1993) claims that "Tansey's work does indeed constitute a kind of chain, a plaited chain or braid, each picture a portion of a metaphorical strand, the strands themselves relatively distinguishable as associated with at least one of three types" (p. 16). Those types include: (1) "the quest: for meaning, for comprehension, for truth. Figures in Tansey's paintings assume poses suggestive of hunting, peering, searching, surveying, scavenging" (p. 16); (2) "conflict or confrontation at a crossroads. People clash, sometimes physically, sometimes psychologically" (p. 16); and (3) images, "drawn from the art world." According to Freeman, "he considers the traditions of art history and their critical assessment suitable for investigation" (p. 16). What is instructive to the art educational researcher is the means through which Tansey arrives at his paintings. He works from a massive archive of clippings whose sources are magazines, illustrated histories of soldiers, armaments, and costumes (Freeman, 1993, p. 17) and he is a voracious reader with a collection of well-underlined books on art, aesthetics, and critical theory.

Tansey has devised an ingenious way for creating paintings in which questions, issues, and images are connected. He has constructed a wheel consisting of three concentric rings on which ambiguous statements are written. The innermost ring consists of nouns such as *apologist, cleanup crew,* and *analyst.* The middle ring contains verbs, actions, and processes such as *destabilizing, de-inventing, mastering, unleashing,* and *scrutinizing.* The outermost ring contains nouns and phrases such as *conceptual cowboy, closet formalists, innocent eye,* and *iconoclasts.* With a spin of the wheel we might read, "clean-up crew scrutinizing the innocent eye." Tansey's most elaborate wheel, made in 1990, is of polished wood with engraved letters. It has 180 entries on each ring, which makes 5,832,000 combinations possible. "By exhibiting the wheel and inviting viewers to spin it, the artist in effect authorizes them to explore the range of ideas available within the vocabulary he provides. 'The wheel also has a double function,' he explains, 'as an art object and game for inventing new metaphors and extending content'" (Freeman, 1993, p. 21).

A Diagram of the Content of Art Educational Research

In my career, I have created matrices to show the content of art education and the behaviors associated with it (Wilson, 1971; Kaupinnen & Wilson, 1981). A more recent paradigm I helped to create is found in the *Early Adolescent through Young Adulthood/Art Standards* (National Board for Professional Teaching Standards, 1994, p. 18). My matrices and paradigms—because they usually consist of one set of classifications in a column on the left side of a grid and another set of classifications in a row across the top of the grid—lack the flexibility and humor of Tansey's wheels. As I studied Tansey's wheel, I wondered if it would be possible to create a circular diagram that shows different components of art educational research and how they might be combined and related to one another in order to generate research content. This is precisely what I now wish to present, with a disclaimer and a caution. First, my wheel for art educational research will neither result in the quirky statements nor afford the playful degrees of freedom found in the random combinations of Tansey's nouns and verbs. Second, one should never assume that research topics are arrived at through random combinations of questions, relations, and topics—although the possibility is appealing. The primary purpose of my wheel is to serve as an aid for thinking comprehensively about the possible content of art educational research.

Figure 1 shows a wheel relating to art educational research. The central circle, with 20 classifications or dimensions of meaning,[5] shows the kinds of basic questions that might be posed about any art educational research topic. Around the central circle, a second ring shows major kinds of relationships[6] which might exist between the various dimensions of meaning (and their implicit questions) and topical classifications of art educational research. The five outer concentric rings list major topical classifications to which research might be directed. In these five rings, the major topics run half way around the circle so that it is possible to dial up a single topic or combinations of two or more of the major topics. I make no claim regarding the comprehensiveness of the diagram. Indeed, I assume that individuals will have different conceptions of the content of art educational research and feel the need to add new components to one or more parts of the diagram.

Dimensions of Meaning

The dimensions of meaning outlined here are much as Kreitler and Kreitler (1976, pp. 26–29) formulated them. In effect, they may be seen as a comprehensive set of questions that might be asked about any referent or topic in or beyond art education. The Kreitlers used descriptive titles to designate their dimensions of meaning, whereas I have chosen to state the dimensions of meaning in the form of questions. In a few instances I have combined two of the Kreitlers' meaning categories into a single category. Examples, which illustrate different aspects of dimensions of meaning, are drawn from the field of art education and usually are derived from topics and sub-topics of the diagram's outer rings. Following are

---

[5]These dimensions of meaning are adapted from the work of Hans and Shulamith Kreitler (1976, pp. 25–34). The Krietlers' initial formulation included 21 dimensions of meaning to which they subsequently added a 22nd, cognitive actions and causes.
[6]Like the dimensions of meaning, these relationships have been adapted from the work of Kreitler and Kreitler (1976, pp. 31–35).

The Second Search

major types of questions that might be asked with respect to art educational research. The numbers in the following sections are meant to assist interpretation of Figure 1.

Twenty Questions Relating to Dimensions of Meaning
1.1 **Of what is this topic or referent a part?** To what system, or in what context is the referent typically found? For example, art museums are part of the art world and art education is a part of both the world of art and the world of education.

Figure 1—The Possible Content of Art Educational Research

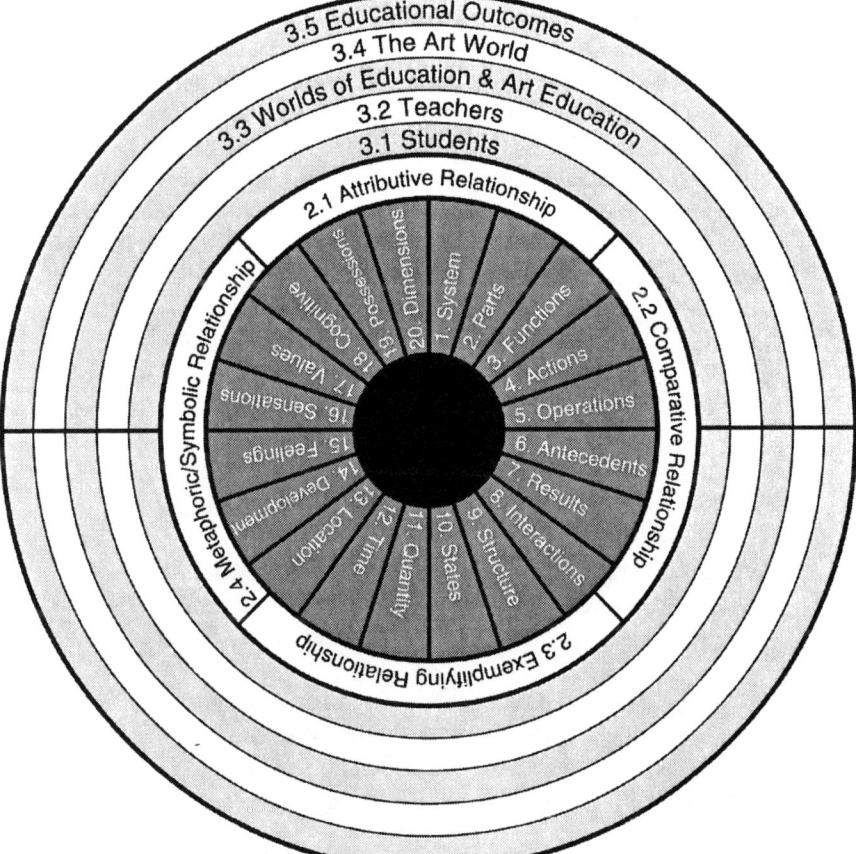

1.2 **What items and parts constitute the referent?** Of what things is the referent composed? Determining the parts of something is one of the most basic steps in research. One of my earliest studies, for example, was to devise a set of categories for classifying the statements individuals make about art (Wilson, 1966).

1.3 **What is the referent's function, purpose, and role?** One of the essential components of inquiry is to determine what a referent does. What, for example, are different roles performed by an art teacher? In this chapter I have already raised questions about the purpose of research in art education and how it influences educational practice.

1.4 **In what actions does the referent engage, what actions does it reflect, and what possible actions might it perform?** What, for example, are different acts in which art teachers engage as they perform different teaching roles? Why is it that older children are more successful than younger children at showing motions and movement in the human figures they draw?

1.5 **How does a referent operate?** In the policy analysis realm of art educational research, we could direct attention to ways in which organizations such as the National Art Education Association or the National Endowment for the Arts provide services to the field of art education.

1.6 **What are the referent's antecedents?** What caused something to occur? In most historical and experimental research, we want to know the prior conditions that affect or shape occurrences and events. We want to know, for example, whether certain initiatives that teachers undertake affect their students' behaviors. We also might raise questions regarding which art educational theories have exerted the greatest influence on how art is taught in schools.

1.7 **What are the referent's consequences?** What are the results that can be traced directly to an antecedent? In what specific ways, for example, does art education affect students' behaviors and attitudes toward art once they leave school?

1.8 **With what does the referent interact?** What are the items, things, people, objects, events, etc. affected by or associated with the referent? In a student's painting, for example, various combinations of sensory qualities, compositional elements, expressive features, subject matter, and symbols interact to reveal meaning.

1.9 **What is the referent's structure?** How do the different subparts of the referent relate to one another structurally? What is the pattern in which the parts are arrayed? In art education, for example, we might inquire into the administrative structure of a school system and the structure of its curriculum. We might look at the way a student's artwork is composed or the way different components of art classrooms are arranged.

1.10 **What are the states and the possible changes in state or status that the referent might undergo?** Just as paint goes from liquid to dry, many other referents in art and art education undergo changes. Questions might be asked about the status of art in the schools or the way its inclusion changes from time to time.

1.11 **In what quantity does the referent exist?** Determining how much or how little there is of something is one the basic features of empirical research. Anything that can be counted has the potential to provide insight into art education. For example, in what quantities do students exhibit certain creativity traits, to what extent do they possess knowledge of facts of art history, how strongly do students believe that art is a useful school subject? About practices in art education, we might ask what percentage of the nation's elementary schools have special art teachers and how much time is allocated to art instruction?

1.12 **What are the referent's temporal characteristics?** What is the time or the times in which the referent exists, has existed, or will exist? This meaning dimension relates to things such as duration, frequency, age, chronology, the factors that are of particular interest to the historians of art education. For example, we might conduct research relating to when the elements and principles of design were first introduced in American art classrooms.

1.13 **In what locations does the referent exist?** What are the usual or unusual places in which something is found? We know, for example, that art education occurs not only in schools, but also in homes, art museums, and camps. In what other locations does or might art education take place?

1.14 **How Did the Referent Develop or Evolve?** What is a referent's past, its history, the patterns of its origins, the manner in which it was formed? What predictions can be made about how it might continue to develop in the future? This dimension of meaning has particular relevance to the history of art education and to young people's artistic growth.

1.15 **What feelings and emotions does the referent have; what feelings or emotions does it evoke?** We often speak, for instance, of a work of art conveying a particular emotional quality, which, in turn, arouses certain feelings and emotions within a viewer.

1.16 **What sensations does the referent have; what sensations does it evoke?** Works of art have sensory qualities such as colors, lines, and textures. Sometimes these sensory qualities actually cause viewers to feel sensations of pain. In art education we might ask questions about the power of certain works to evoke various kinds of sensations in particular viewers.

1.17 **What judgments, opinions, motives, and values does the referent have; what judgments, opinions, motives, and values does it evoke?** Works of art evoke judgments. Art teachers and their students may arrive at very different conclusions about the aesthetic value of a given work of art. Is it differences in teachers' and students' motives and opinions that lead them to judge artworks differently?

1.18 **What cognitive attributes does the referent have; what cognitive responses does it evoke?** Artworks evoke various interpretations; some of those interpretations conflict with one another. Art students' interpretations of artworks may differ from those of their teachers or art critics.

1.19 **What does the referent possess or to whom does it belong?** Museums amass collections of artworks around which educational programs are developed. Schools sometimes develop collections of artworks to use in educational programs.

1.20 **What are the referent's dimensions, weight, and mass?** Although this meaning dimension appears to have limited use in art educational research, one can imagine studies, for example, which might be directed to art classroom dimensions and spaces that lead to the most efficient instruction.

Four types of relationships between and among dimensions of meaning and art educational research topics

When applied to the various topics, subtopics, and referents relating to art educational research, the 20 dimensions of meaning listed above may be used to generate an endless stream of questions. The following questions may be directed to at least four kinds of relationships[7] between or among dimensions of meaning and referents. These relationships include:

2.1 **Attributive relationships.** When an assertion is made that artworks have the potential to alter individuals' views of human purpose, this is an attribution of the manner in which meaning attributed to artworks might function in educational settings to change individuals' conceptions of themselves and their futures.

2.2 **Comparative relationships.** This type of relationship directs attention to the similarity or differences that exist between, for example, art teachers and their students, or between inner city and suburban students.

2.3 **Exemplifying relationships.** In this type of relationship, one instance of something may be used to represent an entire class of things. In a case study one middle school art teacher might, for example, be selected as typical or representative of most middle school art teachers in a school district.

2.4 **Metaphoric/Symbolic relationships.** This final type of relationship consists of illuminating characteristics and qualities of one thing in terms of another. For example, the art classroom can be seen as a theater where teachers and students are actors who play designated roles.

Art Educational Research: An Overview of its Primary Topics and Subtopics

It would be helpful if the realm of art educational research had a readily agreed upon framework so that we could specify things such as its context (1.1), its parts (1.2), and the logical structure of the patterns of relationships (2.1, 2.2, 2.3) among the parts (1.9). As I set out to provide an overview of some of the primary topics and subtopics, I debated whether to begin with the world of art, the student, or the realm of school and schooling. After shuffling things such as students, teacher, curriculum, schools, artworks, and outcomes into various configurations, I could identify no one satisfactory logical starting or ending place. Consequently, I concluded that there is no necessary or sufficient logical structure of primary topics and subtopics that might be associated with art educational research. It is possible, however, to present these topics in a pragmatic structure—one that has

---

[7]Like the dimensions of meaning, these four classifications of relationship are taken from Kreitler and Kreitler (1976, pp. 32–34).

practical utility and perhaps even a certain hierarchical feel about it. Nevertheless, I can imagine that, on other occasions, I might arrange the topics in a different order. I also should note that the set of primary topics and subtopics presented below represents only one of many possible sets which might be constructed and that there is space to list only a few of the subtopics that might conceivably fall under a primary topic.

3.1 **Students and their lives in art.** In the one big goal for art education presented earlier, I suggested that the creation and interpretation of art had the potential to change for the better individuals' conceptions of themselves and their worlds. There are myriad subtopics associated with students of art and their lives in art. The process of coming to know one's self and one's worlds through art is a notably complex matter, and among other things it relates to knowledge of students and their:

- motives for making art-like things in school and outside of school,
- conceptions of art and understanding of things such as the distinctions between "high" art and popular art forms or relationships among behaviors such as pretend-play, story telling, and art making,
- patterns of development in art-making and the influence of parents, culture, society, social class, the popular media, schooling, etc. on their art making,
- cognitive processes relating to understanding complexities of art in its historical and cultural contexts (art history), to processes through which meaning is derived from works of art and to acquiring and applying criteria for judging the merit and quality of different types of art; and to the knowledge, beliefs, skills, attitudes, patterns of reasoning, imagination, creativity, problem-solving abilities, or patterns of cooperative behavior that students acquire through art education and ways they apply them to other school subjects, and
- attitudes and beliefs relating to art programs, art curricula, art teachers, the goals of school art educational programs, the contributions of art to lives during and beyond school.

3.2 **Teachers and how they teach art.** In art education, there is relatively little inquiry into art teachers and their teaching. If an agenda for research into the nature of art teachers were undertaken, it might include topics and issues such as the following:

- types of teachers such as elementary and secondary school art specialists, elementary classroom teachers, college professors, private studio teachers, museum educators, even parents, and the ways they go about teaching; art teachers' motives for becoming art teachers; their knowledge and understanding of art; the extent to which they live their lives in the world of art and the individuals within the art world with whom they associate; their patterns of art exhibition attendance; the social and economic classes from which teachers emerge; their gender; their status within the educational community and society at large; and how teachers design their own living spaces,

- art teachers' interests and abilities relating to making art; the formal and informal conceptions and philosophies of art they possess; their abilities to interpret artworks, including their knowledge of histories and philosophies of art; and their abilities to make inferences about times, places, and peoples on the basis of information found in works of art,
- teachers' conceptions of their students; their understanding of students' artistic development; their ethnic and cultural backgrounds; their understanding of the "cultures" of childhood and young adulthood, adulthood, and older age; and their understandings of the roles that art might play in students' lives during school and beyond,
- teachers' formal and informal philosophies of art education; the sources of those philosophies; their consequences for practice; and the actual and implicit art educational goals teachers posit for their students,
- teachers' classroom behaviors and practices; instructional patterns; the formal and informal curricula they follow; their conceptions of their students' artworks; and the criteria they use to evaluate students' artworks and students' interpretations of art works, and
- how art-teachers-to-be are prepared in various countries; their education in art, general education, and art education; art educational rites of passage they undergo; the processes of professionalization; professional development programs designed for art teachers; and art teachers' out-of-classroom professional activities such as attendance at conferences and workshops, writing for publication, and contacts with colleagues.

3.3 The worlds of art education and education. In topics 3.1 and 3.2, I have already pointed to some of the key players who inhabit the worlds of education and art education. There are many other topics associated with these two complex realms, which are filled with an enormous array of factors, most of which have not been subjected to careful investigation by art educational researchers. These topics include:

- philosophies of art education and education and their relationships; the relationships of philosophies of art education to world views and major systems of value relating to art, education, society, and human purposes; the histories, antecedents, interrelationships, and influences of various philosophies of education and art education; the literature of art education; the individuals who are the originators of art educational philosophies, and their motives, lives, and beliefs; researchers of art education and their research studies;
- art curricula and their relationship to philosophies of education, the goals associated with art curricula, art curricular structures, and their sources and instructional consequences; the legislative and regulatory antecedents and consequences of curricula; the contents of art educational curricula including the texts, works, and concepts around which curricula are organized; relationships among art curricula and the curricula of other subjects; similarities and differences found among art educational curricula of different countries;
- the contexts in which art education is taught—art classrooms, their size, shape, design, and contents; conceptions of the art world which they implicitly or explicitly exemplify, represent, or reflect; and the art settings and contexts to which teachers take or send their students such as art museums and centers, art galleries, artists' studios, libraries;
- the resources used in art education—supplies for making art, textbooks, and reproductions of artworks; commercial publishers and manufacturers of art resource materials and the influences they have on the teaching of art; units of instruction, lesson plans, and other printed materials prepared by teachers; teacher-made tests and examinations;
- the products of art education—artworks students create, their discussions and writings about art, exhibitions of students' artworks and other products, films, and videotapes showing students and teachers in art educational settings;
- regulatory structures—the federal, state, and local laws and regulations that govern things such as arts graduation requirements, the amount of instructional time devoted to art, and art teacher certification requirements;
- processes of art educational change—the nature of change; the forces that lead to new educational initiatives in general education and art education and their relationships; consequences of change initiatives; funding sources for new educational initiatives such as public sources (federal, state, local) and private sources (corporations, foundations, and trusts); and change communities and consortia of institutions that contribute to educational change;

- professional associations and arts advocacy organizations—their purposes and functions, organization, histories, programs, publications; and
- administrative and supervisory structures—the ways art educational programs in schools, museums, and other educational institutions are administered, supervised, monitored, and evaluated; the individuals who administer and supervise arts programs; their backgrounds, values, and methods.

3.4 The world of art. Like the worlds of education and art education, the art world has myriad components whose relationships to one another are highly complex. Becker (1982) for example, elucidates the social web of artists, artworks, collectors, critics, curators, dealers, galleries, museums, and publishers that constitute whole sets of art worlds. Although the world of art extends well beyond the world of art education, there is a large section of jointly shared terrain. For example, artworks and the ideas associated with them form an important part of the content of art education. Moreover, my one big goal for art education relates not just to the art taught in schools but also to the art world beyond school, in which students have the opportunity to live or to visit from time to time. In the subtopics below, I will point to only a few of the components of the world of art that appear to have particular relevance to art education.[8]

- works of art—the major forms in which artworks exist including painting, drawing, performance and installation art, architecture, television and video, comics, product and graphic design, etc.; the classifications of types such as "high" art, "low" and popular art, advertising art, crafts, etc.; individual works of art, for example, Artemisia Gentileschi's *Susanna and the Elders* (1610) and Cindy Sherman's *Film Stills* series; features of works of art such as their sensory, formal, expressive, and stylistic characteristics; subject matter, symbols, themes, and metaphors; their genre such as scenes from everyday life;

---

[8] In a report on a five-year evaluation of six regional staff development consortia sponsored by the The Getty Education Institute for the Arts, I have created a diagram that shows the geography of the art world, its features, and their relationships and described art museum-centered rites of passage that teachers and administrators undergo in a complex professional development program. I have drawn many of the subtopics for this section from that diagram. The report titled *The Quiet Evolution: Changing the Face of Arts Education* will be published by the The Getty Education Institute for the Arts in 1997. Some of the ideas presented in this section also relate to Figure 2 in the *Early Adolescence through Young Adulthood Standards* (National Board for Professional Teaching Standards, 1994, p. 18).

- the creators of works of art—classes and types of artists including fine, folk and self-taught, popular, ecclesiastic, craftspersons, advertising artists, designers, and architects; individual artists and their roles and status; those who taught them, and those whom they taught; the development of individual careers, etc.;
- the processes through which individual works of art are made; the techniques used to form them; the materials from which they are made, etc.;
- the contexts of works of art—their origins, age, history, functions and purposes; their owners; the places in which they are found such as studios, public spaces, homes, museums, and galleries; the economic contexts of art including dealers and collectors, the consumers of art, etc.;
- the types of inquiry and inquirers associated with art, works of art, and artists—art history, art historians, and art historical inquiry; criticism and art critics; archeology and archeologists; sociology and sociologists of art; anthropology and anthropologists who study art; psychology and psychologists who study art and artists; philosophy of art and aestheticians; semiotics and semioticians who direct their inquiry toward art, etc.; and
- the meaning of art and works of art; the functions and purposes of art in society; the interpretations of meaning directed to individual artworks and collections of works of art; and the feelings and emotions artworks arouse, etc.

3.5 Outcomes of art education: lives pervaded with art and the artistically discriminating society.

The outcomes of art education could have been listed under "students of art" (3.1), merely, as one of the consequences of art instruction. In this section, however, I want to extend the outcomes of art education to individuals' lives beyond formal schooling. I wish to emphasize the point that the most important outcomes of school art programs are not achieved while students are still in school. Rather, they are achieved when, having left school, individuals continue to enrich their lives and their society through meaningful and satisfying encounters with art. This topic (3.5) has been created to draw attention to an important area of art educational research that has been largely neglected. That is to say, when it comes to achieving the goals of art education, the bottom line is what individuals, of their own volition, do in the art world. In other words, if art education makes little or no difference to individuals' lives beyond school, then art education has failed to a significant degree.

The Second Search

For many years, art teachers, especially high school art specialists, have consciously directed their most talented students toward the vocational and career possibilities of art. In addition to this important outcome of art education, there are the consequences of art education for the general student. We need to know about the other dimensions of individuals' experiences in art beyond school, which might be affected by art education. These, I think, are the very factors to which educational researchers should attend. The possibilities presented below are merely a first tentative attempt to map the terrain of the types of art-related lives individuals might live.

- active and artistically discriminating laypersons—individuals who use works of art to form their conceptions of themselves, their worlds, their sense of the way society and civilization ought to be and to plan their future lives; the different meanings individuals derive from works of art of various kinds including the "high" arts and popular arts, design arts, traditional and contemporary art; individual interests, social classes, economic status, and other societal factors that shape both the degree of participation in the various worlds of art and the insightful interpretations of works of art, especially individuals and groups whose expected interpretative and participatory artistic behaviors have been altered by various forms of art education;
- leisure time art makers, individuals who spend parts of their lives in the nonprofessional production of art—the kinds of art they make, the meaning it gives to their lives; various functions and purposes of art making; the antecedents and consequences of leisure-time art making; leisure-time art makers' motives, attitudes and beliefs, and the values they hold regarding the things they make; their artistic imaginations and creativity, the amount of time they devote to making art;
- consumers of art knowledge—the individuals who read and respond critically to art criticism, art historical writing, and deliberate and debate about the nature of art and the standards through which the merit and quality of artworks should be determined;
- consumers of artworks—individuals and groups who collect various forms of art, and the degree to which different forms of art education affect individuals' art collecting behaviors;
- creators and consumers of consciously designed interior and exterior environments—individuals who design with sensitivity the spaces in which they live; individuals who read semiotically the meaning of the personal spaces that they design and that others design; individuals who read semiotically public living spaces and public art and apply aesthetic reasoning processes to influence their design; and

- individuals who choose vocations in art—advertising artists, architects, art critics, art gallery owners and employees, art historians, art museum curators, art museum educators, art restorers, art teachers, ceramic artists, fashion designers, filmmakers, graphic designers, interior designers, landscape architects, photographers, print makers, product designers, sculptors, video artists, and performance artists.

Concluding Thoughts about the Topics and Subtopics for Art Educational Research

My guess is that Mark Tansey had about as much fun playfully selecting the items included on his wheel as he did in spinning the wheel to see the kinds of associations it produced and the kinds of suggestions it made regarding possible subjects, topics, and themes for his paintings. In specifying the items to be placed on his wheel, he outlined some of the important parameters of his world of artistic inquiry. We don't know the ways, at least not all the ways, that Tansey uses the wheel to generate ideas for his artworks. We can be fairly certain, however, that once the painter has spun the wheel to generate ideas for his works, his creative challenges have just begun. He undertakes a lengthy process of locating visual sources, and arranging and transforming them in a series of sketches before the act of painting is begun (Sims, 1990).

In my description of the classes of research questions (dimensions of meaning), the primary topics and subtopics for art educational research, and the relationships that might exist among them, I have already engaged in a good bit of cognitive wheel-spinning (both literal and metaphoric). I used the topics of art educational research to exemplify the research questions and then as a way of presenting topics. I have used the dimensions of meaning—somewhat casually, I confess—as a way of actually generating subtopics. Now it is time to use the system created by the wheel in a more systematic manner.

The One Big Research Problem and Its Related Problems: Spinning Wheels, Seeing Relationships, and Planning Research Projects

What I would actually like to do is sketch out the biggest and most important research problem I can imagine. In doing so, I hope to illustrate some of the interrelationships among research questions and topics and also show how research might contribute to achieving the one big goal of art education. As I present this enormous hypothetical research initiative, I will also take the opportunity to link art educational research questions and topics to: (1) research methods and (2) the role of theory and metaphor in art educational research. In effect, the initiative provides an opportunity to illustrate what a complete act of educational research might be.

Statement of the Big Problem for Art Educational Research

As I read David Halle's book, *Inside Culture: Art and Class in the American Home* (1993), I was disappointed, but not surprised, that in a book dealing with the various forms of art individuals collect and display in their homes—art which reveals, among other things, who they are and what they value—there was not a single mention of art education and the ways it might have shaped the subjects' knowledge and tastes relating to works of art. There was, however, a great deal of information about social class, economic status, religion, and their relationships to the works of art individuals write into the texts of their lives. We are left wondering why the researcher didn't pursue the art educational line of inquiry, and if he did, why he didn't present his findings. Were there none? Unfortunately, in this area of vital interest to art education we have virtually no information about how art education affects students' lives once they leave school.

Art educational researchers have confined their attention primarily to the conditions under which art education is offered in schools and to students' achievements while they are still in school. *How does art education affect individuals' lives beyond school?* This is not only one of the most important questions we face, it is also one of the most difficult to answer. If we were to search for answers to this global beyond-school question, it could raise a whole series of in-school research problems that have been ignored by art educational researchers and by art teachers.

Researching the Global Question: Relationships between Parts and Wholes

In researching the out-of-school outcomes of art education we are immediately faced with issues of methodology—of selecting the inquiry processes that have the greatest potential to answer our research questions. We also confront the enormity of a research problem that includes all possible outcomes among all possible subjects within a given population. It is a problem that could be as broad as a sample of all students who have attended all schools in the United States during this century or limited to the students who attended a particular school and who took classes from one art teacher during a particular period of time. In either instance, we would face the challenge of grasping the broad topic and its parts simultaneously. This is what Lewontin (1991) calls:

a third view, one that sees the entire world neither as an indissoluble whole nor with the equally incorrect, but currently dominant, view that at every level the world is made up of bits and pieces that can be isolated and that have properties that can be studied in isolation. Both ideologies, one that mirrors the premodern feudal social world, and the other that mirrors the modern competitive individualist entrepreneurial one, prevent us from seeing the full richness of interaction in nature. In the end, they prevent a rich understanding of nature and prevent us from solving the problems to which science is supposed to apply (p. 15).

An Initial Study, Its Methodology, and the Resultant Puzzle

Seeking answers to the global question of outcomes and the parts of which the global outcome is composed is like accounting for all possible relationships among the major topics and subtopics of art educational research and the dimensions of meaning and questions. This would be equivalent to noting all the possibilities that could result from continually spinning and re-spinning the wheels of the diagram found in Figure 1. The only way I can imagine researching such a complex whole/parts problem is to undertake a qualitative or ethnographic-like study where a sample of individuals is selected and interviews are conducted about their lives in art and the antecedents to those lives. The methodology would be somewhat like that employed by Halle (1993) when he made a random sample of six New York City and Long Island neighborhoods. He contacted individuals, made appointments, observed the art in their homes, and interviewed them. In our hypothetical study, however, the topic, the variables, and their relationships would necessarily be broader than those to which Halle attended.

Let's say that we selected a random sample of individuals to find out about the contributions of school art education to their lives beyond school. Our first question might be global. *Tell me the role that art plays in your life?* Soon, however, we would need to begin asking more specific questions about different kinds of art experiences and the motives that underlie them. The questions might turn to such things as the sources for individuals' values, interests, and beliefs about art; we might explore the social class to which individuals belong and try to determine if those individuals who come from lower social and economic classes were less likely to have social models for participating in the art world than those from higher social and economic classes. We could explore whether or not models for living lives pervaded with art were actually provided in their art classes. We then might explore the assignments individuals were given in their art classes, why they think they did them, and their relationships to their beyond-school art activities. Questions might be directed to the extent to which art teachers were mentors and provided information and models relating to a range of art-world-related modes of being. We also should expect that, during the initial interview process, new issues will emerge from the questions we ask and the answers we receive.

Through a process of analysis of answers to our interview questions, let's assume that we amass a mountain of data about the kinds of relationships that appear either to exist or not to exist between art educational experiences of various kinds of art-related lives individuals might live.

Analyzing Initial Findings. Our findings might take the form of a series of narratives or life stories that exemplify different kinds of lives individuals might live in art. These stories might provide unique insights into the relationships of art education to life. A number of different narratives might exemplify some of the different lives one can live in art and how they came to be. From these exemplifications, we might tentatively conclude, for example, that social and economic class, which provide opportunities for art experiences outside of school, appears to affect beyond-school lives in art more than school experiences. If this were one of our conclusions, it would confirm what we already know from findings from the first National Assessment of Educational Progress in Art (Wilson, 1981). These narratives might also begin to reveal a number of other patterns. They might show, for example, that individuals who, from the time they were very young, possessed both talent and strong desires to draw and create other forms of art (Wilson & Wilson, 1976) were consequently able to overcome social and cultural disadvantages in order to create art and thus live a life in art. In conducting the initial portions of our "second-search," let's assume that, from the narratives and from other patterns of information emerging from our analysis of the data we are able to conclude that in-school art educational experiences were usually not influential in leading individuals to live lives in art, but that in a few cases they were. How do we explain why art education appeared to make a difference to individuals' lives in some instances while in many others it didn't? Now we are faced with a fascinating research puzzle. This is where metaphor and theory construction might come into play.

Searching for explanations: Metaphor and Theory. Early in my research career, I was faced with this very problem of explaining different effects of art schooling. While teaching in Britain during the early seventies, I became fascinated by an art teacher who had created a most unusual classroom. The institutional features in half the room had been transformed into a combination art museum and comfortable living room. The hard institutional surfaces and furniture contrasted with an exquisite Jacobean table and chairs, plants, a white carpet, and art and artifacts that told much of the history of Britain. What happened when working-class teenagers were taught in this environment? I traveled throughout England interviewing former students about their experiences in the classroom and their lives beyond school. Some had become artists and designers with growing reputations; others were collectors of art. A much larger group of former students apparently lived lives virtually unaffected by their art education. I searched for an explanation—a theory which would account for both the students whose lives were changed dramatically by art education and those who lives were virtually unaffected.

After returning to the United States, while attending a meeting of the American Anthropological Association, I heard Victor Turner describe his research in East Africa where he attempted to determine the factors that led to changes in a tribal society. He told of watching the regular, everyday, and structured aspects of the society, noting that changes occurred without his being able to identify their sources. Finally, Turner began to attend to what he called the "anti-structural" aspects of the society—its puberty rites, weddings, ceremonies surrounding the installation of a new leader, and conflicts that led villages to break into smaller units. In these rites of passage, encounters, and other unexpected events he identified the origin of new symbols and behavioral patterns (Turner, 1969).

Listening to Turner's theory of structure and anti-structure, I had an instant flash of insight in which I saw that the beyond-class-time activities of the British art room—the time that teacher and students spent in the classroom before and after school doing things such as eating together, talking about the room's collection of artifacts, entertaining a continual stream of casual visitors and former students, and taking days off from school to visit stately homes and to collect antiques—were either anti-structural or extra-structural. Once I knew what to look for, I could trace most of the changes in students' lives to these extra-structural times (Wilson, 1974). Turner's theory provided the structure from which most of the questions I had raised, and many others I had not thought of, were answered. This finding of explanations to research quandaries through metaphors and others' theories that appear out of the blue is a central feature of imaginative inquiry.[9]

Re-searching for the Answers to Smaller Questions: In-school Art Educational Experiences and Life-beyond-school

As we return to our hypothetical study of the outcomes of art education, we could develop a whole series of speculations about why students fail to carry the things they learn in art classes into their lives. For example, is it because (a) teachers seldom draw connections between art assignments and how they relate to life beyond the classroom, (b) art assignments don't have connections to life, (c) art educational goals and curricula ignore beyond-school outcomes,[10] (d) teachers see no need to make the connections because most students don't care about the connections, (e) the connections between art classroom activities and life are difficult if not impossible to make, or (f) teachers attend mainly to the structural rather than the anti- or extra-structural aspects of art teaching? The list of possibilities could go on and on. Interestingly, the answers to most of these questions about the effects-beyond-school can be sought while students are still in school. Let's examine ways of seeking answers to some of these questions and in the process discuss the research methodologies the questions seem to require. We have a number of interesting choices including qualitative or ethnographic, descriptive or survey, relational or correlational, and experimental and quasi-experimental studies.

What Goes on in the Art Classroom?: A Qualitative Study of the Connections Teachers Make between Art and Life

If we hypothesized that one of the primary reasons students make few connections between art classroom experiences and their lives beyond school is because teachers don't expect them to make connections, then we could test this hypothesis by observing teachers' classroom behaviors. Again, as in our first study of beyond-school lives-in-art, a qualitative study appears a good choice. We could select a sample of elementary, middle, and high school art teachers, make careful observa-

---

[9] A fascinating account of this process is found in the writing of Gould and Lewontin (1979). In a paper titled, "The Spandrels of San Marco and the Panglossian Paradigm: A Critique of the Adaptationist Programme," Gould and Lewontin offered a critique of the adaptationist theory of evolution, which had dominated evolutionary theory for 40 years. This paper, one of the most frequently quoted in recent scientific literature has an entire book devoted to its rhetoric (Selzer, 1993). What is most fascinating to me about the paper is how Gould used his experience of the architecture of San Marco to demolish adaptationist theories. He had set for himself the task of preparing his and Lewontin's critique and while visiting San Marco in Venice he tells us, "I had an epiphany of sorts," as he looked up at the spandrels—the spaces between the arches that support San Marco's domes—and saw them "not 'nooks and crannies left over,' but potential determinants of the entire design." He tells of his "strange feeling of almost manic exhilaration followed by the total calm of understanding" as he saw the implications of his insight for both critiquing and explaining evolutionary theory (Gould in Seltzer, 1993, p. 324).

[10] The National Standards for Arts Education (1995) ignore possible beyond-school outcomes, while the stirring rhetoric introducing the standards deals primarily with beyond-school benefits.

tions of their classroom instruction over a given period of time, and note the number of times they make explicit connections to the beyond-school implications of their assignments.

What if we were to discover that teachers seldom attend to the beyond-school implications of their instruction? This finding could lead to a new set of research issues.

A Survey of Teachers' Beliefs about the Connections between Art Instruction and Beyond-school Art Activities

In qualitative, ethnographic studies it is possible to observe a large number of factors and account for most, if not all, of the major topics, many subtopics and meaning-related questions found in Figure 1. In qualitative studies, however, it is seldom possible to observe more than a small number of cases. Since the sample of cases does not represent a given population, the generalization of findings to the entire population would be inappropriate unless the case studies were linked to a much larger set of related case studies. If we want to be more certain that art teachers in general either make or fail to make connections between art assignments and beyond-school ways of living in the art world, we could develop and administer a questionnaire to a broad representative sample of art teachers.

There is a desirable link between questionnaires and qualitative studies. Preliminary interviews and observations provide topics around which questionnaires may be built. If, for example, an initial qualitative study of 21 teachers showed that high school art instructors were far more likely than middle and elementary school instructors to make connections between classroom art activities and beyond-school art activities, we might wish to see if the findings could be confirmed in a larger sample.

A questionnaire might be prepared containing items with a scale attached to permit respondents to indicate whether they: strongly agree, agree, are undecided, disagree, or strongly disagree with statements such as:

1. Whenever I give my students an art assignment, I point out how it will be useful to them when they are adults.

2. Most art teachers give little thought to showing the relationship between the assignments they give students and the artistic activities in which they might engage once they leave school.

3. It is my goal to show my students that every assignment I give directly to their lives-in-art beyond school.

4. Connecting school art assignments to students' lives beyond school is one of the most important objectives of art education.

There is a deliberate underlying structure to the four items; each deals with a specific belief type. The first is a belief about self, the second a general belief, the third a belief about goals, and the fourth a belief about a norm or value.[11] An individual's actual beliefs would be reflected in a compilation of responses to 30 or 40 items probing different dimensions of art-classroom/life-in-art-beyond-school connections.

If our questionnaire were administered to large enough samples of elementary, middle, and high school art instructors, we might have sufficient data to either confirm or refute our hunches about whether high school teachers are more likely than middle and elementary art teachers to make connections between school art and life.

A Relational Study of the Connections Teachers Make between Art and Life and Students' Beyond-school Activities

Another approach to educational research is to study relationships between two sets of variables. Let's assume, for example, that over the years we have noted that the students of some art teachers, more than those of other teachers, are likely to attend art schools and become artists, art teachers, and art historians. In a pilot study we ask a sample of art teachers to make a list of former students for whom art plays an important part in their lives. These individuals might include, for example, professional artists, collectors, art teachers, or even those who are ardent visitors to art museums. We would probably find that some teachers are able to name dozens of former students with strong interests in art and other teachers who are able to list few or none. Consequently, we decide to administer our questionnaire relating to teachers' beliefs about the importance of connecting classroom assignments to art activities beyond school and then analyze data to determine whether there is a positive relationship between teachers who think it is

---

[11] Kreitler and Kreitler (1976) have shown that questionnaires containing a nearly equivalent balance among these four belief types are far more likely to predict individuals' behaviors than questionnaires that deal with only one or two belief types.

important to relate school art to life and the number of their former students who now live lives connected to art.

In our study we would, of course, need to take into account factors such as the number of years the teachers have taught and the social, economic, and cultural backgrounds of their students. Nevertheless, if we were to find a positive relationship between teachers' beliefs about in-school practices and their students' behaviors beyond school, we would have identified a potent factor affecting whether or not the global goal of art education is achieved.

The Effect of Teachers' School-to-life Connecting Behaviors and Students' Beliefs about Their Lives in Art Beyond School

Experimental research in education has fallen into disfavor of late. One of the primary reasons is that although there are many complex relationships among a large number of variables, in experimental research it is possible to study only a few of these variables that may affect educational outcomes. The careful controls required for experimental studies in education may have little relationship to the "real" world of education. I think, however, that there is still an important place for experimental and quasi-experimental studies in art education. Let's propose a study relating to the effect of a set of instructional variables on students' beliefs about the application of school art learning to their lives beyond school.

In a series of hypothetical qualitative, survey, and relational studies, we have determined a probable link between the instructional activities of some teachers and the beyond-school behaviors of their students. It appears that if teachers continually make connections between their classroom instruction and the possible ways students might use the things they learn in art class when they are adults, there is a greater likelihood that these students will engage in beyond-school activities more frequently than students of teachers who do not make these connections.

We decide to design an experimental study to determine whether these school-to-life connections affect students' in-school beliefs about their future lives-in-art. Groups of elementary, middle, and high school teachers agree to attend a special professional development program in which they study a newly developed "art-to-life" curriculum that employs units of instruction prepared especially to highlight connections between in-school and beyond-school behaviors. After attending the program, most of the teachers agree to teach the special curriculum to all their students. They also agree to give strong explicit emphases to the school-to-life dimensions of the curriculum to randomly selected classes but not to other classes. In other words, their students all get the same curriculum, the same units of instruction, the same content, but some classes are singled out to receive activities and assignments relating to explicit art-to-life linkages while in other classes the linkages are either implicit or non-existent. The instructors teach the curriculum for an entire semester. Their teaching is monitored periodically to determine if they are indeed adhering to the explicit and implicit instructional conditions. The teachers also keep journals and note students' responses relating to the new curriculum.

At the end of the semester all students are given a belief inventory designed to assess the probability that they will engage in art activities beyond school. This inventory has been carefully pilot-tested and it has been shown to distinguish between individuals who are highly disposed to beyond-school art activities and those who are not. If we find that the school-to-life curriculum, reinforced with explicit connections to out-of-school activities, has significant positive relationship to scores on the belief inventory, we will then possess another strong indication of the way in which art education can become more effective by influencing students' lives beyond school.

The Complete Act of Educational Research: Some Brief Conclusions

In this chapter I have tried to illustrate my belief that research in art education should be based on an explicit statement of beliefs about the goals of art education both in-school and beyond-school. I have tried to illustrate what I consider the content of art educational research to be through outlining various kinds of relationships among primary topics, subtopics, and questions derived from a comprehensive set of dimensions of meaning. I have tried to indicate that educational research is more valuable and has a greater chance of influencing art educational practice when relationships are revealed among more rather than fewer dimensions of content. This is why I see qualitative studies conducted in natural classroom settings as extremely useful starting places for art educational research. Observations from qualitative studies, especially if they are illuminated by both conscious theory construction (the process of which would require at least another chapter to outline) and a search for metaphors that explain findings and generate new insights, can make an enormous contribution to our understanding of art education.

My fondness for qualitative research notwithstanding, I value highly survey, relational, and experimental studies. There are also other forms of art educational research about which I have said little. For example, in my evaluation work, I view the art classroom and school as a text to be interpreted much as one might interpret a work of art. Eisner calls this educational criticism (1991). In recent years I have come to see the enormous benefits that come from two quite different forms of analyses; one is analysis of the policies that govern art and educational institutions and the other is semiotic analyses (Bal & Bryson, 1991) of various art and art educational contexts. Finally, I see the need to ground virtually every research study in historical and philosophical contexts. I think the various approaches to education research complement one another. When we employ several simultaneously or in series our chances for understanding art education increase.

In this chapter I have tried to show that the questions we formulate shape the kinds of research methodologies we employ. The questions should come first and issues of methodology follow. In my series of mostly hypothetical illustrations of research, I have tried to show that the complete act of art educational research is achieved not through the completion of one study; rather, it is composed of a whole series of studies encompassing many related questions, problems, and research methodologies. I believe the art educational content-wheel shown in Figure 1, (and its reference to the way Mark Tansey arrives at his painting topics), has its greatest utility in reminding researchers and consumers of research of the many different interactions of topics and questions that merit a second-search and of how much research there is yet to do.

References

Bal, M., & Bryson, N. (1991). Semiotics and art history. *The Art Bulletin, 73* (2), 174–208.

Barthes, R. (1985). Day by day with Roland Barthes. In M. Blonsky (Ed.), *On signs* (pp. 98–117). Baltimore: Johns Hopkins University Press.

Becker, H. S. (1982). *Art worlds.* Berkeley, CA: University of California Press.

Clark, G. A., Day, M. D., & Greer, W. D. (1987). Discipline-based art education: Becoming students of art. *The Journal of Aesthetic Education, 21*(2), 129–193.

Danto, A. (1992). *Mark Tansey: Visions and revisions.* New York: Harry N. Abrams.

Dow, A. W. (1899). *Composition.* New York: The Baker and Taylor Company.

Eisner, E. W. (1991). *The enlightened eye: Qualitative inquiry and the enhancement of educational practice.* New York: Macmillan.

Freeman, J. (1993). *Mark Tansey.* Los Angeles: Los Angeles County Museum of Art.

Gould. S. J., & Lewontin, R. C. (1979). The spandrels of San Marco and the Panglossian paradigm: A critique of the adaptationist programme, *Proceedings of the Royal Society of London, Series B: Biological Sciences, 205,* 581–598.

Halle, D. (1993). *Inside culture: Art and class in the American home.* Chicago: University of Chicago Press.

Kauppinen, H., & Wilson, B. (1981). *Kuvaamataidon didaktiikka.* Helsinki, Finland: Otava.

Kreitler, H., & Kreitler, S. (1972). *Psychology of the arts.* Durham, NC: Duke University Press.

Kreitler, H., & Kreitler, S. (1976). *Cognitive orientation and behavior.* New York: Springer.

Lewontin, R. C. (1991). *Biology as ideology: The doctrine of DNA.* New York: HarperCollins.

National Board for Professional Teaching Standards. (1994). *Early adolescent through young adulthood/art: Standards for national board certification.* Detroit, MI.

National Standards for Arts Education (1995). Reston, VA: Music Educators National Conference.

Sims, P. (1990). *Mark Tansey: Art and source.* Seattle, WA: Seattle Art Museum.

Smith, W. (1872). *Art education, scholastic and industrial.* Boston: James R. Osgood and Company.

Selzer, J. (1993). *Understanding scientific prose.* Madison, WI: University of Wisconsin Press.

Sully, J. (1896). *Studies of childhood.* London: Longmans, Green, and Company.

Turner, V. W. (1969). *The ritual process: Structure and anti-structure.* Chicago: Aldine.

Wilson, B. (1966). An experimental study designed to alter fifth and sixth grade students' perceptions of paintings. *Studies in Art Education, 8*(1), 33–42.

Wilson, B. (1971). Evaluation of learning in art education. In B. S. Bloom, J. T. Hastings, & G. F. Madous (Eds.), *Handbook on formative and summative evaluation of student learning,* (pp. 499–558). New York: McGraw-Hill.

Wilson, B. (1974) The other side of evaluation of art education. In G. Hardiman & T. Zernich, (Eds.), *Curricular considerations for visual arts education: Rationale, development and evaluation,* (pp. 247–276). Champaign, IL: Stipes.

Wilson, B. (1981). The triumph of American culture over the art educational establishment: Findings from the U.S. National Assessment of Educational Progress in Art. *The product of a process: A selection of papers delivered at the 24th INSEA World Congress, Rotterdam, the Netherlands.* Amsterdam: De Trommel.

Wilson, B., & Wilson, M. (1976). Visual narrative and the artistically gifted. *The Gifted Child Quarterly, 20*(4), 432–447.b

Qualitative Forms of Research Methods

The purpose of this chapter is to: 1) discuss the nature of qualitative inquiry; 2) explore different kinds of qualitative inquiry; 3) explain the role of interpretation; 4) present various participant observation stances; 5) offer ways of gaining access and achieving reciprocity; 6) review stages of qualitative research; 7) suggest practical procedures related to research methods as well as research writing; 8) present sociocultural problems; and 9) give future alternatives for qualitative research. Specifically, stages of qualitative research to be described are data collection, content analysis, and comparative analysis. Practical suggestions for analysis will include such examples as computer programming, icon and color coding of concepts, focus groups and key informants, and spreadsheets for comparative and cross-site analysis.

What is Qualitative Inquiry?

An inquiry is simply a question, but as a process it invites a series of questions. A major guiding question can be a simple one, for example, "What is art teaching like on a Navajo Reservation?" This question is open-ended, experiential, and invites a metaphoric response and vivid portrayal. Sub-questions also can be used; such as, "What types of instructional behaviors do Navajo teachers use?" Some questions come from a review of the literature, while others emerge in the process of conducting qualitative research.

According to Eisner (1991), qualitative research is the search for qualities—the characteristics of our experience. We translate these qualities through our chosen representation form and conceptual outlook. Six features of qualitative study are

MARY STOKROCKI
Arizona State University

that it is 1) field-focused, 2) constructed so that the researcher is an instrument, 3) interpretive in nature, 4) expressive in language, 5) highly detailed, and 6) persuasive (Eisner, 1991).

Qualitative inquiry is a systematic process of describing, analyzing and interpreting insights discovered in everyday life (Wolcott, 1994). Similar to quantitative research, qualitative methods begin with [empirical] observation of a phenomenon and its characteristics. In qualitative studies, the logic of inference is one of directly observed comparison, resulting in new insights and reclassifications, rather than strict numerical comparison and classification (Willis, 1978). This form of research *generates* theory and extends our particular understandings, rather than *generalizing* about them (Glaser & Strauss, 1967). Lincoln and Guba (1985) and Stake (1988) refer to qualitative research as naturalistic inquiry, which is a careful study of human activity in its natural and complex state. Finally, qualitative inquiry broadens our field of knowledge or refutes our accepted beliefs through comparisons with other cases. Qualitative types of research depend on personal, social, and idiosyncratic meanings that are valued for themselves.

What are the Different Kinds of Qualitative Inquiry?

Qualitative research includes four main types of inquiry including ethnography and microethnography, phenomenology, educational criticism, the case study, and social critical theory to name a few. For other types of qualitative research, such as historical and narrative inquiry and ethnomethodology (Sevigny, 1978), see Denzin and Lincoln's (1994) *Handbook of Qualitative Research.*

Ethnography, according to Wolcott (1988), is both process and product; a picture of a group's "way of life" (p. 188). Ethnography is an inquiry process carried out by a person from a point of view based on experience and knowledge of prior research. Anthropologists try to understand the significance or meaning of an experience from the participants' views. Some researchers also use the term ethnography to refer to all techniques used in fieldwork, not a single method (for example see Stuhr, 1986).

Microethnography is the study of a smaller experience or a slice of everyday reality, such as instruction. Microethnography is the process of data collection, content analysis, and comparative analysis of everyday situations for the purpose of formulating insights (Smith, 1978). In my studies, the focus is on teaching as a way to understand a culture. For example, I used several microethnographic procedures in my study of teaching preadolescents during a nine-week sequence (Stokrocki, 1988).

Phenomenology is the study of an experience and its essences. Ingarden suggests that all phenomenological as well as aesthetic experience is "a composite process having various phases and a characteristic development that contains many heterogeneous elements" (Willis, 1978, p. 43). This method is a line-by-line search for essential statements and an in-depth thematic analysis of them (van Manen, 1984). Beittel (1973) and his students were the first to publish their phenomenological photographic investigation of and dialogue on creativity with artists in a drawing laboratory. Another good model of phenomenological inquiry is Jeffers' (1992) explanation of how a group of preservice teachers in an elementary art methods course made sense of their aesthetic decision-making experience. The final result of writing and re-writing ended in a new phenomenological text of intersubjective experience. Such a text may take new metaphoric forms, such as a parable or play. For instance, my dissertation research structure was based on a play format that included setting, characters, opening scene, subsequent acts, climax, and denouement (Stokrocki, 1982). In this way, I was able to reveal the unfolding of my own and my co-students' comprehension of our pottery class. East-West philosophical pottery tradition, which the teacher Kenneth Beittel explored, became clearer to me as my research progressed.

In *Educational Criticism,* Eisner (1991) bases his methodology on aesthetic criticism, which consists of descriptive, analytic, and thematic stages. In his evaluation stance, Eisner questions not only sources of school problems but their symptoms as well. In previous writings, he claimed that educational connoisseurs had final judgment. His stance since has changed to include the participants' views and opinions of the researcher's ideas. In educational criticism, polyphonic opinions should exist side-by-side, similar to the "rashomon effect," described in literature and in film. The purpose of this type of research is the expansion of perception, based on Deweyan ideas, and the enlargement of understanding.

Case Study, which originated in psychology, is research that depicts a problem in all "its personal and social complexity," according to Stake (1988, p. 256). It is a search for an understanding of an idiosyncratic, complex case. When conducting a case study, Stake warns us to set limits in the beginning and widen them as we later interrelate different components. Most researchers only gradually come to realize which issues are best to construct their stories. An issue may emerge as a classification; for example, a staff person who calls students either "hoarders or sharers." An issue also may evolve as a contingency, one thing consistently coexisting with another; for example, "whenever the child cried, the teacher became busy with other children" (Stake, 1988, p. 259). (For recent examples of case study research methods, see Blaikie, 1994 and Chen, 1993.)

Social Critical Theory calls for critique of research. Personal perceptions, meanings, and value systems underlie all research and need to be flushed out. Reconceptualists earlier argued for reorganizing art education around human consciousness and political action (Pinar, 1975). All research involves interpretation and proceeds from conjecture to refutation. Thomas (1993) offers critical ethnography as "a type of reflection that examines culture, knowledge, and action" (p. 2). This kind of research exposes hidden assumptions, agendas, and power centers that repress communication. Some qualitative research tends to be more subjective and even self-critical at times (Mason, 1988), while other types are more objective and reveal the obvious, yet taken-for-granted, metaphoric structures of an institution (see Sikes, 1992).

What is Interpretation?

Interpretation is a process of translation, which is as old as the *Bible* itself. Many types of interpretation exist: psychological, historical, legal, religious, and symbolic. The process of interpretation is similar to a detective searching for clues and establishing facts. Interpretation is concerned with uncovering the multilayered meanings of a phenomenon and understanding them more deeply. According to Bleicher (cited in Stokrocki, 1983), "understanding is the recognition and reconstruction of meaning through language." Meaning is a conveyed intention of established social significance, personal interest, and all its suggested qualities. Meaning involves the subjective realm of existence and continues beyond the author and his/her audience towards the universal. Interpretation starts with concrete perceptions and delves into hidden preconceptual aspects. For example, the ability to interpret is quite natural and is manifested from the beginning of an experience, as when you walk into a room and perceive it to be cold. You are translating your study in English and bound by an anthropological lens as opposed to a psychological one. Your task is to achieve a deeper interpretation.

Eisner (1991) defines interpretation as a process of explaining the meaning of an event by putting it in its context, making the experience vivid, identifying its prior conditions and potential consequences, and providing reasons for practices. For example, what are the different meanings of a wink or a blink—one has a message and the other does not. Interpretations are good guesses or suppositions.

The process of interpretation is simply one of logical questioning, as in a dialogue. The system begins with good conjectures, supporting material, and proceeds with refutations of incorrect meanings, according to Popper (cited in Stokrocki, 1983). Interpretation occurs simultaneously with description. When interpreting, remember to: 1) state your pre-understandings of the phenomenon and explain its context; 2) realize [state] that your information is probably true; 3) seek totality and coherence of meaning in your description; 4) search for the human meaning of the phenomenon and all its etymological, traditional, and philosophical meanings; and 5) apply your findings to your own life and state how the experience has changed you. Maitland-Gholson and Ettinger (1994) explain interpretive decision making as it relates to selected examples in art education. They examine different interpretive research roles in order to: 1) construct meanings directly from participants' words and actions [phenomenology], 2) uncover hidden norms and biases through consensus of insiders and outsiders [critical theory], 3) disclose patterns of power and behavior through linguistic analysis [interpretive analytics], and 4) uncover changing ideological meanings [deconstruction].

I use the anthropological work of Geertz (1973) as the theoretical framework for my studies. To interpret a culture is to understand what participants say about it. Geertz calls it "thick description." He states that "A culture is concretely, an open-ended, creative dialogue of subcultures, of insiders and outsiders, of diverse factions" (cited in Clifford, 1988, p. 46). Dialogue is a process of questioning and a give-and-take comparison of ideas, as researcher, participants, and outside reviewers together search for significant or hidden insights (Gadamer, 1975). Interpretation is an historical understanding, because cultures are always in dynamic transition.

What is Participant Observation and Its Stances?

Participant Observation is a process of describing, analyzing, and interpreting an everyday activity to understand it more fully (Glaser & Strauss, 1967). Pohland (1976) and Spradley (1980) call it multi-person, multi-method, and multivariable. I have added the fourth aspect *multidimensional* (Stokrocki, 1986). Participant Observation implies that the researcher is learning from people and not just studying them. The researcher is the prime tool for gathering data. One can be a complete observer, a full participant, or a half participant and half observer. Sevigny (1978), as well as many other researchers, calls a combination of all three stances *triangulation*, a sociological process of viewing a situation from all three stances. You can also achieve triangulation by using different research techniques. For instance, in Sevigny's (1978) study of five university drawing courses, he incorporated audiotapes, interviews, and diary writing. He also warns that accepting the full participant stance and not relating the perspective of the observer has its consequence of refusal of the observed to grant permission to use the study. Wolcott (1988) suggests that triangulated techniques are helpful "for cross-checking, or for ferreting out varying perspectives on complex issues and events" (p. 192).

Triangulation increases validity by incorporating at least three different viewpoints and methods. Developing a good memory also is important. In my research, some of the Navajo people subtly criticized me because they felt that writing everything down meant that I did not learn my lessons well. Qualitative researchers, therefore, must explain their evolving logic behind their selection of methods (Smith, 1978; Stokrocki, 1991).

How Do I Gain Access and What About Reciprocity?

Gaining access, a process of seeking permission to conduct a study, can be formal or informal. For example, in her complicated negotiations with Japanese art educators to observe an individual school, Mason (1993) describes weeks of formalized meetings to determine the scope of her study and to insure that the situation would be the best possible one to observe. Inherent in this protocol is the Japanese mandate that the situation be excellent, which filters out any comparison or views of less then perfect situations.

In contrast, after failure to reach possible research sites through Arizona State University's Center of Indian Education, I found a more informal network that could provide me with potential sites. The process began with a reference from the state art consultant and continued with casual introductions at regional art education meetings on the Navajo Reservation. At times, in order to obtain signed consent to even conduct the study, it took nearly six months to convince Navajo superintendents of my earnestness and fair representation. They wanted to see the completed report. Gaining access mainly involved establishing a sense of trust.

At times, gaining access may consist of a simple letter on school stationery that states, "The ___ School System grants permission to ___ to conduct research on ___ in the ___. The information will become part of the curriculum." Include a copy of a previous study and/or your research proposal. Participants, including students, however, have the right to refuse to cooperate and to change their minds at any time during the research process.

Furthermore, refer to the people that you study as *participants*, not *subjects*. Terms like *subjects* are demeaning. The ethics or rules of conduct regarding qualitative research are changing as researchers form alliances with participants in trying to understand specific situations and make recommendations. Through such interactions both parties become equal in status.

Qualitative research assumes reciprocity—an exchange of favors. Some reason should be given to participants for their cooperation in your research (Patton, 1990, p. 253). Reasons can vary from a feeling of importance at being observed, useful feedback, pleasure from interactions with the observer, or payment for completing some task.

What Are the Stages of Qualitative Research?

Qualitative research unfolds in three stages: *data collection, content analysis,* and *comparative analysis* (Strauss & Corbin, 1990). Hypotheses need not be stated in the beginning of a participant observation assessment, but will be generated throughout the study (Glaser & Strauss 1967; Glaser 1978; Glaser, 1992). Most qualitative researchers are not interested in forming universal generalizations, but in generating concepts or insights for future use. There are many ways of conducting qualitative research. Let's explore the following stages of qualitative research.

Data collection is a process of recording an event and gathering pertinent information. Following are some suggestions for collecting data. Start by writing first impressions, making a space map, called a *sociogram*, which requires following participant interactions and recording field notes to include dates and times and dialogues and gestures among participants. Use both audio (or video) tape recording as well as field notes that can be backup in case the electronic equipment fails. Photographs may add vividness to your research, but you can also sketch participants' artworks or artmaking in progress. Conduct a *sociocultural profile* by asking questions about the racial and economic background of the setting and its participants. Write to the Department of Commerce or local Chamber of Commerce for a community profile. Gather cultural documents such as a school mission statement, course of study, art curriculum, and art handouts for further interpretation. Reconstruct data that may be lacking such as a curriculum sequence or lesson plan objectives.

Transcribe your notes, other pertinent information, and findings into separate documents on the computer. Keep a running calendar of visits and events. Data should include site, date, class time, lesson description, and students' age levels, grades, class memberships, gender, and race. Note non-verbal behaviors and timing of events, called *time frequency*, which may be set approximately every five minutes. Anonymity is important. Use pseudonyms or initials of participants; otherwise, obtain signed and dated permission for release of participants' and school names. How many classes or how much time should you spend observing and analyzing? I use a rule of thumb of spending at least ten sessions once a week. Wolcott (1988) suggests one year or one complete cycle.

Ethnographic interviewing is a systematic process of asking questions in the form of a natural dialogue. Some interviews are highly structured in advance and others are more conversational (James, 1994). Since participants often do not take questionnaires seriously, it is advisable to follow-up questionnaires with informal interviews. Some questions may be open-ended but will need prompts to elicit information. For example, the question "what is art?" may need the following prompts: "drawing, creativity, expression, and other?" A good way to approach participants is to ask them to teach you about their educational situation so that you in turn can train university preservice teachers who will be visiting their institution. It is important to find key informants who are participants and appear willing to cooperate with you and give you extra information and insights.

Content analysis is a process of forming convincing suppositions, called propositions, from data and their content (Krippendorf, 1980). A supposition is a probable explanation. Some researchers borrow categories from previous research; other categories may emerge from the data in metaphoric forms. Write down evolving questions on an event at the beginning of your study and include them as assumptions. Keep a running account of how they change. Then compare them with evidence obtained over time. For example, on the Navajo reservation, the slow pace of classroom time overwhelmed me. I kept asking "What's happening?" and had to get coffee from the office to stay awake. I needed to slow down and focus my attention on specific actions, such as mere attending and sitting in silence (Stokrocki, 1995). Coming out of Cleveland's active, inner-city schools, I found it difficult to adjust to the Navajo's extreme quietness or nonaction. The Navajo believe that sitting and thinking is doing something. The students, however, produced marvelous artworks and the silence and reflection had a calming effect on me. Wolcott (1994) believes that self-criticism, as I just described, is a significant methodological finding.

Qualitative Forms of Research Methods

The stage of *content analysis* is used in discovering concepts (abstract ideas) and themes. Some concepts, such as lecturing, are simple, while other concepts, such as teaching, are complicated. A researcher must start the content analysis procedure with sorting categories. Bogdan and Biklen (1992) suggest the following starter categories: setting, participant views, process, activity, passages, stages, behaviors, and methods. These categories are *conceptual clusters*. An example of clustering concepts is putting all types of evaluation, scanned from your transcripts, into one category called appraisal instruction. These include examples such as testing, journals, checklists, and individual conferences. Thus, the researcher reduces all his/her field notes into simpler and more abstract codes. When doing content analysis, be sure to define all the categories and concepts.

Van Manen also suggests a line-by-line search of your field notes or documents for essential statements that later form themes (cited in Jeffers, 1992). Furthermore, I encourage using color, icon, or marginal codes to stand for the concepts. Make a key to explain your codes and colors and keep copies of your original transcripts.

To store and track data and to assist in my coding, I use the computer software program called "Hyperqual" (Padilla, 1993; See Figure 1). Although the program stores the information and helps you "tag and stack" it into files, you still have to do the hard work of analysis. Later, you can highlight your major findings throughout your final report.

Look for informal patterns or emerging concepts, such as repetitive words or ideas that are often hidden.[1] Temporarily use a simile or a metaphor to describe an emerging concept. A metaphor is a figure of speech that interrelates dissimilar things. In my study of Beittel's class, for instance, I noted how his off-the-cuff remarks, available to those nearest him, contained valuable instructional information. Emerging concepts may be part of the taken-for-granted folkways that you hardly notice. The Navajo, for example, consider silence or prolonged attention as valuable learning experiences. In certain cultures, listening and watching are more

---

[1] For example, keep running lists of instructional words, such as *kinds of appraisals:* flash (praise), inprocess, test, quiz, grading, checklist, matching, fill-in-the blanks, self-evaluation, art criticism, and assessment; *kinds of instruction:* lecture, demonstration, examples, discussion, questioning, debate, slides, and field trips.

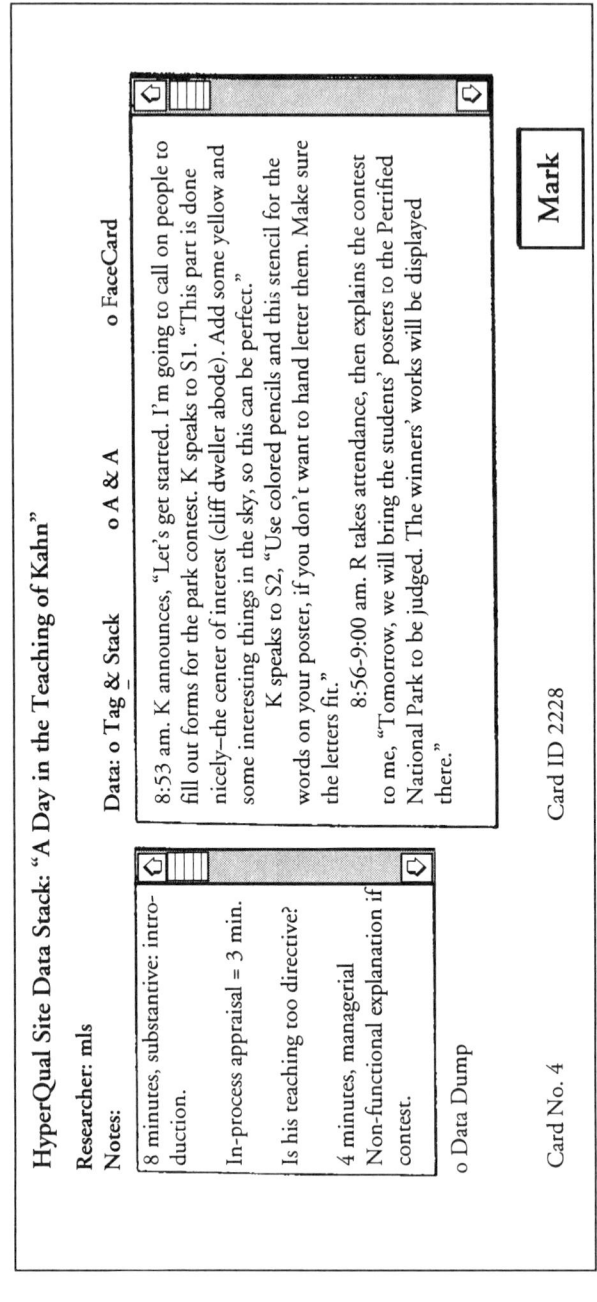

Figure 1
An Example of a Printout Using Software "Hyperqual"

[Note: Explanation of terms: mls=mary lou stokrocki; "Tag & Stack" button = select and put data chunks into files with a new tag or label; Data Dump = create/print separate files; Mark = to index this card like a bookmark.]

Qualitative Forms of Research Methods

Table 1

An Example of Time Sampling of T's High School Art I Instruction

Class Session	Substantive min. %	Managerial min. %	Appraisal min. %	Studio/Nonfunctional min. %	Total min. %
2/28/91					
period 1	5	5	0	40	50
period 2	5	3	3	39	50
3/1/91					
period 1	2	5	3	35	50
period 2	0	5	5	39	50
period 3	0	5	10	35	50
	(ART 1: pointillism, introduction to graduation cover design)				
period 4	(painting plant still life)				
period 5	(lunch)				
period 6	(prep)				
period 7	(ceramics)				
Total	12 min.	23 min.	21 min.	188 min.	
Average	3 min.	5 min.	4 min.	38 min.	50 min.
	6%	10%	8%	76%	100%

Note:
Substantive instruction is the introduction of new art content to the entire class.
Managerial instruction is the control of student behavior and classroom functioning.
In-process appraisal is the informal monitoring and guiding of student process and product.
Studio/nonfunctional instruction is that which is not related to the lesson, such as joking and interruptions.
Dominant Finding-Nonfunctional instruction; 76% of class time; thus teacher may be a *laissez-faire* instructor.

important than questioning. These kinds of concepts often are delivered informally and based on everyday language.

How do you know if you have found something important? Importance can be determined by frequent recurrence or emotional intensity. Qualitative researchers sometimes use quantitative measures, such as counting and time sampling. Time sampling is a process of measuring the frequency of an activity with a stop watch or tape recorder (Barker, 1968). In qualitative research, anything that occurs more than 50% of the time is frequent and important; for example, when a category is saturated with several examples it becomes worthy of attention (Bogdan & Bilken, 1992; Glaser & Strauss, 1967). Look for different dimensions of that category as well. Record this frequency of instruction in a chart. (see Table 1.)

Qualitative researchers also infer social significance, defined as the emotional impact of an event on participants. The participants may report an affective occurrence, such as a raku ceremony and celebration, as totally overwhelming. In my study of Beittel's pottery class, for example, students reported their experience as one of *communitas*, a state in which the social interactions were so special that they reached a stage of sacramental sharing, involvement, and creativity (Stokrocki, 1982). I suggest that you do not throw away any of your evidence; it may become significant later for a comparative study.

To start reporting, use an outline and make a table, graph, diagram, or chart to explain the process you arrived at to capture your data. Something as simple as a condensed checklist is quite handy for researchers to scan a large amount of information. For other ways of qualifying data see Miles and Huberman (1984). Then write up your report or essay. Do not forget to include sections on your mission statement, objectives, course of study, unit, and/or lesson plan. Ethnographers use a simple formula, such as a *paragraph construction,* for writing individual findings. In the first sentence, mention your conceptual finding. In the next sentence, define the concept. Then give a few examples of dialogue or anecdotes from the transcripts. In the last sentence summarize what you learned new about the concept. An example of reporting a finding follows.

Let me use a *laissez-faire* type of instruction to illustrate the workings of content analysis. Laissez-faire instruction is basically a noninterference teaching method that is used on the Navajo reservation. Because of the slow pace at the high school level, teaching seemed more laissez-faire. The instructor daily reviewed the ongoing lesson or briefly introduced a new project for approximately five minutes out of a 50-minute class session. [Refer to Table 1.] Mr. T wrote instructions on the blackboard and displayed art examples. He used excess time for coordinating extracurricular events. Mr. T challenged advanced students with photocopied lessons from Hubbard and Zimmerman's (1982) *Artstrands*. The instructor confessed, "I am laissez-faire because someone told me not to interrupt these kids so much when they are working. They are independent learners. I have an open-door policy, if they need help, they ask" (Stokrocki, 1995).

Look for alternative suppositions or explanations. For example, I reported this teacher's instructional style as laissez-faire in several of my observations. I checked for his interpretation and he agreed that he wasn't going to change. I looked for probable reasons: 1) he is sick or lazy; 2) it's his first year of teaching in this school and he is too busy adapting to this situation; 3) it's Friday and springtime, and he is preparing for the annual art show; or 4) he is teaching Native American students, who prefer independence and dislike questioning. You can report all the reasons and give the most probable explanations. Notice that the last explanation comes from a review of the literature (More, 1989). Here is where you step into the next research stage, that of comparative analysis.

How to Start Writing?

Wolcott (1988) suggests that you write your first draft while at the site; then you can ask more questions and fill in the gaps while there. Describe the context, participants, program, schedule, etc. Simply write the story. Some people need an outline; others start with a stream-of-consciousness writing style. I transcribe my field notes into the computer as I work and code simultaneously. Beginners need to show and separate the transcripts from the coding. Don't worry about grammar at first. Use major headings and subheadings throughout your research writing. State the limits of your study: time, person, site, malfunctioning equipment, and other problems.

How do you know when your study is complete? When the categories become saturated with several examples, you can estimate that you are temporarily finished. Due to space limitations for journal articles, three examples for each finding may be adequate. You will need to limit your focus later and some categories will become insignificant to be mentioned only briefly. To present information clearly, James (1994) uses charts, cognitive maps, diagrams of interviews, critiques, and lectures.

Table 2

A List of Findings

Contextual:
Improved quality [certified] and quantity of art teachers, but shortage of Navajo art teachers.
Students more non-traditional, bilingual, low socio-economic.
*Most teachers pleased with their supplies and facilities, but crowded due to expanding enrollments.[Collapse this insight into the next]
*Most teachers pleased with their teaching schedules and administrative support.
Lack of attendance a major problem at all high school levels.

Curricular:
A wide range of school missions existed.
Cultural continuity more evident at elementary level.
Vocational training major at high school.
Art programs mostly studio based, male-dominated: 3-D arts popular in West and 2-D arts, in the East.
**SNA art appreciation occasionally accompanied studio lessons.
Some artworks offensive.

Instructional:
Most substantive instruction began with sequenced demonstration and repetition of actions and words.
Facilitator teaching style and in-process appraisal instruction was dominant at all levels.
Relaxed control and teasing.

Preferential: Student art and learning
Older students were reticent in public discussion, whereas younger students seemed more confident.
Students' imagery was predominantly imitative, realistic, and eclectic.
Students preferred independence and observational learning style due to their strong recognition memory.
Deep concentration and seasonal lack of it.
^Reading comprehension problematic and helped through journalizing.
[* Collapse these findings and ^ remove the insignificant.]
** SNA refers to Standard Native American

Table 3

Comparative Analysis

Standard Native American	Standard American/European
[in common]	
traditional	non-traditional
preservation of tradition	**cultural change**
noninterference	interference-progress
small schools, little funding	rapid enrollments, federal funds
[improved facilities, small crowded]	
shortage of SNA art teachers	more Anglo and male teachers
[all certified]	
[wide range of schools and their missions]	
cultural emphasis at elementary	vocational at secondary
culture teacher	specialists
attendance — high school problem	
[art program: studio fine arts dominant]	
3D art preferred in west (Hopi)	2D art preferred in east
[influence of watercolor, perspective]	
[male-dominated curriculum]	
weaving introduced earlier	
borrowed beadwork & dream catchers	
[SNA art appreciation occasionally with studio lesson]	
taboo images [popular culture tolerated]	
teaching as showing(demonstration)	**teaching as lecture & questioning**
facilitator teaching style	directive teaching style
relaxed control and teasing	teacher controlled
informal, in-process appraisal	formal appraisal
perceptual learning style	**conceptual learning style**
HS students independent & observational learning	
no high school public discussion	public discussion
{discussion now at elementary level}	
draw from memory	**draw what you see**
2-dimensional, copied realistic images	3-D realistic drawing from still life
more outlined and flat color	more shading

(Highlighted words are major comparisons)

What is Comparative Analysis and How Do you Do It?

Comparative analysis is a process of interrelating findings or explanations in one class session or several class sessions to form suppositions (propositional insights). Interrelation consists of both *internal analysis* (within your own study) and *external analysis* (comparisons with other cases and the related literature). If you compare two or more of your observed, class sessions, you are using *internal comparative analysis*. When you include evidence from related research or local experts to support your interrelated findings, you are using *external comparative analysis*. Present your proposition, give an internal example (to refresh the reader's memory), and add external support. State that your findings are tentative, exploratory, incomplete, or working hypotheses. To start comparative analysis, I suggest the following:

Use a chart or check list. If you use the Hyperqual (Padilla, 1993) software computer program, "tag & stack" all your subheadings or findings into one file. Merge some of the findings into a more inclusive file. Interconnect them as on a bulletin board. Then make a contrasting chart. On one side, put your explanatory finding, and on the other side place opposite or alternative ones (see Tables 2 and 3). Remember that you are looking for possible explanations or interpretations to make sense of your data. In this way, you can interrelate the data and gain more insights into your inquiry.

Report your comparative findings by using the same paragraph formula as discussed above. The paragraph will be longer and expand into a section. An example follows:

In-process appraisal instruction was the dominant form of instruction at all levels (on the Navajo Reservation). In-process appraisal is the individual monitoring of work in process with alternative suggestions (Sevigny, 1978). The Anglo and Navajo art teachers interacted more with their elementary students than their secondary students. For example, "D," the new Anglo teacher at the primary level (CPS) and "W", the new Navajo elementary art teacher (MFES), spent nearly 50% of their time informally appraising students at work. More specifically, both "L's" (CBS) and "D's" (CPS) lessons on watercolor painting devoted 30 minutes, out of 40 minutes, to individual attention. They constantly reminded students to use water first. "M" further directed, "You don't want to see the edges of the watercolor lines." He suggested that another student use a bigger brush. Later, he suggested to a third student to blend in some orange color while the leaf was still drying. Appraisals, however, were most often flash comments: "That's different or neat!" (Stokrocki, 1995).

A *focus group*, which marketing researchers often employ, consists of a small group of informants who meet to discuss only a few questions or findings. The focus group is particularly helpful in culturally diverse situations (Krueger, 1994; Sikes, 1992). Similar to inter-judge or inter-rater reliability, a group of external local experts or outside art teachers can verify, refute, or add to your interpretation.

Other studies provide external comparison. For example: Erickson and Mohatt (1982) first videotaped and studied communication differences in Native American and Anglo teachers. They noticed that Native American teachers spent most of their time circulating the room and giving individual attention. In comparison, I found in my study (Stokrocki, 1995) that all teachers, both Native American and Anglo, evaluated students' progress privately, informally, and mostly based on effort.

Comparisons with extreme cases can strengthen your findings, build or generate new insights, and lead to grounded theory (Glaser & Strauss, 1967). An extreme case is a situation where a practice failed or where it was problematic, such as "the class from hell" or teaching junior high students (Stokrocki, 1988). Report issues in a chart that feature pros and cons. You are also doing cross-cultural comparative analysis, if you compare two teachers from different cultures. You can record the contextual or cultural differences through similar research found in a review of the literature. Finally, you can generate grounded theory from preliminary lists of propositions or hypotheses (Glaser & Strauss, 1967). For example, Ritenour (1983) collected data through unstructured taped interviews of 12 artists, from which he generated a list of qualifications (conceptual categories: time, social, environmental, and conflict) and preliminary propositions. He later revised the propositions and reported them both in a running theoretical discussion and as a list of conclusions. The extreme cases in this study evolved from personal and family conflicts that resulted in major lifestyle changes.

How to Write Conclusions

Conclusions are significant findings that you discovered about the concepts in the title of your study. Some qualitative researchers list major propositions and others generate them differently. I pin up my entire study on a bulletin board to track major concepts (in my title or in my research questions) and color code them throughout my paper. My recent paper (Stokrocki, 1995), for example, "A Microethnographic Study of Art Teaching on the Navajo Reservation," begins with a section explaining the concepts in the title (microethnographic, art, teaching, & Navajo). At the end of my paper, I check to include what I learned about these concepts. What you are doing at this point in your research is condensing or collapsing the data further. You can include conflicting results here (see Table 3).

If you can't find significant conclusions, review and raise questions about related concepts or theories, send your paper for review and solicit suggestions, and invite collaboration and competing opinions (Wolcott, 1994). Be honest about what you did not find and what microethnographic methods did not work. Mention that future research is needed and in what areas such research is needed.

What is Cross-Site Analysis and How Do You Do It?

If you compare several qualitative sites, you are doing external comparisons or *cross-site analysis*. *Cross-site analysis* is a process of interrelating findings from several contexts to generate themes which may be used to develop new theory (Miles & Huberman, 1984). Cross-site analysis also increases generalizations that reassure researchers that themes and problems in one setting are not entirely unique. For example, I am the sole author of my cross-site analyses (Stokrocki, 1989). Other researchers may compile their individual case studies in one volume for readers to compare (Day, Eisner, Stake, Wilson, & Wilson, 1984), or a review team may compare the findings of the previous studies in one document (McLaughlin & Thomas, 1984).

Cross-site analysis is a constant comparative method of developing theory analytically that is generating categories and their properties (Glaser, 1978). Steps entail the following: 1) start to gather information, 2) search for major issues or patterns in the information that become the central categories, 3) look for several examples of these categories, 4) describe and explain these categories, while looking for new ones, 5) interrelate social processes to develop an evolving model, and 6) employ sampling and coding devices to focus the analysis on the central categories (adapted from Bogdan & Biklen, 1992).

More specifically, I have been using a Macintosh spreadsheet software program called "MicroExel," which has numbered lines and in which you can set up working categories. I use it as a kind of shorthand to track my concepts and cross-check the frequency of my findings as well. I use several spreadsheets to manage my data in this way.

What is the Future of Qualitative Research?

Narrative Storytelling

Barone (1992) argues for translating research data into "morally persuasive" stories and other narrative forms to make research more accessible to the general public. He notes the historical work of Charles Dickens and Kidder's (1989) more recent book, *Among Schoolchildren,* as convincing examples that stirred change in education. Art educators have also interpreted their research data into different experiential formats, such as a parable (Mason, 1980), a play (Stokrocki, 1982), personal cultural histories (Zurmuehlen, 1990), and tales of women's lives (Kellman, 1992/93). Wolcott (1994) suggests such different representational modes as the mystery, chronicle, life-cycle, and the Roshoman effect (a story told from three viewpoints). I translated my ethnographic research experiences on the Navajo Reservation into a story of "A School Day in the Life of a Young Navajo Girl: A Case Study in Ethnographic Storytelling" (Stokrocki, 1994). I changed my researcher voice into that of a young Navajo girl to paint a picture of the changing context and I added the actual transcript description of a clay lesson through her point of view introducing it as her favorite class. I later discussed such inherent issues as authenticity, authority, religious differences and cultural dynamics, representation and negotiation, and changing gender differences. I encourage you also to translate your research into some qualitatively visual and verbal art form.

Collaborations and Methodological Mix

The future of qualitative research will entail a collaboration of polyphonic voices of teachers, researchers, graduate students, and others who are trying to understand an educational experience. Bogdan and Biklen (1992) regard such attempts as *action research*, "the systematic collection of information that is designed to bring about social change. The researcher is actively involved in the study's cause" (p. 223). *Action research* often involves teachers as actively involved in the research process (May, 1993).

Art experiences go beyond mere schooling and now encompass all folkways and forms of life-long learning. Research begins with understanding and ends in social action. The future will see the mix of various qualitative and quantitative methods to suit particular questions and sites (Wolcott, 1988). As our computers become more sophisticated and are able to handle large information data bases, research methods will become complex. At times, research results end in policy decisions and at other times they simply enlighten our knowledge of idiosyncratic events.

References

Barone, T. (1992). A narrative of enhanced professionalism: Educational researchers and popular storybooks about school people. *Educational Researcher, 21* (8), 15-24.

Barker, R. (1968). *Ecological psychology: Conceptual methods for studying the environment.* Stanford, CA: Stanford University Press.

Beittel, K. (1973). *Alternatives for art education research.* Dubuque, IA: Wm. C Brown.

Blaikie, L. (1994). A case study on art education in a township high school in South Africa: Donatello in Kwa Mashu — It's absurd. Seminar for Research in Art Education *Abstracts of Research Presentations.* Baltimore: MD: Maryland Institute, College of Art.

Bogdan, R., & Biklen, S. (1992). *Qualitative research for education* (2nd ed.). Boston: Allyn and Bacon.

Chen. M. F. (1993). Art, culture, and Chinese-American students: An on-going case study at a Chinese community-based school. In Zurmuehlen (Ed.), *Working papers in art education* (pp. 3-21). Iowa City, IA; University of Iowa.

Clifford, J. (1988). *The predicament of culture.* Cambridge, MA: Harvard University Press.

Day, M., Eisner, E., Stake, R., Wilson, B., & Wilson, M. (1984). *Art history, art criticism, and art production: An examination of art education in selected school districts.* Santa Monica, CA: Rand for the Getty Center for Education in the Arts.

Denzin, N., & Lincoln, Y. (Eds.). (1994). *Handbook of qualitative research.* Thousand Oaks, CA: Sage.

Eisner, E. (1991). *The enlightened eye: Qualitative inquiry and the enhancement of educational practice.* New York: Macmillan.

Erickson, F. & Mohatt, G. (1982). Cultural organizations of participation structures in two classrooms of Indian students. In G. Spindler (Ed.), *Doing the ethnography of schooling* (pp. 132-174). Prospect Heights, IL: Waveland.

Gadamer, H. G. (1975). *Truth and method.* New York: Continuum.

Geertz, C. (1973). *The interpretation of cultures.* New York: Basic Books.

Glaser, B. (1978). *Theoretical sensitivity: Advances in the methodology of grounded theory.* Mill Valley, CA: Sociology Press.

Glaser, B (1992). *Basics of grounded theory analysis.* Mill Valley, CA: Sociology Press.

Glaser, B., & Strauss, A. (1967). *The discovery of grounded theory.* Chicago: Aldine.

Hubbard, G., & Zimmerman, E. (1982). *Artstrands: A program of individualized art instruction.* Chicago: Waveland Press.

James. P. (1994). The construction of learning in a sculpture studio classroom: An ethnographic study. (Doctoral dissertation, University of Minnesota, 1994). University Microfilms # 9424315.

Jeffers, C. (1992). Research as art and art as research: A living relationship. *Art Education, 46* (5), 12-17.

Kellman, J. (1992/93). Threads between worlds: Multiculturalism in a Guatemalan [Mayan] school. *Journal of Multicultural and Cross-cultural Research in Art Education, 10/11,* 101-110.

Kidder, T. (1989). *Among schoolchildren.* Boston: Houghton Mifflin.

Krippendorf, K. (1980). *Content analysis: An introduction to its methodology.* Beverly Hills, CA: Sage.

Krueger, R. (1994). *Focus groups: A practical guide for applied research.* Thousand Oaks, CA: Sage.

Lincoln, Y., & Guba, E. (Eds.). (1985).*Naturalistic inquiry.* Beverly Hills, CA: Sage.

Maitland-Gholson, J., & Ettinger, L. (1994). Interpretive decision making in research. *Studies in Art Education, 36* (1), 18-27.

Mason, R. (1980). Interpretation and artistic understanding (Doctoral dissertation, The Pennsylvania State University, 1980). *Dissertation Abstracts International, 41* (05A), 2002.

Mason, R. (1988). *Art education and multiculturalism.* New York: Methuen.

Mason, R. (1993). Artistic achievement in Japanese junior high schools. *Art Education, 47* (1), 8-19.

May, W. (1993). "Teachers-as-researchers" or action research: What is it, and what good is it for art education? *Studies in Art Education, 34* (2), 114-126.

McLaughlin, M. W., & Thomas, M. A.. (Eds.). (1984). *Art history, art criticism, art production. Vol. 1: Comparing the process of change across districts.* Santa Monica, CA: Rand.

Miles, M., & Huberman, M. (1984). *Qualitative data analysis: A sourcebook of new methods.* Newbury Park, CA: Sage.

More, A. (1989). Native American learning styles: A review for researchers and teachers. *Journal of American Indian Education* — Special issue [no number], 15-27.

Padilla, R. (1993). *Hyperqual II*, v.1. software and the *Hyperqual User's Guide*, v.5.0; revised edition; 3327 N. Dakota, Chandler, AZ 85225.

Patton, M. (1990). *Qualitative evaluation and research methods* (2nd ed.). Newbury Park, CA: Sage.

Pinar, W. (1975). *Curriculum theorizing: The reconceptualists.* Berkeley, CA: McCutchan.

Pohland, P. (1976). Participant observation as a research methodology. *Studies in Art Education, 13* (3), 4-24.

Ritenour, J. (1983). Art production by selected artists. As effected by personal and family relationships. (Doctoral dissertation, Arizona State University, 1983). DAI-A 44/02.

Sevigny, M. (1978). A descriptive study of instructional interaction and performance appraisal in a university studio art setting: A multiple perspective. (Doctoral dissertation, The Ohio State University, 1977). *Dissertation Abstracts International, 38,* 6477-A.

Shumaker, E. (1986). What did they say? A content analysis of Art Education, 1948-1984. *Art Education, 34* (6), 35.

Sikes, M. (1992). Interpreting the Heard Museum as a metaphoric structure: A critical and ethnographic study (Doctoral dissertation, Florida State University, 1992). *Dissertation Abstracts International, 53* (3), 694-A.

Smith, L. (1978). An evolving logic of participant observation, educational ethnography, and other case studies. In L. S. Shulman (Ed.). *Review of Research in Education, 6* (pp. 316-377). Ithasca, IL: I.E. Peacock for the American Educational Research Association.

Spradley, J. (1980). *Participant observation.* New York: Harcourt, Brace, Jovanovich.

Stake, R. (1988). Case study methods on educational research: Seeking sweet water. In R. Jaeger (Ed.). *Complementary methods for research in art education* (pp. 253-273). Washington, DC: American Education Research Association.

Stokrocki, M. (1982). Spheres of meaning: A qualitative description and interpretation of an art learning environment (Doctoral dissertation, The Pennsylvania State University, 1981).*Dissertation Abstracts International, 42 (08), 3394-A.*

Stokrocki, M. (1983). Interpretation theory: Its meaning and application to art education. *Canadian Review of Art Education Research, 10,* 13-25.

Stokrocki, M. (1986). The dimensions of an art learning environment. Journal of *Art Education, 39* (2), 18-21.

Stokrocki, M. (1988). Teaching preadolescents during a nine-week sequence: The negotiator approach. *Studies in Art Education, 30* (1), 37-46.

Stokrocki, M. (1989). A cross-site analysis: Problems in teaching art to adolescents. *Studies in Art Education, 31* (2), 106-117.

Stokrocki, M. (1991). A decade of qualitative research in art education: Methodological expansions and pedagogical explorations. *Visual Arts Research, 17* (1), 42-51.

Stokrocki, M. (1994). A school day in the life of a young Navajo girl: A case study in ethnographic storytelling. *Art Education , 47* (4), 61-69.

Stokrocki, M. (1995). An exploratory microethnographic study of art teaching in one Navajo public school system: The Anglo view of Running Water. In H. Kauppinen & R. Diket (Eds.). *Trends in art education from diverse cultures* (pp. 181-191). Reston, VA: National Art Education Association.

Strauss, A., & Corbin, J. (1990). *Basics of qualitative research: Grounded theory procedures and techniques.* Newbury Park, CA: Sage.

Stuhr. P. (1986). A field research study which analyses ethnic values and aesthetic/art education: As observed in Wisconsin Indian community schools. Paper presented at the American Education Research Association. San Francisco. [ERIC ED276540]

Thomas, J. (1993). *Doing critical ethnography.* Newbury Park, CA: Sage.

van Manen, M. (1984). *Doing phenomenological research and writing.* Monograph No. 7. Edmonton: University of Alberta.

Willis, G. (1978). Qualitative evaluation as the aesthetic, personal, and political dimensions of curriculum criticism. In G. Willis (Ed). *Qualitative evaluation: Concepts and cases in curriculum criticism* (pp. 2-18). Berkekey, CA: McCutchan.

Wolcott, H. (1988). Ethnographic research in education. In R. Jaeger (Ed.). *Complementary methods for research in art education* (pp. 187-206). Washington, DC: American Education Research Association.

Wolcott, H. (1994). *Transforming qualitative data.* Thousand Oaks, CA: Sage.

Zurmuehlen, M. (1990). *Studio art: Praxis, symbol, presence.* Reston, VA: National Art Education Association.

Historical Research Methods in Art Education

Sound historical inquiry requires thorough, painstaking compilation of facts, critical reading of both primary and secondary sources, careful notetaking, and establishment of chronologies documenting *who* did *what where* and *when*. Well-written historical accounts also require attention to *why*, development of a narrative interpretation of facts that makes them meaningful and explains their significance to readers who are distant from the events recorded. Historical research has two sides, with two different but complementary sets of skills.

Historical accounts of American art education began to be written soon after Walter Smith left Massachusetts in 1883 to return to England. Perhaps the earliest chronicler was Isaac Edwards Clarke whose four-volume congressional report on *Art and Industry* shaped subsequent interpretations (Clarke, 1885, 1892, 1897, 1898; Efland & Soucy, 1991; Soucy, 1990) .

In an 1893 paper for the International Congress of Art Instruction held in Chicago in conjunction with the World's Columbian Exposition, Mary Dana Hicks (1895) described three stages in the growth of American art education: first, teaching drawing as a means of improving industrial products; second, teaching drawing as a means of developing mental abilities; and, third, providing a broader art instruction with an aesthetic focus to help students perceive and express "the beautiful." These historical accounts by Clarke and Hicks represent two different approaches to historical research. We can describe Clarke's approach as that of a compiler and Hicks as a shaper.

MARY ANN STANKIEWICZ
Independent Scholar & Consultant

Clarke focused on gathering historical facts. He collected and reprinted documents that he judged important to the development of fine and industrial art education in the United States. Clarke's compilation has the appearance of objectivity. His four volumes with their numerous appendices seem so comprehensive that most historians of art education have used the documents he reprinted as primary sources without considering that certain values governed his selection (Efland & Soucy, 1991). Clarke can be regarded as an early example of a *positivist* or *scientific historian* of art education. Scientific historians, often followers of the 19th century German historian Leopold von Ranke, believe that it is possible to tell what *really* happened in the past by collecting facts and presenting them in chronological order. Scientific historians, like Clarke, perform a great service by compiling and editing collections of primary sources (Gottschalk, 1969); however, they tend to ignore the fact that their apparently objective history is the result of a process of selection in which some facts are chosen and others ignored.

Hicks, on the other hand, was less interested in compiling documents and historical facts than in shaping the past for present use. This approach has been labeled *historicist* and attributed to Wilhelm Dilthey, another 19th century German who was both a philosopher and historian. Dilthey argued that we are all part of history, and that no one can stand outside of history (as scientific historians seem to claim to do) discovering and documenting objective facts about the past. He argued that historians must imaginatively and empathetically enter the point of view of a past era or person; understanding the past is the result of imaginative re-creation, not the automatic outcome of collecting facts. Dilthey and his followers also believed that historians were constrained by contemporary values; thus, all research on the past was governed by contemporary needs. In her 1895 paper, Hicks used her understanding of two decades of changing rationales for art education practice in order to develop a justification for the place of art in public schooling. Many other art educators since Hicks' day have used the history of art education to justify certain practices over others.

Not only was Hicks putting the past in service of present needs, but she was creating an overarching interpretive framework, a modest version of the grand schemes conceived by historians like Spengler and Toynbee (Barzun & Graff, 1977). Documenting past facts was less important to Hicks than finding meaning in them. Hicks focused on the interpretation of the past in an attempt to make past ideas and events meaningful by putting them into the context of an overarching pattern and explaining their usefulness to present problems.

Historical Research Methods and Methodologies for Art Education

Although historians of art education, in the century since Clarke and Hicks, often have leaned toward either compiling facts or shaping interpretive patterns, the best historical research does both. The methods of history are both scientific and artful (see Table 1 for an overview of historical research processes). My goals in this chapter are: (1) to help those interested in writing art education history better understand how history of art education is related to other forms of history, particularly to history of education and art history; (2) to suggest ways to identify fruitful topics for historical research; (3) to discuss primary and secondary sources and their uses in historical research; (4) to explain issues of authenticity and credibility in historical research methods; and (5) to discuss questions of interpretation and narrative, the art of history. I will use examples from my own research as well as citations from selected writings on art education history.

This chapter is not definitive; it is meant to be suggestive and provocative. Anyone interested in serious research into the history of art education would benefit from reading history and reflecting on the approaches and strengths of other historians. Courses in historical research methods, history of education and its methods, art history and methods, oral history, and the study of material culture

---

Table 1

Overview of Historical Research Processes

I. Select a topic to research
   A. Look for gaps and anomalies in written histories of art education
   B. Choose a topic that is personally meaningful and significant to the field of art education
II. Compile facts from primary and secondary sources
   A. Read written sources; listen to oral testimonies; look at pictures, ephemera, objects and artifacts
   B. Establish the authenticity and credibility of sources
   C. Prepare chronologies, i.e., charts showing what happened when
III. Write a narrative that interprets the facts through a meaningful story that will hold a reader's interest

are all useful in providing tools that can be adapted to the specific needs of art education history. This chapter is only a beginning.

What Is History of Art Education?

Just as art education is sometimes considered a hybrid discipline, related to both art and education, so history of art education has ties both to history of education and art history. Art education is concerned with the theory and practice of teaching and learning in the visual arts. Thus, some histories of art education may be thought of as a subset of curriculum history within general education, for example, Efland's *History of Art Education* (1990) and Wygant's *School Art in American Cultures, 1820-1970* (1993). However, recent history of education, following Cremin's (1977) broadened definition of education, has moved beyond the history of curriculum, biographies of past educational leaders, or even histories of school systems and other educational institutions. One challenge facing revisionist historians of education has been to extend the definition of education beyond schools and school systems without becoming "hopelessly adrift" in a world where every aspect of socialization can be considered a form of education (Kaestle, 1988, p. 64).

Although art teaching and learning often occur in K-12 schooling or in post-secondary institutions, art education is not limited to those sites. Art education can be found in museums, community centers, and social service agencies that provide afterschool and vacation programs for young people. Art education can serve people of all ages in settings that range from nursery schools through senior centers. Adult art education programs can be offered at work sites or in jails and prisons. Although some art programs at hospitals or drug rehabilitation facilities are more therapeutic than educational, art education can be found in these settings as well. All of these programs can provide starting points for historical research. Papers presented at the 1985 and 1989 Penn State conferences on the history of art education have addressed art education in Victorian periodicals and professional journals, in woman's clubs and the military, via radio and through exhibitions (Amburgy, Soucy, Stankiewicz, Wilson, & Wilson, 1992; Wilson & Hoffa, 1985). Just as educational historians have shifted their attention beyond the schoolhouse walls, so have historians of art education.

While art education history may have a breadth similar to educational history, its focus is more clearly defined because it addresses the visual arts. Some researchers may regard their work in history of art education as a subset of history of education, with similar interests and goals, however, the relationship of art education history to art history is more tenuous. Art history has traditionally focused on high quality works created within a fine arts tradition by recognized artists (Kultermann, 1993; Roskill, 1976). Some art historians develop comprehensive lists and descriptions of work by individual artists. Some practice connoisseurship, attributing works to artists based on the careful study of details in the art work. Other art historians analyze subjects and symbols, practicing iconography and iconology respectively as they move from describing and classifying subjects to identifying "the deeper meaning or content of a work of art" (Kleinbauer & Slavens, 1982, p. 76). There are documentary art historians as well as object-centered art historians. The former may use research methods that are more like those of historians in general, rather than methods such as connoisseurship or iconography which are specific to art history (Belting, 1987). In recent years the practice of art history has been influenced by psychology, Marxism, feminism, critical theory, and developments in literary criticism, such as semiotics and deconstruction (Minor, 1994; Rees & Borzello, 1986).

History of art education may be grounded in aesthetic assumptions similar to those which have provided theoretical bases for the art historian. On the other hand, historians of art education have the freedom to examine art-related objects which fall outside the purview of high art. Historians of art education have tended to focus more on the role of art in the education of nonartists than on changes in the education of artists. Historians of art education are more apt to study children's drawings than masterpieces created by artists.

Nonetheless, there are points of contact, and points where more contact would be desirable. Some art educators have paid more attention to the juvenalia of past artists than have art historians; their knowledge of children's artistic development helps them understand these youthful works in a different way than the art historian (Pariser, 1985, 1995). When art historians study art schools and academies, historians of art education can help them place these specialized institutions into larger educational contexts. An art historian might wonder about Walter Smith's contribution to the diffusion of the aesthetic movement in the United States; an historian of art education can explain why Smith was brought to Massachusetts and his impact on art instruction (Stein, 1986). Korzenik's *Drawn to Art* (1985b) looks at how children in one 19th century family learned to draw and how they became artists. The two boys and one girl in the Cross family were not major figures in American art. Thus, their story would probably have fallen outside the interests of most art historians, but Korzenik's book is now a recognized contribution to both American art history and history of art education. An historian of art education can also look at the development of art history instruction with an alternative perspective than that of the art historian who assumes that the teaching of art history began at Harvard, Princeton, and Yale, excluding smaller liberal arts colleges, women's colleges, and secondary schools (Stankiewicz, 1994). Historians of art education can help broaden perspectives and interpretations of art historians.

Historians of art education can learn from art historians as well. Historians of art education can examine how school art relates to movements in fine and commercial art, to folk and ethnic arts, drawing on art historical research on genres, periods, and styles. They can pay closer attention to visual qualities of school art, of reproductions, of work created by artists whose art education may have been far from mainstream academic traditions. Historians of art education also might think about examining art works by art educators and comparing their written and visual work. Graduate students interested in exploring history of art education as a research area should look to art history not just for content, but also for methods of conducting research. The new art history looks outside traditional fine art boundaries; feminist and Marxist art historians are sources of alternate interpretive frames for art education history.

While art education history has close ties to history of education and to art history, it has the potential to be genuinely interdisciplinary when researchers draw on intellectual and cultural history, the study of material culture, American studies, cultural studies, labor history, feminist history, and other disciplines. Historians of art education have relied on secondary sources from intellectual history for many years, tracing ideas developed by intellectuals through general education into art education (Efland, 1990: Stankiewicz, 1984, 1987). More recently historians of art education have examined art education in the context of popular and high culture, the current events of a period, and larger social spheres (Wygant, 1993). More work in history of art education as related to cultural history is needed. Historians of art education in search of histories that capture the realities of the classroom have begun to use material objects as catalysts for research and as sources of information (Korzenik, 1983), but more research is needed here as well (Lubar & Kingery, 1993; Schlereth, 1982). The fields of American studies and cultural studies (Wolff, 1984) are growing domains of knowledge; historians of art education can benefit from using writings in these areas as secondary sources and investigating current interests in these fields. For example, labor history is useful for art educators who want to look at the past in relation to industrialization and issues of class. Feminist history has much to offer a field in which the majority of practitioners have been women while the historically recognized leaders were men. Collins and Sandell (1984) have suggested that

Historical Research Methods and Methodologies for Art Education

the current status of art education resulted, at least in part, from a tendency to regard art as a feminine interest in a social context which devalues both art and women. The aspiring historian of art education should begin by exploring at least one area of special-interest history in order to become familiar with alternative interpretations of the past and how other historical researchers conduct their work.

Oral history has grown out of the work of ethnographers and folklorists. It differs from most of the approaches above because it offers a methodology that can be applied to various areas of history, rather than existing as an area of content itself. Art educators have been using audio and videotapes to record biographies of leaders in the field for several years (Garber, 1993; Smith, 1995), but oral history can also record the voices of local art educators or stories of how everyday people learned the visual arts (Stankiewicz & Zimmerman, 1985; Zimmerman & Stankiewicz, 1982). Oral history provides a useful counterbalance to research methods based on art history, because it tends to focus on ordinary people, traditional ways of doing things, and stories and beliefs that sometimes are taken for granted or devalued when compared with elitist approaches to art and culture that focus on higher social classes, avant-garde trends, and intellectual theories.

What Is the Question?

There are many possible topics for historical research in art education. The challenge lies in asking questions that will make past events meaningful to contemporary audiences. The best topics are those which allow the researcher to build on personal interests (after all, you will be living with the study for quite a while) and to explore issues that have continuing significance for the field. Korzenik (1985a; 1995) has suggested that students look for empty spaces in the chronology of art education, then begin to ask questions about topics that might fill in the gaps. She emphasizes the personal stake that her graduate students have developed in their research topics, pointing out that interest in some topics increased or declined depending on trends in local schools from 1973 to 1993. Bolin (1995) recommends that researchers take time to reflect on their choices of topics, asking themselves, among other questions, why they selected specific topics and what significance the topics might have for others.

In contrast with Korzenik's (1985a) recommendation to identify "empty holes" in art education's past, Efland has argued that often a research problem or question comes "from a perceived anomaly" (1995, p. 57). In my own experience, both thin places in the written history of art education and odd pieces that do not seem to fit the expected pattern of the fabric of written history are indications of a topic in need of research. For example, Efland mentions that public schools in the late 19th century "came under the domination of the middle class" (1990, p. 147), but does not provide evidence for this assertion nor explain why the middle class began to dominate schooling. Given the assumption that drawing was introduced into Massachusetts public schools in 1870 for the working classes, a shift to art education for middle-class students indicates both an anomaly and an empty hole in need of research.

Bolin (1995) describes doing history as an interactive process. Historical research (what I have referred to as compiling the facts) goes hand-in-hand with historical inquiry (shaping those facts into a meaningful narrative). During this process, questions usually arise that will lead to new projects. Often, new research problems will emerge from applying present theories to past events. For example, Apple (1990) suggests that curriculum researchers ask ideological questions as they study contemporary schooling. These same questions can fruitfully be asked when one is doing research into past curricula and may result in new questions and research problems, as the researcher's growing understanding leads to recognition of previously unnoticed holes and anomalies.

Detective Work: Primary and Secondary Sources

Historians have long made a distinction between primary and secondary sources. Primary sources are those created by participants in the events studied. They can include personal journals or diaries, letters, student art works, photographs of art educators and their classrooms, lesson plans, publications such as professional periodicals or conference proceedings, curriculum documents, and other oral, written, or visual sources. The rule of thumb is that documents created closer to the time of the event studied are likely to be more reliable than later versions (Gottschalk, 1969). However, as I shall discuss, primary sources must be regarded critically even when they appear to be authentic and credible.

Secondary sources are those written about an historical event after the fact and must be treated even more cautiously and critically. For example, Clarke (1885) reprints an 1875 letter from Walter Smith to John Eaton, U. S. Commissioner of Education, describing his proposed program for industrial art education in Massachusetts. Smith's letter in the Appendix to Clarke's report may be considered a primary source for its content, but any discussion of Smith and his work in Massachusetts written by Clarke in his chapters is a secondary source.

Historians identify at least four ways to use secondary sources. First, they may provide contextual information on the place or period so that each historian does not have to start from a blank canvas. Next, secondary sources are mines of information for other sources, both secondary and primary. Often a bibliographic essay will list the archives used, perhaps describe the collections, or acknowledge the archivist by name. This information is valuable in preparing research plans. Third, secondary sources may be used to suggest hypotheses or potential interpretations; here is where Bolin's interactive process of historical research and historical inquiry begins to bear fruit. Fourth, sometimes a secondary source will include a direct quotation from an original source that cannot be found. Although it is better to locate the primary source and make sure it really says and implies what the secondary source says it does, a researcher can cite the secondary source and also indicate that it contained a quotation from an original source.

Locating written primary and secondary sources depends on knowing how to use libraries and archives effectively (Stankiewicz, 1982). Library catalogs, whether card catalogs or on-line versions, provide preliminary information on books and periodicals. Reference materials can help the researcher locate facts, find archival collections, locate authoritative secondary sources, and lay the groundwork for extended research. Just as a good detective should gather a variety of forms of evidence in order to solve a case, historical researchers must compile historical facts before determining what shape the narrative will take. Facts for history of art education, however, do not reside only in books or written archival records. The historian of art education should read extensively, but also be comfortable with oral history methods that require listening (Ives, 1974), and with methods from art history or material culture studies that require careful looking and interpretations from images, objects, and other visual sources (Handlin, 1979). Oral history archives, rare book rooms, print and photograph collections, museums with their archives and libraries can all be sites for the detective work of historical research. Many historians of art education develop their own collections of primary and secondary source materials, haunting used book stores in search of treasures. Korzenik (1985b) found an extensive collection of family papers and artworks through her connections with an antique dealer. As she describes her initial sight of the collection, she reminds us that it was only because of her prior research that she understood the potential significance of the Cross papers.

While historians have been working with private collections, archives, libraries, and museums for hundreds of years, historians of art education in the late 20th century have access to computer-assisted resources. From my home computer, with a modem and link to the Internet, I can access on-line library catalogs in other states. I can download and print a paper copy of an ERIC Digest that gives me a quick overview of current developments in educational theory and practice or a document from ERIC/Art. I can locate recent newspaper or magazine articles that might be useful secondary sources. If my computer has multimedia capabilities and a connection to the World-Wide Web, I can vicariously visit the city where an archive or museum is located, perhaps even learn more about the museum's collections and its hours. I have used my computer, modem, and on-line service to plan a trip to the Library of Congress, even reserving the books I needed in advance. Computers, fiber-optic networks, and other technological advancements will have a powerful impact on the detective work of historical research, an impact that cannot be predicted at this point. These technologies, and their capabilities for putting information into new forms and creating new images, will make the historian's traditional methods of internal and external criticism even more important.

Questions of Method: External and Internal Criticism

Historical research traditions center around two major methods of inquiry: *authenticity* or *external criticism*, and *credibility* or *internal criticism* (Barzun and Graff, 1977; Bloch, 1953; Gottschalk, 1969; Hockett, 1955; Nevins, 1962; Tuchman, 1981). *External criticism*, used to verify the authenticity of sources, requires examining whether a primary source is the kind of document it appears to be, whether it is genuine, as well as determining what the author was trying to communicate. *Internal criticism* examines the believability of the source, the author's meaning, the truthfulness of the testimony, and the competence of the witnesses.

One of my first encounters with a problem of authenticity occurred during a repeat visit to an archive. When I first started work on this particular project, the papers I was working on had not been completely processed, that is, prepared for the use of researchers. Although much of the material had been organized in folders by categories, some boxes contained correspondence in unopened envelopes and materials in the forms in which they had been brought into the archive. By my second visit, the work of processing had moved forward, inspired, I like to think, at least partly by my interest in the collection. Several newly processed letters had been placed in correspondence files dated in the 1950s. As I read these letters, they rang false. The content suggested that people whose friendship had begun around the time of the First World War were writing as if places and events from that period were recurring in the 1950s. The envelopes and postmarks that had helped me date some of the unprocessed material had been removed in processing, but I could locate correspondence from the 1920s with clearly established dates and demonstrate to the director of the archives that the material had not been accurately filed. The authenticity of letters had been put into question by a processor unfamiliar with European conventions for postmarking and dating letters.

The Henry Turner Bailey (1865-1931) Papers at the University of Oregon have given me opportunities to practice internal criticism.[1] These papers are a wonderful source for the historian of art education; the university acquired published materials along with unpublished documents, so several versions of lectures and articles can be compared. Bailey also kept a personal diary and sketchbooks, as well as a professional journal in which he recorded business trips, meetings, and other details of his work. As I read through Bailey's diaries, professional journals, and correspondence, I noticed that his accounts of specific events differed, depending on whether he was writing to a friend, writing a report for his supervisor, or writing for himself. Which account should I believe? I needed to think about why Bailey might have wanted to present the same event in different lights to different audiences. Was one account the true one or did all the versions contain some element of truth? In the case of Bailey's battles over drawing books with John Spencer Clark and Louis Prang, I could compare how Prang and Clark had dealt with one of Bailey's predecessors, Walter Smith who was the first Massachusetts supervisor of industrial drawing. The process of historical inquiry and the methods of internal criticism led me to speculate on the role of self-interest in the development of art education and on tensions between commercial profits and public benefits (Stankiewicz, 1986).

Questions of Narrative: Interpretation and Story

Historical research often has been described as both an art and a science. Historians and philosophers who make this distinction label the gathering and compilation of facts as the scientific aspect of history. Shaping historical facts into a coherent, meaningful, and significant narrative through questioning, the process Bolin (1995) referred to as historical inquiry, is the art of writing history. When I took a graduate course in historical research methods, the professor, a respected

---

1 Research on the Bailey Papers was initially funded through a National Endowment for the Humanities Travel to Collections Grant during the winter of 1986. In 1995, I returned to the University of Oregon due to a summer fellowship from The Oregon Humanities Center.

medieval historian, explained that many people assume that the most time-consuming part of doing history is the process of collecting facts. Actually, according to Professor Roberts, both research and writing should be given about equal time. Too often apprentice historians fail to give themselves enough time to develop a meaningful interpretation and write the story so that a reader who is not an expert can understand its significance.

White (1978) has argued that the meaning and significance of any written history resides in its status as a story and in the language used to tell that story. Is the historian writing a romance, a comedy, a tragedy, or a satire? What type of explanation does the historian prefer? What ideological position does the historian take in trying to help readers understand the ethical and social implications of the story? What types of figurative language does the historian tend to use in telling the story? Just as expert teachers use analogies and metaphors to make ideas clear to students (Sternberg & Horvath, 1995), so most historians use figures of speech as they attempt to make their stories meaningful and engaging. According to White, categories of plot, explanation, ideology, and figurative language can be used to analyze written history and its narrative status. Although White applied his very dense, scholarly analysis to existing works of history, his model can be useful in thinking about the process of writing history of art education (Stankiewicz, 1995).

White emphasizes the art of history. Like Dilthey (Gardiner, 1959) and others, White believes that all historians are making interpretive decisions throughout their process of research and inquiry. Clarke (1885) selected certain events for inclusion in his report to Congress on art education; another author might have selected different events, based on different assumptions about the potential role of art education in the post-Civil War republic. Although Clarke's four volumes have been used as primary sources for much history of art education, it is important to remember that they were an interpretation of raw data just as much as Hicks' three historical periods were an interpretation of the past quarter century based on her understanding of art education.

White's model is useful for writers of art education history because it suggests questions that should be asked during the process of interpretation:

• What type of story do I want to tell about these events?

• What explanatory model do I follow in developing my explanation of the past?

- What are my beliefs about society and morality? Do I accept the status quo or want to use my historical work to change it?

- Does my use of figures of speech make the narrative more meaningful? Do I use metaphors effectively?

History is judged on its literary form as well as on its factual accuracy. Tuchman (1981) argues that historians must be artists, creative writers who can provide background information while keeping the story moving and maintain the reader's interest in a plot where the outcome is usually known. Korzenik (1985b) incorporated inventive scenes, speculation based on fact and probability, into her account of 19th century drawing instruction. Although she had no concrete evidence that the Cross children had access to a drawing book at home, she imagined them around the kitchen table, drawing and talking about the things they made. Korzenik explains that her description is imaginative, but art educators will recognize that the passage is grounded in the insights of an experienced teacher.

Conclusions

Although past historians of art education have tended to focus either on compiling facts and establishing chronologies of past events, or on shaping an interpretation of the past to justify present theory and practice, meaningful histories of art education require both compiling facts and shaping interpretations. Historical researchers in art education can strengthen their skills by drawing on a variety of other disciplines. Interdisciplinary research can not only suggest alternative interpretations, but also broaden the types of questions researchers examine and the types of histories they write. While art educators can learn from their colleagues in other fields, perspectives specific to art education history may also contribute to greater understanding of how art has functioned in social institutions and in the larger culture.

References

Amburgy, P., Soucy, D., Stankiewicz, M. A., Wilson, B., & Wilson, M. (1992). *The history of art education: Proceedings from the second Penn State conference, 1989*. Reston, VA: National Art Education Association.

Apple, M. W. (1990). *Ideology and curriculum* (2nd ed.). New York: Routledge.

Barzun, J., & Graff, H. F. (1977). *The modern researcher* (3rd ed.). New York: Harcourt Brace Jovanovich.

Belting, H. (1987). *The end of the history of art?* (C. S. Wood, Trans.). Chicago: University of Chicago Press.

Bloch, M. (1953). *The historian's craft.* New York: Vintage.

Bolin, P. (1995). Matters of choice: Historical inquiry in art education. In P. Smith (Ed.), *Art education historical methodology: An insider's guide to doing and using* (pp. 44-52). Pasadena, CA: Seminar for Research in Art Education/Open Door Publishers.

Clarke, I. E. (1885). *Art and industry. Part I, Drawing in Public schools.* U.S. Senate Report. 46th Cong., 2nd sess., Vol. 7. Washington, DC: Government Printing Office.

Clarke, I. E. (1892). *Art and industry. Part II, Industrial and manual training in public schools.* U.S. Senate Report. 46th Cong., 2nd sess., Vol. 7. Washington, DC: Government Printing Office.

Clarke, I. E. (1897). *Art and industry. Part III, Industrial and technical training in voluntary associations and endowed institutions.* U.S. Senate Report. 46th Cong., 2nd sess., Vol. 7. Washington, DC: Government Printing Office.

Clarke, I. E. (1898). *Art and industry. Part IV, Industrial and technical training in schools of technology and in U.S. land grant colleges.* U.S. Senate Report. 46th Cong., 2nd sess., Vol. 7. Washington, DC: Government Printing Office.

Collins, G., & Sandell, R. (1984). *Women, art, and education.* Reston, VA: National Art Education Association.

Cremin, L. A. (1977). *Traditions of American education.* New York: Basic Books.

Efland, A. D. (1990). *A history of art education.* New York: Teachers College Press.

Efland, A. D. (1995). Historical research methods for art educators. In P. Smith (Ed.), *Art education historical methodology: An insider's guide to doing and using* (pp. 62-69). Pasadena, CA: Seminar for Research in Art Education/Open Door Publishers.

Efland, A. D., & Soucy, D. (1991). A persistent interpretation: Art education historiography and the legacy of Isaac Edwards Clarke. *History of Education Quarterly, 31,*(4), 489-511.

Garber, E. (1993). On the importance of remembering women art educators. In K. G. Congdon & E. Zimmerman (Eds.), *Women art educators III* (pp. 196-212). Bloomington, IN: Mary J. Rouse Memorial Foundation at Indiana University and NAEA Women's Caucus.

Gardiner, P. (Ed.) (1959). *Theories of History.* New York: The Free Press.

Gottschalk, L. (1969). *Understanding history* (2nd ed.). New York: Alfred A. Knopf.

Handlin, O. (1979). Seeing and hearing. In O. Handlin, *Truth in history* (pp. 227-251). Cambridge, MA: Harvard University Press.

Hicks, M. D. (1895). Does art study concern the public schools? *Proceedings of the International Congress no Education of the World's Columbian Exposition.* New York: National Educational Association.

Hockett, H. C. (1955). *The critical method in historical research and writing.* New York: Macmillan.

Ives, E. D. (1974). *The tape-recorded interview.* Knoxville, TN: University of Tennessee Press.

Kaestle, C. F. (1988). Recent methodological developments in the history of American education. In R. M. Jaeger (Ed.), *Complementary methods for research in education* (pp. 61-80). Washington, DC: American Educational Research Association.

Kleinbauer, W. E., & Slavens, T. P. (1982). *Research guide to the history of western art.* Chicago: American Library Association.

Korzenik, D. (1983). Art education ephemera. *Art Education, 36*(5), 18-21.

Korzenik, D. (1985a). Doing historical research. *Studies in Art Education, 26*(2), 125-128.

Korzenik, D. (1985b). *Drawn to art.* Hanover, NH: University Press of New England.

Korzenik, D. (1995). Looking back on twenty years of graduate students' historical research. In P. Smith (Ed.), *Art education historical methodology: An insider's guide to doing and using* (pp. 35-43). Pasadena, CA: Seminar for Research in Art Education/Open Door Publishers.

Kultermann, U. (1993). *The history of art history.* New York: Abaris Books.

Lubar, S., & Kingery, W. D. (Eds.). (1993). *History from things: Essays on material culture.* Washington, DC: Smithsonian Institution Press.

Minor, V. H. (1994). *Art history's history.* Englewood Cliffs, NJ: Prentice-Hall.

Nevins, A. (1962). *The gateway to history* (rev. ed.). Garden City, NY: Anchor Books.

Pariser, D. (1985). The juvenalia of Klee, ToulouseLautrec and Picasso: A report on the initial stages of research into the development of exceptional graphics artistry. In B. Wilson & H. Hoffa (Eds.), *The history of art education: Proceedings from the Penn State conference* (pp. 192-202). Reston, VA: National Art Education Association.

Pariser, D. (1995). Lautrec—Gifted child artist and artistic monument: Connections between juvenile and mature work. In C. Golomb (Ed.), *The development of artistically gifted children: Selected case studies* (pp. 31-70). Hilldale, NJ: Lawrence Erlbaum.

Rees, A. L., & Borzello, F. (Eds.). (1986). *The new art history*. London: Camden Press.

Roskill, M. (1976). *What is art history?* New York: Harper & Row.

Schlereth, T. J. (Ed.). (1982). *Material culture studies in America*. Nashville, TN: The American Association for State and Local History.

Soucy, D. (1990). A history of art education histories. In D. Soucy & M. A. Stankiewicz (Eds.), *Framing the past: Essays on art education* (pp. 3-31). Reston, VA: National Art Education Association.

Smith, P. (Ed.). (1995). *Art education historical methodology: An insider's guide to doing and using*. Pasadena, CA: Seminar for Research in Art Education/Open Door Publishers.

Stankiewicz, M. A. (1982). Searching out women art educators of the past. In E. Zimmerman & M. A. Stankiewicz (Eds.), *Women art educators* (pp. 96-112). Bloomington, IN: The Mary J. Rouse Memorial Fund and the NAEA Women's Caucus.

Stankiewicz, M. A. (1984). "The eye is a nobler organ:" Ruskin and American art education. *Journal of Aesthetic Education, 18*(2), 51-64.

Stankiewicz, M. A. (1986). Drawing book wars. *Visual Arts Research, 12*(2), 59-72.

Stankiewicz, M. A. (1987). Beauty in design and pictures: Idealism and aesthetic education. *Journal of Aesthetic Education, 7*(4), 63-76.

Stankiewicz, M. A. (1994). Virtue and good manners: Toward a history of art history instruction. In C. H. Smyth & P. M. Lukehart (Eds.), *The early years of art history in the United States* (pp. 183-193). Princeton, NJ: Department of Art and Archaeology, Princeton University.

Stankiewicz, M. A. (1995). So what: Interpretation in art education history. In P. Smith (Ed.), *Art education historical methodology: An insider's guide to doing and using* (pp. 53-61). Pasadena, CA: Seminar for Research in Art Education/Open Door Publishers.

Stankiewicz, M. A., & Zimmerman, E. (Eds.). (1985). *Women Art Educators II*. Bloomington IN: The Mary J. Rouse Memorial Fund and the NAEA Women's Caucus.

Stein, R. B. (1986). Artifact as ideology: The aesthetic movement and its American cultural context. In D. B. Burke, J. Freedman, A. C. Frelinghuysen, D. A. Hanks, M. Johnson, J. D. Kornwulfs, C. Lynn, R. B. Stein, J. Toher, & C. H. Voorsanger, *In pursuit of beauty: Americans and the aesthetic movement* (pp. 22-51). New York: Rizzoli.

Sternberg, R. J., & Horvath, J. A. (1995). A prototype view of expert teaching. *Educational Researcher, 24*(6), 9-17.

Tuchman, B. W. (1981). *Practicing history*. New York: Ballantine Books.

White, H. (1978). Interpretation in history. In H. White, *Tropics of discourse* (pp. 51-80). Baltimore: Johns Hopkins University Press.

Wilson, B., & Hoffa, H. (Eds.). (1985). *The history of art education: Proceedings from the Penn State conference.* Reston, VA: National Art Education Association.

Wolff, J. (1984). *The social production of art.* New York: New York University Press.

Wygant, F. (1993). *School art in American culture. 1820-1970.* Cincinnati, OH: Interwood Press.

Zimmerman, E., & Stankiewicz, M. A. (Eds.). (1982). *Women art educators.* Bloomington, IN: The Mary J. Rouse Memorial Fund and the NAEA Women's Caucus.

Reading and Interpreting Research Journal Articles

You are not alone if you have struggled to read a research journal article and found yourself at a loss for drawing any meaningful conclusions from what you have read. The purpose of this chapter is to help guide you through reading and interpreting the contents of professional journals, particularly those that contain research information about art education. In many cases, research journal articles fall into established categories and are presented in recognizable formats. By identifying these aspects of research articles, you can make progress toward understanding their content.

Why Should We Publish and Read Research Journal Articles?

By publishing research, we are adding to the body of new knowledge in the field. When developing new ideas or planning new investigations, researchers must be familiar with previous research. Such research is most accessible when it is published in the form of journal articles. In fact, research is not really complete until it is published in scholarly journals and shared with a professional community. Thus, familiarity with existing literature allows us to know what research has been done, to build on existing work, and contribute something new to the field (APA, 1995).

By reading and evaluating research, we are able to stay current with important trends in art education. Most new information in the field comes directly

JUDITH SMITH KOROSCIK
The Ohio State University

ELIZABETH KOWALCHUK
The University of Kansas

from research published in journals and presented at professional meetings (Katzer, Cook, & Crouch, 1991). Reading research articles in original contexts allows us to interpret and use the most relevant aspects of investigations in our teaching and in further studies we conduct. Being able to read and assess original research is particularly important for art teachers who may have little contact with other specialists, and, yet, have questions about their own teaching or what their art students have learned.

Chapter Overview

After a general introduction to various types of journal articles, two sample articles will be discussed, illustrating how research reports can be analyzed to determine the significance of their findings for theory and practice. These two research studies have a common theme but exemplify alternative research methods. Both studies are *empirical* (derived from observation or experiment). However, one is *descriptive* in nature (an empirical observation without intervention) while the other is *predictive* (an investigation in which experimental methods are used to examine intervention effects). One study is based on qualitative evidence alone, while the other study contains both qualitative and quantitative elements. The discussion of these research journal articles will focus on the following questions:

- What is the scope of the research problem and research questions discussed in the article?

- What research methods did the author(s) use to examine the variables under investigation?

- How can the reported findings be interpreted in light of the research methods used?

- What can be concluded about the findings of the study and their significance for theory and practice in the field of art education?

Types of Research Journal Articles

It is important to first recognize that there are many forms of research. You can become acquainted with a range of research methods by reading other chapters in this book. For convenience, we provide a summary of different forms of research and examples of journal articles that use each of these forms of research (see Tables 1 and 2).

Different forms of research methods are used because not all research questions are alike. Some questions require descriptive methods, while other questions require experimentation or philosophical analyses. Journal articles reflect these differences. With some practice, you should come to recognize at least four types of research articles: *reports of original research, review articles, theoretical articles, and commentaries.* Distinguishing between types of articles and research methods is useful because each has a purpose as well as limitations. Readers of scholarly articles must have a working knowledge of how research design and methods affect conclusions that can be reached from research.

Reports of original research. The range of original research found in art education literature is quite extensive. It includes reports of historical, philosophical, ethnographic, case study, survey, experimental, and multi-method or triangulated studies (see Table 2). The common feature of all such reports is that they present the outcome of a scholarly investigation which offers new evidence that often sheds light on a specified research problem.

Published reports of original research are typically organized to reflect stages in actual research processes (APA, 1995). Usually, but not always, original research includes sections labeled as follows:

- **Scope of the Study:** An introductory statement about the purpose of the study, generally takes the form of an explanation indicating the need for the study and background to the research problem investigated. Commonly contains a review of literature summarizing previous research relating to the study.

- **Methods:** A description of research methods used to conduct the study, including a description of any participants, location of the study, and procedures used to gather evidence.

- **Results and Discussion:** A description of gathered evidence and interpretation of findings in relation to previous research and known practice.

- **Conclusions:** The statement of concluding arguments based on the findings of the study, and a discussion of their implications for theory and practice in art education.

It is important to note that when research reports deviate from these discretely labeled sections, they often contain the same kind of information in a similar sequence. With practice, readers familiar with the typical content of these sections will be able to recognize them even when they are not labeled as such.

Review articles. Critical evaluations and summaries of previously published materials are referred to as review articles. Such articles often identify gaps or inconsistencies in the literature that need further examination (see Table 1). In addition, review articles can present relevant literature from another field as a way of addressing or clarifying a current problem. For instance, Sullivan's (1993) review titled, *Art-Based Art Education: Learning that is Meaningful, Authentic, Critical and Pluralist,* focuses on recent research in psychological inquiry and educational reform as well as contemporary art theory as a way of informing current art education practice. In contrast to reports of original research, review articles are arranged by relationship rather than by steps in the inquiry process (APA, 1995).

Theoretical articles. Although often similar in structure to review articles, theoretical articles refer to original research findings only when they inform an issue under discussion (see Table 1). In these articles, authors typically present a new theory or refine a prevailing hypothesis by drawing on existing literature. By using logical arguments, an author may also examine existing theory to highlight or recommend the use of one theory over another (APA, 1995). For example in his article titled, *Defining and Structuring Art Criticism for Education,* Anderson (1993) draws upon earlier art criticism and art theory to propose a definition and method of structuring art criticism in an educational context (p. 199).

Commentaries. Some journal articles seem more like essays than research articles. Among such articles are commentaries (refer to Table 1). Usually shorter than the previous types of articles, commentaries invite dialog by pointing out issues that have been or should be addressed in published articles. Although they do not replace the need for original research, commentaries can advance the field by stimulating debate on a topic that needs further examination. Such articles typically convey an author's opinion, and they invite a response much the same way that a newspaper editorial or letter-to-the-editor provides an interactive forum for debate. For instance, Dufrene (1994) stimulated such a debate over the classification of art stimuli used by Erickson (1994a).

Take note of why there are different forms of research articles. As you can see, research in art education necessarily requires a variety of research methods and is written in a variety of recognizable forms. It is essential to note that the choice of

Reading and Interpreting Research Journal Articles

Table 1
Types of Research Journal Articles

Article Type	Description	Example	Purpose or Problem Addressed in Example
REPORTS OF ORIGINAL RESEARCH	Relate outcomes of empirical or non-empirical scholarly inquiry. Includes reports of historical, philosophical, ethnographic, case study, survey, experimental &/or multi-method studies.	Erickson, M. (1994b). Evidence for art historical interpretation referred to by young people and adults. *Studies in Art Education, 35* (2), 71-78.	Reports on results of a descriptive study that examined responses of over 800 participants (aged 6 to adult) to works of art in order to determine the variety of historical understandings that could be formed.
REVIEW ARTICLES	Offer critical evaluations and summaries of previously published materials organized around a central research topic or concept. Can identify relations, contradictions &/or inconsistencies in the literature or introduce existing area of literature to a new audience (APA, 1983, p. 21).	Sullivan, G. (1993). Art-based art education: Learning that is meaningful, authentic, critical and pluralist. *Studies in Art Education, 35* (1), 5-21.	Examines recent research in psychology and education as well as contemporary art theory and practice to suggest implications for art education.
THEORETICAL ARTICLES	Ordinarily, present a new theory by drawing on existing literature. May trace the development of a theory in order to refine or expand theoretical constructs.	Anderson, T. (1993). Defining and structuring art criticism for education. *Studies in Art Education, 34* (4), 199-208.	Draws upon earlier art criticism and art theory to propose a definition and a method of constructing art criticism in an educational context.
COMMENTARIES	Concisely written, sharply focused responses to issues that have been or should be addressed in published scholarly articles. Typically conveys author's opinion. May stimulate debate on an issue.	Dufrene, P. (1994). A response to Mary Erickson. *Studies in Art Education, 35*(4), 252-253. Erickson, M. (1994a). Erickson responds. *Studies in Art Education, 35*(4), 254.	Points out inconsistencies and difficulties in Erickson's report concerning the placement of artworks in a Western or Non-western category framework while suggesting alternative comparative artworks. Thanks previous commentator for feedback while noting that "some readers may value learning about what I've discovered regarding the development of art historical understandings, in spite of the artworks selected for participants' interpretation" (p. 254).

Table 2
Types of Original Research Used in Art Education

Research Method	Description	Art Education Example	Purpose or Problem Addressed in Example
HISTORICAL INQUIRY	The systematic collection, evaluation, synthesis, and interpretation of data related to past events.	Stankiewicz, M. A. (1992). From the aesthetic movement to the arts and crafts movement. *Studies in Art Education, 33*(3), 165-173.	Outlines primary factors connecting both the Aesthetic Movement and the Art and Craft Movement to art education while arguing that "quest for simple cause-and-effect explanations of the history of art education need to be replaced by more complex interpretations of past events" (p. 172).
PHILOSOPHICAL INQUIRY	The analysis of key features of a concept or discipline with purpose of adding to or articulating relevant paradigm within the field.	Chanda, J. (1993). A theoretical basis for non-western art history instruction. *Journal of Aesthetic Education, 27* (3), 73-84.	Argues the need for new teaching models that will provide alternative methods of thinking about and looking at art.
ETHNOGRAPHIC RESEARCH	The investigation of the cultural systems of a particular group or people. A type of descriptive research.	Campanelli, M., Stuhr, P. L., & Barger-Cottrill, S. (1990). Trails: A drug and alcohol prevention program utilizing traditional Indian culture and artistic production. *Journal of Multicultural and Cross-Cultural Research in Art Education, 8* (1), 18-28.	Introduces use of art education for rehabilitative purposes by describing results of interviews conducted with four Wisconsin Native Americans focusing on a drug and alcohol prevention program operating on 11 Wisconsin reservations.
CASE STUDY RESEARCH	The observation and description of an individual (person, group, district, school, etc.) or limited set of individuals in order to make generalizations about a wider population.	Zimmerman, E. (1992). A comparative study of two painting teachers of talented adolescents. *Studies in Art Education, 33* (3), 174-185.	Compares the practices of two art teachers of talented young adolescents in summer art classes to determine the characteristics of successful art teachers of the talented.
SURVEY RESEARCH	The description of the characteristics of a large group of people from a smaller representative sample collected at a particular point in time.	Stone, D. (1993). The secondary art specialist and the art museum. *Studies in Art Education, 35* (1), 45-54.	Examines how secondary art specialists use art museums; what benefits and problems they encounter; how comfortable they feel teaching in this setting; and, how they view school and museum relationships.
EXPERIMENTAL RESEARCH	Generally, the study of cause and effect relationships. Controls or manipulates independent variables to predict changes or to study outcomes.	Cupchik, G. C., Shereck, L, & Spiegel, S. (1994). The effects of textual information on artistic communication. *Visual Arts Research, 20* (1), 62-78.	Reports on two experiments that examined participants' responses to artworks before and after being given stylistic and contextual information.
MULTI-METHOD OR TRIANGULATED RESEARCH	The combination of one or more of the above methods. May include use other descriptive or relational methods (i.e., action research, ex-post facto, etc.).	Anglin, J. M. (1993). Three views of middle school art curriculum. *Studies in Art Education, 35* (1), 55-64.	Describes the art curricula of 40 middle schools through a combination of content analysis, interviews, and observations.

research methods is not arbitrary but dictated by the nature of the questions the investigator is attempting to answer.

A Closer Look at Two Research Articles

What follows is an in-depth review of two research reports (Koroscik, Short, Stavropoulos, & Fortin, 1992; Short, 1995). We could have chosen any two articles for comparison, but in our experience journal readers often struggle most with reports of original research—particularly those that present empirical findings. The papers we will examine are empirically-based, which simply means that the researchers used systematic means to gather new evidence about real-world experiences or phenomena. By the end of this review, you should have a better understanding of how empirical studies inform us about art education problems and practices. We hope this review will serve you well as a preparation for reading research articles of all kinds. You also should be better prepared to assess what you read in other reports of empirical research.

To begin, you will need enough background information to recognize an empirical study when you read one. Many people think that is easy to do because all empirical reports contain quantitative evidence represented in statistical terms. Although sometimes this is true, it is important to know that some empirical studies, in fact increasing numbers of empirical studies in art education, report findings that are qualitative in nature. Being able to distinguish between qualitative findings and quantitative data does not in itself enable you to conclude that an article is a report of empirical research. For instance, sometimes historical investigations provide statistical information, but they are not empirical studies. Moreover, it is often assumed that all experimental research is based on quantitative evidence, but this is not always the case.

For something to be empirically-based, it must be derived from observation or experiment. The purpose of empirical observation is to *describe* what is found without trying to change it. We often refer to this as a form of *descriptive research*. At other times, we want to go beyond description. Our research interest is to predict how something might be different if we changed (or manipulated) the way it is at present. When researchers change things, they do it selectively and with some purpose in mind—normally to find out whether they can improve upon the status quo with an intervention of some kind. This form of empirical study is called *experimental research*.

Figure 1 illustrates the basic differences between these two forms of empirical research. Notice in the case of descriptive or observational studies, the research question of "What is?" drives the study. In experimental or predictive empirical research, the research question of "What could be?" is under investigation. The purpose of both forms of empirical research is to look for the ways an experience or phenomena can vary from and influence something else. Empirical researchers often refer to those things that vary as *variables*—of which there are essentially two kinds, dependent and independent variables. In a well designed study, the selection of variables closely corresponds to the research questions that frame the investigation. Although the term *variable* (or *factor*) is less commonly used by researchers who conduct descriptive studies, the examination of variables is nevertheless central to all forms of empirical research. For comparative purposes, it is useful for readers of empirical research articles to look for factors that have been investigated even if they have not been labeled as variables.

Keep in mind that the central focus of an empirical study is the *dependent variable(s)* because the purpose of the investigation is to assess whether and how much this variable depends on something else. In an observational study, the objective is to gather as much evidence as possible to identify possible influences on the dependent variable. You might think of this as casting a wide net to detect what fish co-exist in a single body of water. Or you might be interested in what kinds of fish were caught last month in three different locations. In an experimental study, you might be fishing in the same body of water; however, your aim is to study cause-and-effect relationships. For instance, you might set out to discover what bait is most effective for catching coho salmon in Lake Michigan. You are especially interested in comparing the effectiveness of three varieties of bait to discover which of these *independent variables* causes the best effect (i.e., the number and quality of fish caught, the *dependent variable*). By design, you have limited your experiment to the study of only three types of bait and to coho salmon. Your choice of bait is based on earlier observations and experiments by other fishers of coho salmon. The focus on only three varieties of bait enables you to look at causes and effects in close detail, but it also limits what you will be able to discover in a single experiment. Therefore, your research plan might be to conduct a number of experiments, each with a limited focus. In that way you can manageably investigate how the same or different bait might be used to catch coho salmon and other fish in Lake Michigan. Related studies might be planned for other fresh water lakes.

As this illustration suggests, observational and experimental empirical research can go hand-in-hand. They serve complementary but different purposes because

Reading and Interpreting Research Journal Articles

Figure 1. *A comparison of approaches to empirical research.*

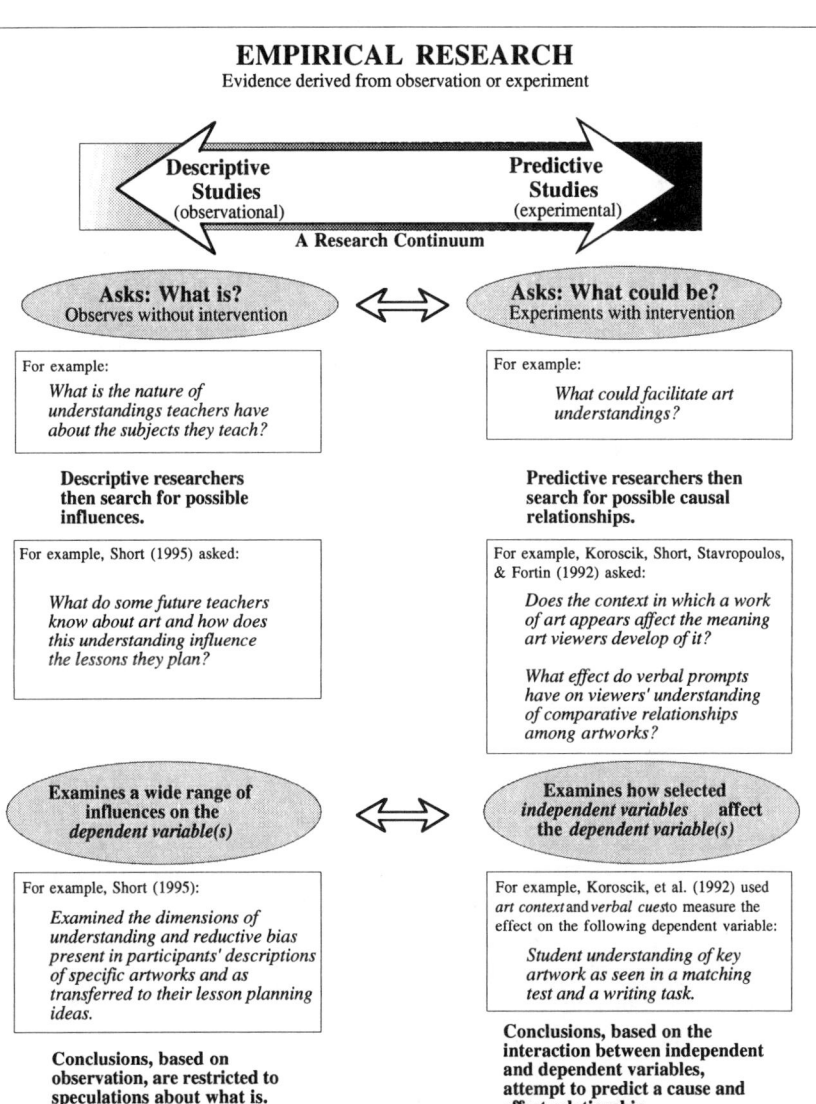

they inform different research questions. This is why an essential first step in reading a research article is to identify the research questions being asked. In our previous examples, did the author set out to answer the question, "What are the varieties of fish that live in Lake Michigan?" or was the point of the study to investigate "Which one of three varieties of bait is best for catching coho salmon in Lake Michigan?" Both are valuable questions, but they require different empirical methods. Readers of original research reports must bear this difference in mind when reading and assessing the value of any journal article.

The research articles discussed below illustrate how two forms of empirical research were used to study the experience of understanding art. The report by Short (1995) presents the findings of a series of descriptive case studies. The article by Koroscik, Short, Stavropoulos, and Fortin (1992) refers to an experimental investigation. What do these articles tell you about understanding works of art? How can you determine that these two reports of original research are empirically-based? Many people assume that the best way to proceed is to read each article sequentially from beginning to end. Instead, we recommend following a somewhat nonlinear approach. The remainder of this chapter provides an outline of steps you might take to read and interpret research articles (see Appendix A for reprints of the two articles).

What is the Scope of the Research Problem and Research Questions Discussed in Each Article?

Refer to the title. It may seem obvious, but the first step we recommend in reading a journal article is to closely examine its title. The title of a research report should guide you toward identifying the scope of the study by introducing the research questions and the major variables under investigation.

What can you detect from reading the titles of the two articles by Koroscik et al. (1992) and Short (1995)? Based on the titles alone, what do you think the research questions of each study might be (see Figure 2)? Try rewording the titles as research questions to make them more meaningful. These are the questions we came up with when we reworded the title of Short's article:

- What do future art teachers understand about art?

- How do future art teachers' understandings of art come into play when they think about teaching?

The title of Koroscik et al.'s study can be reworded as follows:

- How is the understanding of art affected by the contextual framework in which it is examined?

- What function do comparative contexts and verbal cues have on understanding art?

It is acceptable if the questions you generate are somewhat different. The point of the exercise is to begin to question what you read in order to fully grasp what the authors of a research article had in mind when they designed their study. If you don't understand the purpose of a study, you will be unable to make sound judgments about the choice of research methods and significance of the findings.

Upon a closer look at an article's title you should be able to identify the variables that were investigated. In the article by Koroscik et al., it should be clear that the dependent variable is "understanding art" and the independent variables are "comparative art contexts" and "verbal cues" (see Figure 2). What you don't know from reading the title is whose understanding of art was investigated nor what dimensions of art understanding were examined. The title of this article does however provide enough information to suggest that it relates to Short's article in which "understanding domain knowledge" is linked to "pre-service art teacher specialists."

Read the abstract. Most research articles contain an abstract which we recommend reading next. Concisely written in an established format, abstracts indicate the following: (a) the nature of the research questions investigated, (b) who participated in a study, (c) the research methods used, and (d) the scope of major findings. By reading the abstracts prepared by Koroscik et al. and Short, you can quickly compare the scope of each study as summarized in Table 3.

This cursory review confirms that the two studies are linked by a shared purpose to investigate the nature of understandings about art. Both studies include college students as participants, but Short employed descriptive, case study methods to research the higher-order thinking of prospective art teachers. In contrast, Koroscik et al. used experimental methods to predict how selected art viewing situations or interventions (comparative art contexts and verbal cues) may help or hinder the interpretation of art meanings held by undergraduate non-art majors. The findings of both studies indicate that understanding art is complex and cog-

Figure 2—Excerpts from Short (1995) and Koroscik et al. (1992).

STUDIES in Art Education
A Journal of Issues and Research
1995, 36 (3), 154-169

Copyright by the
National Art Education Association

Understanding Domain Knowledge for Teaching:
Higher-Order Thinking in Pre-Service
Art Teacher Specialists

Georgianna Short

Cherry Creek School District #5
Englewood, Colorado

This study investigates the higher-order thinking and subject matter understanding of pre-service art specialists. The relationship between art specialists' subject matter understanding and instructional choices is also examined. Individual case study research was conducted on 18 prospective art teachers from a large midwestern state university. The participant-volunteers were visual art or art education majors in the final stages of course-work. Qualitative data were triangulated from a series of oral interviews, lesson-planning activities, personal biographies, university transcripts, and self-reports. The data analysis revealed that only some pre-service art teachers exhibited the higher-order thinking or in-depth understanding expected of specialists in visual art. Most future art teachers displayed overly simplistic thinking, shallow understandings, and superficial domain knowledge. The findings suggest the content knowledge and art understandings possessed by pre-service art teacher specialists should not be taken for granted. Successful completion of required coursework does not guarantee higher-order thinking or deep understanding of the domain. Implications for teacher preparation are discussed.

In recent years there has been growing concern that teachers do not know or understand enough about the subjects they teach. As early as 1983, reports such as *Nation at Risk: The Imperative for Educational Reform* alleged that deficiencies in the subject matter knowledge and understanding of teachers are responsible, in part for a decline in the quality of what American students know. Authors of the report question how much subject matter understanding prospective teachers can possess when most come from the nation's "bottom quarter of graduating high school and college students" (National Commission for Excellence in Education, 1983, p. 22). These teacher candidates are then subjected to teacher preparation curricula "weighted heavily with courses in educational methods at the expense of courses in subjects to be taught" (NCEE, 1983, p. 22).

STUDIES in Art Education
A Journal of Issues and Research
1995, 33 (3), 154-164

Copyright by the
National Art Education Association

Frameworks for Understanding Art: The Function of
Comparative Art Contexts and Verbal Cues

Judith S. Koroscik, Georganna Short, Carol Stavropoulos
The Ohio State University
and
Sylvie Fortin
The University of Quebec at Montreal

The purpose of this investigation was to study contextual variables that influence the understanding of works of art. A key artwork was introduced to college students with other works of art in three different comparative contexts (same-artist vs. same-theme vs. interdisciplinary). Verbal contextual conditions (cued vs. non-cued) were also manipulated to show whether students rely on explicit verbal prompts to find relationships among works of art. The results of a multiple-choice matching test and an open-ended writing task indicate both types of contextual variables can have a strong impact on what a student looks for and thinks about when examining a work of art. Verbal cues can prompt students to elaborate on possible art meanings. Comparative art contexts containing familiar ideas can reduce the occurrence of misunderstandings if those ideas are explicitly identified for students. These and other findings have a direct bearing on how educational interventions might be structured.

One of the most important characteristics of intelligence is the ability to transfer previously acquired knowledge to new learning situations (Bransford, Sherwood, Vye, & Rieser, 1986). In order for students to make use of their cognitive resources, they must find meaningful connections between their existing knowledge and whatever they are attempting to understand (Prawat, 1989). Research has shown that transfer is highly context-dependent because much of what a student understands is embedded in the original learning context (Perkins & Salomon, 1988). Studies in reading comprehension have shown that readers often derive meanings of texts by scrutinizing surrounding contexts for semantic cues (Bransford & Johnson, 1972; Carrell, Karracsak, & Coyle, 1984). Verbal contexts can provide meaningful cues for comprehending texts, and conversely, the understanding of pictures can be influenced by verbal contextual cues (Warren & Flurri, 1982). Verbalizations of picture content during art viewing experiences (Barrett, 1985; Koroscik, Gerber, & Baxter, 1987; Koroscik, Osman, & DeSouza, 1988). What remains in question is how the presence of one

Table 3
An Overview of Research Methods and Findings

Study Components	Short (1995)	Koroscik et al. (1992)
RESEARCH QUESTIONS	What do future art teachers understand about art? How do these understandings influence the art lessons they plan?	Does the context in which a work of art appears affect the meaning art viewers develop about the art work? What effect do verbal prompts have on viewers' understanding of comparative relationships among works of art?
RESEARCH METHODS	Descriptive, multiple case study	Experimental
VARIABLES	Degree of understanding and reductive bias present in pre-service teacher's descriptions of artworks and art content in lesson plans.	Independent Variables: Art Context (3 levels) & Verbal Cues (2 levels) Dependent Variables: Participants' understandings as measured by a matching test and a writing task.
PARTICIPANTS	Undergraduate art education students (N=18) enrolled at a large midwestern university in an art education methods course which included a teaching practicum, the Saturday Art Workshop.	Undergraduate students (N=120) enrolled in a course on contemporary art at a large midwestern university.
MAJOR FINDINGS	Despite their status as advanced learners, many pre-service art teachers in this study "demonstrated overly simplistic thinking, shallow understandings and superficial domain knowledge" (p. 167).	The context in which an artwork is viewed influences the understandings that are formed. Verbal cues are effective in helping students "synthesize their ideas across works of art" (p. 167). Problems in understanding artworks can be the result of students' prior knowledge and/or knowledge seeking strategies.

nitively demanding. The occurrence of misconceptions, simplistic thinking, and shallow understandings can be found even among adult learners.

Scan the introductory paragraphs. The purpose of a study will become even clearer as you review the opening paragraphs of a research article. At this point, you should also begin to grasp the "big picture" or theoretical framework of an investigation and the background to the problems under examination. It is important to gain a sense of the bigger research context and prior investigations because the design of a study and interpretation of its findings depend on this understanding. A well designed investigation builds upon an existing body of research literature. Identifying that connection is an essential step in understanding how the present study sheds new light on the problem investigated. Presumably, the problem is not altogether new to the field, so it is to be expected that an author will cite earlier works in order to offer pertinent background information.

What can you determine about the scope of the study from scanning the beginning paragraphs of the article by Koroscik et al.? As before, you might try rewording the text into research questions. Here are the questions we prepared for each of the first three paragraphs. What questions can you add?

- Paragraph 1: If research on reading comprehension has shown that readers often determine meanings of a text by scrutinizing its surrounding context for semantic cues, does the presence of one artwork next to other works of art make any difference in the way meanings are understood by art viewers?

- Paragraph 2: Can novice art viewers be prompted to search for art meanings in greater depth by simply manipulating how a work of art is displayed in comparison to other works of art?

- Paragraph 3: If contextual variables drive an art viewer's choice of search strategies, in what way does that choice contribute to expanding the individual's knowledge base and later aid in the transfer of any new art understandings?

Note that all of these questions seek to predict cause and effect relationships among variables. They ask, "What could be?" rather than what now exists. The research intent is to explore how change in art understandings can be brought about.

Observe that the study by Koroscik et al. is based on earlier research about reading comprehension as well as on prior research in art education, including previous studies by the first author. Since the introduction to the article is very brief, the reference citations are important indicators of background research and the theoretical perspective relating to the study under consideration.

The introduction to Short's article is also just three paragraphs long. What questions come to mind as you read the introductory section of her article? How do your questions compare with the ones we list below?

- Paragraph 1: How much subject matter understanding can we expect prospective teachers to possess when most come from the nation's bottom percentile of high school and college students?

- Paragraph 2: How has the issue of teacher preparation training been discussed in the recent literature on educational reform?

- Paragraph 3: If strong links have been found between instructional decision-making and a teacher's subject matter understanding, will student learning improve dramatically if teachers know more about what they are teaching? How much more do they need to know?

These questions provide a general introduction to the topic of Short's article, but they should not be interpreted as the actual research questions she investigated. Rather in the first paragraph, Short is setting the stage for her investigation as well as justifying that her topic is relevant. Unlike the questions we inferred from the introduction to Koroscik et al.'s article, which are predictive or experimental in nature, Short's introduction does not provide any clues about the research direction she chose to take. You must read on to discover that Short's empirical study was undertaken to investigate "What is?".

Short writes at length to inform readers about the theoretical basis of her research. To get a sense of the theoretical issues she explores, scan the headings and subheadings of her article. You will find her concern was to investigate the understanding of art as an *ill-structured domain*. That term is used to mean that art "concepts vary in meaning from one application to the next" (p. 115). This lack of consistency and predictability make the visual arts domain more demanding to understand than "well-structured" domains (such as mathematics) which are largely rule-based and thus highly predictable. Since preservice teachers in well-structured domains have been found to be lacking in their depth of domain knowledge, Short questions whether even greater comprehension difficulties are prevalent among future art teachers. Her principal interest is to discover whether preservice art teachers engage in the "strategic mismanagement of complexity involving various forms of oversimplification" (p. 157). Her research questions can be summarized as follows:

- What do future art teachers know and understand about art?

- How are their personal understandings of art expressed in the lessons they plan to teach?

Short's purpose is to describe how preservice teachers think and what they already know about art in order to make observations about their ideas for lesson planning. Her research questions do not call for experimentation with an intervention to study cause-and-effect relationships.

Examine the references. It may come as a surprise to learn that everything you need to fully understand a research article is not contained in the article itself. You also must consider the broader context of the report you are reading in order to determine the scope of a study and the contribution of its findings to existing research literature. Authors help readers identify that context by including a list of references. The abbreviated citations that appear in the body of the article are referenced in detail at the end of the report. This information will allow you to find each reference if you choose to do so.

Some readers actually look up every publication referenced in a research article. Then, they also check the references of those cited publications as well. You probably will not do this unless you are conducting your own study or writing a review article. However, we recommend that you check the list of references as soon as you begin to read an article. Take note of the list of authors and the titles and dates of their works. If you compare the references cited by Koroscik et al. and Short, you should find several similarities. This is to be expected since the topics of both articles are related. Another reason is that Short was a contributor to the study by Koroscik et al., and it is safe to conclude that Short's research direction builds on that earlier work.

Why do you suppose the list of references is longer in Short's article than the one published by Koroscik et al.? One explanation is that Short's article provides an extensive discussion of the theoretical literature. Much of the literature she cites refers to *reductive bias,* a learning problem that has not been discussed earlier

Reading and Interpreting Research Journal Articles

in the art education literature. In order to help readers understand how reductive bias compares with other facets of cognition, Short gives a thorough list of related research articles from outside the field of art education. Koroscik et al.'s paper requires fewer references in part because the study reported is one of a series of investigations. It is important that Koroscik et al. cited at least the most recent of those previous investigations so readers can see how one study compares with another. Because this study is one of a series of investigations Koroscik has conducted, it is to be expected that she would discuss broader theoretical issues at length in another article. By checking the reference list, you will indeed find articles of this kind. Also note that Short's reference list points the way for finding another theoretical article by Koroscik (1992).

What Research Methods Did the Authors Use to Examine the Variables Under Investigation?

After identifying the scope of a research article, you will want to consider the exact methods used by the authors to gather new evidence (or data). This is an essential step in your review of an empirical report because the value of any empirical evidence depends on how it was collected. You should also seek to determine whether the selection of research methods by an author actually corresponds to questions he or she set out to investigate. Be aware that sometimes authors claim to have gathered new evidence to inform a particular research question, but their choice of methods invalidates their findings. Your ability to assess the correspondence between research questions and methods rests on the extensiveness of your knowledge of empirical methodologies. Nevertheless, any reader of a research report can make some judgment about the selection of data collection methods. To begin, we suggest searching for answers to the basic questions of who, what, when, where, and how, as we explain below.

Who? Can you identify who participated in the studies by Koroscik et al. and Short? Although the participants in both investigations were students attending a large midwestern public university, how did they differ? Among other things, you should observe a difference in the participants' educational experiences. Short recruited undergraduate seniors and post-graduates in the visual arts who were seeking art teacher certification. All 18 of the participants in Short's study were enrolled in a 10-week teaching practicum which preceded their student teaching. In contrast, Koroscik et al. recruited 120 undergraduates who were enrolled in an introductory course on contemporary art. The participants in this study were drawn from a wide range of undergraduate majors, not from a pool of visual arts students.

You might also observe that the participants in the study by Koroscik et al. were randomly assigned to six different experimental groups of 20 students each. This grouping was planned as part of the experimental design. In contrast, the students in Short's investigation were descriptively compared as individual case studies. The individual cases were later categorized, but this did not entail grouping the participants ahead of time so different experimental conditions could be tested.

What? Next, you might ask what materials the researchers used to gather their empirical evidence. Determine what was brought into the research setting for the participants to consider. Can you detect whether any new research tools were developed to record observations or to collect experimental data?

In our two illustrations, you can observe that the authors' choice of materials involved the careful selection of artworks. Short used a printed reproduction of *Olympia* by Edouard Manet to collect descriptive evidence. A secondary set of 20 art reproductions also was used. Koroscik et al. focused their data collection around reproductions of *The Birthday* by Marc Chagall. The experimental design also called for the development of three comparative art viewing contexts. In the same-artist context, *The Birthday* was shown with reproductions of other paintings by Chagall. In the same-theme context, reproductions of paintings with similar subject matter were presented with *The Birthday*. And in the interdisciplinary context, *The Birthday* was displayed with a variety of artforms (including a videotaped dance performance) all of which were influenced by Chagall's work.

When? The duration of a study is another facet to consider in your review of research methods. When did the participants in the Koroscik et al. investigation examine *The Birthday* in its various comparative contexts? Did the participants make their responses in one sitting or over a longer timeframe? How long and how many sessions did Short's investigation require? Often descriptive empirical studies continue for several weeks or months. Longitudinal studies can take place over many years. The narrow focus of experimental investigations usually demands less time but repeated experiments. (Remember, we said that the study by Koroscik et al. was one of a series of experimental investigations.) What can you detect about the time spent by participants from reading the articles by Koroscik et al. and Short? We list our observations about the two studies below. Did we miss anything important?

- Short required each participant to engage in three interview sessions over a 12-week period. The length of each session varied from one person to the next because they were allowed to respond to the interview questions at their own pace.

Short also gathered lesson plans that were written independently by the participants over a 5-week period.

- Koroscik et al. asked their participants to attend one of several experimental sessions, each of which lasted about 30 minutes.

Koroscik et al. presented artworks at one-minute intervals until all works were simultaneously in view for a total of six minutes. During this time an open-ended writing task was completed by the participants. The participants then were allowed as much time as they needed to view the artworks in order to complete a multiple-choice matching test.

Where? It is also important to consider where a study is conducted. We mentioned above that the studies by Short and Koroscik et al. both took place at a large public university in the midwestern United States. Can you find any additional information about the research site? Where did Short conduct her one-on-one interviews? Although we can't be sure from the report, it seems safe to conclude that it was in some quiet location because the interviews were audio-taped and later transcribed. We can also conclude that the participants wrote their lesson plans wherever they normally write lesson plans. Short's research design did not require writing the plans on-site in her presence.

The report by Koroscik et al. informs us that the experimental sessions were held in "an art classroom [presumably on the university campus] that provided minimal distraction from extraneous stimuli" (p. 156). Some detail is given about the way the classroom was organized and lit for the experiment. A limited number of participants were tested at once in order that all could easily see the art reproductions which were projected as slides or viewed on a video-tape.

How? A final question to ask about research methods should be considered in two parts. First, you need to know how the researchers gathered their new evidence. Second, you need to ask how the evidence was analyzed.

At this stage in your review of the articles by Short and Koroscik et al., you will have already determined that the two studies are both empirical investigations. You know that Short used descriptive methods to make observations about preservice art teachers, whereas Koroscik et al. used experimental methods to predict cause and effect relationships between art contexts and art understandings. You must now look closer to determine precisely how the researchers organized the collection of their empirical evidence. What procedures or protocols did they follow to examine variables? How was the content and sequence of each study conducted? What was said and done throughout the study by the participants and the investigators? We highlight a few of these data collection procedures below. What can you add to this *list?*

- Short used several methods (triangulated procedures) to gather descriptive evidence, including tape-recorded interviews, written lesson plans, and the participants' university transcripts.

  The interviews with participants were conducted by Short in three sessions. Interview I focused on Edouard Manet's painting, *Olympia,* to reveal the preservice teachers' understandings of the work and its possible use in an art lesson. Supplementary information about *Olympia* was made available to the participants during this interview if they chose to consider it. In Interview II and III, the participants were asked to make a personal selection from an array of other artworks and discuss their thoughts about how any of the works chosen might be integrated into a lesson plan. The participants were not given the opportunity to review supplementary materials.

  The participants in Short's study were also asked to prepare written lesson plans to be used for a four-week unit of instruction. The plans included an explanation of "how lesson concepts would be introduced, how students would apply the new concepts, and how lesson content would be summarized for students in concluding activities" (p. 160).

- In the experimental study by Koroscik et al., participants were introduced to artworks one at a time at one-minute intervals in a randomized sequence. All students were shown *The Birthday* by Marc Chagall, which was compared with three other works of art. The comparative artworks differed depending on whether a student had been randomly assigned to the same-artist context, the same-theme context, or the interdisciplinary context. After all artworks in a context were simultaneously in view, students were instructed to write about the works (i.e., the open-ended writing task). Half of the students were prompted to write about the common characteristics of the works (the verbal-cued condition). All other participants merely were instructed to write down their thoughts about the works of art (the verbal non-cued condition). After three minutes, the participants were asked to stop writing. Then half of the students (i.e., those in the cued-condition) were briefly cued about the nature of the artworks' similarities. The other half of the students (i.e., those in the non-cued condition) simply were told that they could continue writing about the artworks for a few more minutes.

After the open-ended writing task was complete, Koroscik et al. asked all of the participants in their study to complete a multiple-choice matching test about *The Birthday*. This test was designed to gather evidence about the students' understanding of the painting in terms of its visual characteristics (formal dimension), subject matter content (descriptive dimension), and expressive qualities (interpretive dimension).

After you have a good sense of how the researchers gathered their data, you will want to consider the procedures they used to analyze that evidence. You might picture the authors holding several boxes full of test booklets, written lesson plans, audio tapes, questionnaires, and other forms of evidence. Next, you should find out what the authors did with the contents of those boxes. Ask how they sorted through all the materials they acquired during the course of their study. Where did they begin with their data analyses and what directions did they take? Think about what you might add to our list of observations.

- Short first used qualitative methods to analyze all the data she gathered. She sorted the data by using "an open coding process to identify and categorize informational units within the data for each case study" (p. 160). By first identifying the "smallest piece of information...that can stand by itself," Short could then group related units into a single category. She identified several categories of student responses by distinguishing between those about an artwork's formal, descriptive, historical or cultural, aesthetic, or critical dimensions. Next, Short counted the number of dimensions present in each student's response from transcripts of the three interview sessions and written lesson plans.

  In order to assess the presence of reductive bias, Short compared each dimension of student responses to those found in the body of published literature by art scholars. After comparing individual participants in this way, Short compared every student to every other student for a cross-case analysis.

- Koroscik et al. used statistical analyses to compare student responses to the multiple-choice matching test. A comparison was made in the students' ability to understand the formal, descriptive, and interpretive dimensions of *The Birthday*. The design of the matching test allowed the researchers to quantify test scores for this purpose.

The procedures Koroscik et al. used to analyze the open-ended writing test were both qualitative and quantitative in nature. First, the researchers performed a content analysis to detect the extent to which the verbal cue and comparative art context led students to write more about the formal, descriptive, or interpretive dimension of *The Birthday*. Second, the quality of the participants' written responses was examined to detect occurrences of any misunderstandings. This was done by comparing each student's response to the body of published literature about *The Birthday*. The frequency of misunderstandings was then totaled so a comparison could be made between the verbal-cued and non-cued conditions and among the three comparative art contexts. Finally, the researchers examined the syntax of written responses by studying whether the students who seemed to struggle most in understanding *The Birthday* had a pattern of writing that differed from the others. This syntactical analysis included assessing the frequency of writing lists of words versus writing paragraphs or combinations of both.

You might observe that there are some similarities between the data analysis procedures used by Koroscik et al. and Short. Both studies involved qualitative and quantitative analyses to examine student responses to the formal, descriptive, and interpretive dimensions of art. Do you think the authors of these two articles used the terms "formal, descriptive, interpretive dimensions" in the same way? Why does Short name additional dimensions of art understanding? Sometimes researchers use the same language but attach different meanings to it. Is that the case here? If the data analyses seem alike in your comparison of the two articles, in what ways are they different? Consider the fact that one article is a report of a multiple case study, whereas the other presents the findings of an experimental investigation.

Sometimes readers without much research experience shy away from reading articles that report findings in statistical terms. Keep in mind that it is not essential for you to determine the appropriateness of the statistical procedures used at this point. Instead, concentrate on understanding the steps taken to systematically gather and examine the data. Think about how you would repeat or accurately replicate the study based on the authors' description. In descriptive research, authors (almost always) refer to a method of data analysis by citing the acknowl-

Reading and Interpreting Research Journal Articles

edged expert on the procedure (e.g., Miles & Huberman, 1984; Lincoln & Guba, 1985; Spradley, 1980). If a statistical test is used to analyze experimental data, authors will name the procedure (e.g., analysis of variance tests, chi-square analyses, Newman-Keuls' tests, and factor analyses). You can then go to statistical research methods texts for more information about these methods of data analysis if you wish (e.g., see Linton & Gallo, 1974).

How Can the Reported Findings Be Interpreted in Light of the Research Methods Used?

The findings of a research study are sometimes taken on face value. Readers may assume it is sufficient to look for bottom line results without questioning whether the findings are valid and reliable. Other readers may think that because an article appears in print, it presents cohesive and infallible results. Unfortunately this is not always the case.

Assessing the reliability and validity of a study can encompass a lengthy, in-depth review on your part. If such a review is beyond your interest or ability, you can take a less comprehensive approach but still be in a position to make informed judgments about the findings of a study. One of the most important things you can do is question whether the evidence gathered in a study actually informs the problem under investigation. What did the researchers set out to investigate? Is there any correspondence between the research methods used and the research questions asked? Did Koroscik et al. use research methods that truly reveal something about art understandings? Can Short claim to have gathered evidence about reductive bias in preservice teachers? We provide partial answers to these questions.

- Short set out to examine whether future art teachers are afflicted with reductive bias tendencies that impair their personal understanding of artworks and restrict their ability to effectively plan art curricula. She claims to have gathered evidence that preservice art teachers vary a good deal in the degree of reductive bias that influences their understanding of artworks and lesson planning. Based on data collected during interviews, from written lesson plans, and from other descriptive data collection methods, Short differentiates between student teachers who are most reductive, moderately reductive, and least reductive. Short explains this differentiation in terms of the qualities and number of connections made about works of art. The most reductive participants could only express art understandings along one dimension (most typically about an artwork's formal properties). At the other extreme, the least reductive participants were able to identify and relate as many as six dimensions of art. Short provides concrete examples of the three reductive bias categories by directly quoting the preservice teachers who participated in the study.

- Koroscik et al. set out to investigate whether even subtle differences in art viewing conditions can affect the understandings of artworks. By controlling and manipulating the situation in which students viewed art, Koroscik et al. claim to have identified two powerful variables related to art understanding and misunderstanding: comparative art contexts and verbal cues. These claims are based on written evidence expressed by college-aged students in response to a multiple-choice matching test and open-ended writing task. Koroscik et al. found that they could predict how students would search for art meanings depending on the choice of artworks surrounding a key artwork. The direction of students' searches for meaning was found to correspond to the nature of the comparative art context. The evidence gathered in the study also indicates that comparative contexts have an even greater impact on understanding art works when accompanied by verbal cues. Without verbal cues, students adopt more diverse and less productive search strategies. By analyzing the syntax of student responses, Koroscik et al. claim to have found evidence to explain why verbal cueing aids understanding and lessens misunderstanding about art works.

What Can be Concluded About the Findings of the Study and their Significance for Theory and Practice in the Field of Art Education?

In completing your review of a research report, you will want to question the significance of the study. Ask whether the findings of the investigation are truly important to the field of art education. Researchers often refer to this as the all important "So what?" question. Answering the question is not as easy as it may seem. Although it doesn't require much effort to express a simple opinion, providing good reasons why a research study is indeed valuable, or not, requires some degree of background knowledge. Ideally, readers should have strong backgrounds in both the practical and theoretical aspects of art education. Those who lack adequate knowledge of research methods, prior research findings, and the theoretical bases found in the literature review are not in good positions to judge the merits of an investigation. Likewise, readers who are novice art educators or who are misinformed about the nature of practice in the field may draw inappropriate conclusions. Readers should merely be cognizant of their own limitations as they attempt to assess the contributions of a study. To begin that assessment, you might review the final sections of a research report. For example, consider what Short and Koroscik et al. claim about the significance of their research. We highlight some of those **conclusions** below.

- Short argues that while her descriptive research was limited to a select number of artworks and only 18 preservice art specialists, the evidence she gathered "represents patterns of understanding" that "offer a glimpse into what may prove to be a problematic area in the education of preservice art teacher specialists" (p. 168).

  Short insists that art teachers need to possess in-depth knowledge of art in order to be effective in the classroom. The descriptive findings she reports are not encouraging about the quality of art teacher preparation. Short found that "despite their advanced learning status and visual art specialization, the majority of preservice teachers [who participated in her study] demonstrated overly simplistic thinking, shallow understandings, and superficial domain knowledge. Their instructional decision-making, as reflected in lesson plans, exhibited similar characteristics" (p. 167).

  Short urges art educators to conduct more research on art teacher preparation in order to "gain additional insight into how future teachers think about and understand the domain, and why some future teachers obtain substantive domain understanding while others fail to do so" (p. 168).

- Because art teachers routinely present works of art to students, Koroscik et al. argue that more thought should be given to how those art viewing displays are organized. Their research findings provide strong evidence that contextual variables, such as comparative art contexts and verbal cues, impact two inter-related facets of art cognition: (a) a student's ability to extend his or her existing knowledge base, and (b) the student's choice of knowledge-seeking strategies (or search strategies).

  Koroscik et al. also argue that art educators need to consider both facets of cognition when designing educational interventions in schools and museums. The researchers insist that more attention should be paid to contextual variables when planning art viewing experiences in order to foster deep understandings of art and reduce common occurrences of misunderstandings. They point to quantitative and qualitative evidence of contextual effects to support their claim that even subtle changes in contextual conditions can make a difference in student understanding.

Koroscik et al. also urge art educators to make careful choices of student assessment tools. The researchers found that multiple-choice matching tests are of limited usefulness in assessing depth of understanding. "Open-ended writing tasks were found to be more useful, but analysis of them is extremely time intensive" (p. 164). Instead of trying to assess a full range of learning outcomes, Koroscik et al. recommend a sharper focus, such as an evaluation of students' successes in comprehending selected key ideas.

After considering the author's arguments, you may want to draw your own conclusions. Are you convinced that Short and Koroscik et al. have provided adequate reports of new evidence in support of their conclusions? Can you detect any gaps between the research methods and reported findings? Do you think the authors have made strong arguments about the importance of their research to the field of art education. How would you answer the "So what?" question based on your reading of each article?

Summary

With some effort and experience, you are certain to discover the relative value of any research journal article you read. Your understanding will advance further as you broaden your knowledge of research methods, published literature, and art education practice.

The most important advice we can offer is that you question everything you read. Ask about the purpose of the study, the need for the investigation, and the type of variables under investigation. Question whether the design of the study corresponds to the research questions that frame the investigation, and ask whether the design builds upon prior research and presents an inclusive theoretical context. Determine whether the choice of data collection and analysis procedures is in line with the problems under investigation. Ask what more is needed to draw informed conclusions about the study.

Try to avoid making judgments about the importance of an investigation until you have made a good effort at finding out why a researcher has chosen to investigate a problem in a certain way. Remember that by reading and evaluating research, you will stay current with important trends in art education. You may even consider conducting research yourself or in partnership with others. Moreover, you will be able to learn from other professionals and avoid spending valuable time reinventing the wheel of art education theory and practice.

References

American Psychological Association. (1995). *Publication manual of the American Psychological Association* (3rd ed.). Washington, DC: Author.

Anderson, T. (1993). Defining and structuring art criticism for education. *Studies in Art Education, 34* (4), 199-208.

Anglin, J. M. (1993). Three views of middle school art curriculum. *Studies in Art Education, 35* (1), 55-64.

Campanelli, M., Stuhr, P. L., & Barger-Cottril, S. (1990). A drug and alcohol prevention program utilizing traditional Indian culture and artistic production. *Journal of Multicultural and Cross-Cultural Research in Art Education, 8* (1), 18-28.

Chanda, J. (1993). A theoretical basis for non-Western art history instruction. *Journal of Aesthetic Education, 27* (1), 73-84.

Cupchik, G. C., Shereck, L., & Spiegel, S. (1994). The effects of textual information on artistic communication. *Visual Arts Research, 20* (1), 62-78.

Dufrene, P. (1994). A response to Mary Erickson. *Studies in Art Education, 35* (4), 252-253.

Erickson, M. (1994a). Erickson responds. *Studies in Art Education, 35* (4), 254.

Erickson, M. (1994b). Evidence for art historical interpretation referred to by young people and adults. *Studies in Art Education, 35* (2), 71-78.

Katzer, J., Cook, K. H., & Crouch, W. W. (1991). *Evaluating information: A guide for users of social science research* (3rd ed.). New York: McGraw Hill.

Koroscik, J. S. (1992). Learning in the visual arts: Implications for preparing art teachers. *Arts Education Policy Review, 94* (5), 20-25.

Koroscik, J. S., Short, G., Stavropoulos, C., & Fortin, S. (1992). Frameworks for understanding art: The function of comparative art contexts and verbal cues. *Studies in Art Education, 33* (3), 154-164.

Lincoln, Y. S., & Guba, E. G. (1995). *Naturalistic inquiry.* Beverly Hills: CA: Sage.

Linton, M., & Gallo, P. S. (1974). *The practical statistician: Simplified handbook of statistics.* Monterey, CA: Brooks/Cole.

Miles, M. B., & Huberman, A. M. (1984). *Qualitative data analysis: A sourcebook of new methods.* Newbury Park, CA: Sage.

Short, G. (1995). Understanding domain knowledge for teaching: Higher-order thinking in pre-service art teacher specialists. *Studies in Art Education, 36* (3), 154-169.

Spradley, J. P. (1980). *Participant observation.* New York: Holt, Rinehart, & Winston.

Stankiewicz, M. A. (1992). From the aesthetic movement to the arts and crafts movement. *Studies in Art Education, 33* (3), 165-173.

Stone, D. (1993). The secondary art specialist and the art museum. *Studies in Art Education, 35* (1), 45-54.

Sullivan, G. (1993). Art-based art education: Learning that is meaningful, authentic, critical and pluralist. *Studies in Art Education, 35* (1), 5-21.

Zimmerman, E. (1992). A comparative study of two painting teachers of talented adolescents. *Studies in Art Education, 33* (3), 174-185.

APPENDIX A-1

Reprinted from *Studies in Art Education*, *36*(3), 154-169.

Understanding Domain Knowledge for Teaching: Higher-Order Thinking in Pre-Service Art Teacher Specialists

Georgianna Short
Cherry Creek School District #5
Englewood, Colorado
and
The Ohio State University

> This study investigates the higher-order thinking and subject matter understanding of pre-service art specialists. The relationship between art specialists' subject matter understanding and instructional choices is also examined. Individual case study research was conducted on 18 prospective art teachers from a large midwestern state university. The participant-volunteers were visual art or art education majors in the final stages of coursework. Qualitative data were triangulated from a series of oral interviews, lesson-planning activities, personal biographies, university transcripts, and self-reports. The data analysis revealed that only some pre-service art teachers exhibited the higher-order thinking or in-depth understanding expected of specialists in visual art. Most future art teachers displayed overly simplistic thinking, shallow understandings, and superficial domain knowledge. These findings suggest the content knowledge and art understandings possessed by pre-service art teacher specialists should not be taken for granted. Successful completion of required coursework does not guarantee higher-order thinking or deep understanding of the domain. Implications for teacher preparation are discussed.

In recent years there has been growing concern that teachers do not know or understand enough about the subjects they teach. As early as 1983, reports such as *Nation at Risk: The Imperative for Educational Reform* alleged that deficiencies in the subject matter knowledge and understanding of teachers is responsible, in part, for a decline in the quality of what American students know. Authors of the report question how much subject matter understanding prospective teachers can possess when most come from the nation's "bottom quarter of graduating high school and college students" (National Commission for Excellence in Education,

1983, p. 22). These teacher candidates are then subjected to teacher preparation curricula "weighted heavily with courses in 'educational methods' at the expense of courses in subjects to be taught" (NCEE, 1983, p. 22).

In a effort to rectify the situation, *Nation at Risk* (1983), together with *Nation Prepared: Teachers for the 21st Century* (1986), *Tomorrow's Teachers: A Report of the Holmes Group* (1986), *America 2000: An Educational Strategy* (1991), and *Goals 2000: Educate America Acts* (1994) call for the restructuring of educational standards for future teachers. New standards would require teacher candidates to "demonstrate competence in an academic discipline," including in-depth understanding of instructional content (NCEE, 1983, p. 30).

Recent evidence suggests strong links exist between a teacher's subject matter understanding and the instructional decisions he or she make about course structure, textbook selection, and lesson content (Grossman, Wilson, & Shulman, 1989; McDiarmid, Ball, & Anderson, 1989; Shulman & Grossman, 1987). Consequently, increasing the subject matter understanding of future teachers is likely to improve their ability to promote thinking, reasoning, and understanding in children (U.S. Department of Education, 1991, 1993).

Understanding in Well-Structured and Ill-Structured Domains

Understanding subject matter content can be more difficult in some domains than in others. For example in mathematics and physics, the problems faced by students contain well-defined underlying patterns (Shulman, 1992). Therefore, these domains are considered examples of "well-structured" domains because concepts are based on laws, axioms, and theorems which can be applied to a variety of situations with predictability and consistency (Efland, 1995; Spiro, Vispoel, Schmitz, Samarapungavin, & Boerger, 1987). Predictability and consistency in the application of basic principles makes problem-solving and learning less difficult (Feltovich, Coulson, Spiro, & Dawson-Saunders, 1992).

Understanding in Ill-Structured Domains

In contrast, the visual arts domain can be considered "ill-structured" because concepts vary in meaning from one application to the next (Efland, 1995). For instance:

> One can learn to recognize paintings in the French Impressionist style by certain gross stylistic indicators such as the use of vibrant color, sketchy brush strokes that capture fleeting impressions of a moment, the illusion of outdoor lighting, and the depiction of life in informal or recreational situations such as outdoor cafes, boating scenes, and the like. Though one may recognize these as outward features of the style, it would be difficult to interpret the meaning or significance of individual works by these attributes alone. Each is a separate case and is subject to varied interpretations" (Efland, 1993, p. 28).

Lack of prescriptive solutions in the visual arts suggests that the development of art understandings may be more demanding than the development of understandings in other fields of study.

Definition of Subject Matter Understanding in Ill-Structured Domains

A useful definition of subject matter understanding within ill-structured domains, such as the visual arts, has been offered recently by researchers who study learning and understanding. They define in-depth understanding in ill-structured domains as: "acquiring and retaining a network of concepts and principles about some domain that accurately represent key phenomena and their interrelationships and that can be engaged flexibly when pertinent to accomplish diverse, sometimes novel objectives" (Feltovich, Spiro, & Coulson, 1993, p. 181).

Knowledge base. According to this definition, in-depth understanding requires a substantial knowledge base. Components of a person's knowledge base include accurate factual and conceptual knowledge as well as paradigms for organizing and guiding inquiry within the domain (Feltovich, Spiro, & Coulson, 1991; Grossman, 1990; Prawat, 1989).

It is now thought that an individual's knowledge base is organized as a cognitive network (Feltovich et al., 1991; Nickerson, 1985; Prawat, 1989). Within this network, fragments of information are connected via interchangeable links (Nickerson, 1985; Prawat, 1987; Spiro et al., 1987). Connective links must be flexible to allow fragments of knowledge to move about and reassemble according to the needs of particular application contexts (Spiro et al., 1987, p. 4).

Cognitive strategies. A person's ability to selectively adapt elements of his or her knowledge base for a specific application involves using cognitive strategies to think about and solve problems, make decisions, and/or generate interpretations (Feltovich et al., 1991; Koroscik, 1992; Prawat, 1989). Some situations may demand strategies where *identical* elements in the knowledge base are reassembled to fit the requirements of different learning situations (Spiro, Coulson, Feltovich, & Anderson, 1988). Other situations may require strategies where *different* elements in the knowledge base are assembled to provide new perspectives on the same learning problem (Glaser & Chi, 1988; Prawat, 1989). Each of these strategies requires cognitive flexibility, indicates higher-order thinking, and denotes in-depth domain understanding (Bereiter & Scardamalia, 1986; Feltovich et al., 1991; Glaser & Chi, 1988; Spiro et al., 1988).

Understanding the Subject Matter of Visual Art

Works of art can represent a variety of complex ideas (Barrett, 1994; Danto, 1981; Goodman, 1984). Comprehending the complexity of and differences between these ideas requires a deep understanding of domain knowledge (Barrett, 1994; Koroscik, 1982, 1992; Wolcott, 1994). In-depth art understandings can be obtained from considering internal information such as formal qualities and descriptive content together with external or contextual considerations including historical background and cultural setting (Barrett, 1994; Danto, 1981; Wolcott, 1994).

The way in which internal considerations of formal elements and descriptive information can relate to interpretation and deeper understanding of artworks may be found in a theoretical model researched and developed by Koroscik (1982). In this model, artworks, embodying six different levels of information, are identified and defined along with their corresponding depth of understanding. In Koroscik's model, viewers begin with an examination of an artwork's structural elements (formal qualities and principles of art) and representational features (descriptive content) which provide the basis upon which meanings and symbolism can be determined. Since meanings may be accessed only by considering relationships between structural and representational features, focus restricted to formal qualities or descriptive content cannot provide deeper understanding.

Experts in the areas of art criticism, art history, and studio production are familiar with the importance of formal qualities and descriptive content to understanding works of art. They are also aware that understanding can be deepened through investigation of historical, political, social, and cultural contexts (Barrett, 1991, 1994; Preziosi, 1989; Zutter, 1990). In interpreting and evaluating works of art, each of these domain experts considers:

- formal qualities and relationship of formal qualities to compositional structure
- descriptive content
- expressive features and related symbolism
- historical/cultural context and authorship
- reasoned interpretation and/or judgment
- aesthetic considerations
- critical discourse

Pre-Service Teachers' Understanding of Domain Knowledge

Recently, some teacher educators have expressed concern about the content knowledge and understanding of students preparing to teach in their respective fields of study (Ball & Feiman-Nemser, 1988; Grossman, Wilson, & Shulman, 1989). Current research evidence suggests pre-service teachers across subject areas often successfully complete required course work but lack understanding of course material. For example, findings in the areas of math, science, history, and reading suggest that future teachers in those domains frequently display superficial understanding of underlying processes and concepts, are unable to connect related information together, reject principles that contradict popular "common sense" views, and impulsively apply formulistic solutions to problems even when results are meaningless (Arditzoglou & Crawley, 1990; Ball, 1990; Fleury & Bentley, 1991; O'Brien & Stewart, 1990; Paget, 1989).

Reductive Bias

The research team of Feltovich, Spiro, Coulson, and Anderson (1988-1993) study problems of learning and understanding. They describe these and related comprehensional difficulties as manifestations of *reductive bias*, defined as a "proclivity toward the strategic mismanagement of complexity involving various forms of oversimplification" (Feltovich, Spiro, & Coulson, 1988, p. 5).

Reductive bias in learning. Studies indicate that students in institutions of higher learning find the volume of information and conceptual complexity of university coursework overwhelming and difficult to manage, frustrating efforts to understand (Feltovich et al., 1988). In these situations, learners frequently simplify information in various ways to make understanding easier (Feltovich et al., 1988-1993). While simplified information may be easier to understand, it is incomplete and often inaccurate. Incomplete, inaccurate information can cause conceptual misinterpretation and result in misconceptions (Feltovich et al., 1988, 1991).

Reductive bias in teaching. The tendency to over-simplify information in various ways also can be found in daily teaching practices. For example, it is common to simplify concepts for beginners and build complexity gradually (Feltovich et al., 1988). Complexity at introductory stages is avoided because both teachers and students find it overpowering and difficult (Feltovich et al., 1988; Glaser, 1984, p. 96). Simplified presentations, in contrast, are thought to facilitate student learning and make teaching easier.

Simplified instruction is often reinforced by selected teaching supplements. In required textbooks for example, the content, supporting diagrams, and illustrations often contain over-simplified views supportive of instructional practices (Feltovich et al., 1988). Further, materials designed to provide hands-on experience and working knowledge of particular concepts are frequently selected on the basis of availability rather than on the basis of properties unique to concepts under study (Feltovich et al., 1988). When taken together, these educational practices represent a "conspiracy of convenience" to make complex subject matter simple (Spiro et al., 1987). The problem is that such procedures interfere with learning in advanced stages when students are expected to comprehend the inter-related nature of concepts, understand context-dependent exceptions, and respond flexibly to the requirements of differing situations (Feltovich et al., 1991).

Preparation of Pre-service Teachers in the Visual Arts

After at least four years of sustained study of the visual arts, pre-service art teachers can be considered *advanced learners* in the domain (for further discussion on advanced learners see Spiro et al., 1988). Considerable formal instruction has provided them with opportunities to examine works of art through historical, cultural, critical, philosophical, and technical perspectives. Increased art knowledge and experience with a variety of perspectives should allow these prospective teachers to achieve a measure of expertise in the ways they approach, understand, and discuss works of art. Indeed, art teachers are considered resident experts in their schools. They are expected to understand the complexity of artworks themselves, and be able to provide classroom experiences that foster similar understanding in their students. However, if art teachers in advanced stages of learning are affected by reductive bias, they may make curricular decisions that encourage patterns of thought and action in pupils that do not correspond to domain precepts. Such practice is of concern since art teachers frequently have autonomy in the areas of curriculum planning and implementation in their schools and are solely responsible for what students understand about visual art (Koroscik, 1992).

One way to determine what future teachers specializing in visual art know and understand about the domain is to ask them to discuss works of art and plan related art lessons for students. Responses can then be examined for factual or conceptual information, higher-order thinking, and in-depth understanding.

Method
Design

Qualitative methods were used in a multiple case, replication design to explore the understanding of future teachers specializing in the visual arts. In a comparative or multiple case study design, triangulated qualitative evidence is collected in a number of different but related case studies (George, 1979; Yin, 1991). "Each individual case study consists of a 'whole' study in which convergent evidence is sought regarding the facts and conclusions for the case; each case's conclusions are then considered to be the information needing replication by other individual cases" (Yin, 1991, p. 57). Because evidence is collected from a number of different case studies and compared, findings are often considered more robust than those derived from studies of solitary cases (Yin, 1991).

Participants

Pre-service art teacher volunteers (n=18) from a large midwest state university participated in this study. The group of volunteers included both undergraduate seniors and post-graduate students specializing in visual art. All were seeking teacher certification. The participants were enrolled in a Saturday art workshop for children, a 10-week practicum required for graduation. Enrollment in this on-campus practicum is contingent upon completion of required coursework and electives in the College of the Arts and the College of Education.

The Saturday workshop provides pre-service art specialists with an opportunity to apply subject matter knowledge and pedagogical skills they have already acquired to actual teaching situations with elementary and secondary students prior to student teaching. During this stage of their professional development, future teachers' understanding of visual art and lesson-planning tends to reflect learning obtained through university coursework and past personal experiences with works of art. Thus, insight into how these advanced learners understand the domain of visual art and how they integrate and transform what they have learned into instructional planning for school-age children is made possible.

Materials

Researcher-selected work of art. A color reproduction of the painting *Olympia* (1863) by Edouard Manet served as one focus of this investigation (see Figure 1). *Olympia* was chosen because it: (a) is pivotal in the history of Western art (Clark, 1984; Gronberg, 1988; Rey, 1986); (b) contains sufficient complexity to be understood on a variety of different levels; (c) is included in survey courses on Western Art required of pre-service teachers; and (d) appears in well-known textbooks on the history of Western art (Arnason, 1986; Feldman, 1987).

Figure 1. Musée d'Orsay, Paris, *Olympia*. 1863. Oil on canvas. 130.5 x 190 cm appeared approximately at this point in the originial article of *Studies in Art Education, 36*(3), 160).

Artworks of choice. A group of 20 color art reproductions (varying in time period, style, artist, and culture) served as a second focus of the study. Subject matter of all 20 artworks was the human form. These reproductions were divided into two groups of 10, matched according to style, artist, culture, or time period.

Procedures

To examine what this group of future teachers understood about visual art, data were triangulated from tape recorded interviews, written lesson plans for the Saturday art workshop, self-reports, autobiographies, and college transcripts.

Interviews. Three one-on-one, tape-recorded interview sessions were conducted with each future teacher over a 12-week period. Interviews followed a written protocol using general and non-directive questions to allow future teachers to "represent themselves in their own terms" (Lofland, 1974, as cited by Merriam, 1991, p. 68).

In Interview I, the pre-service teachers were presented with a color reproduction of *Olympia* and given as much time as they needed to discuss the painting in detail. Two pages of written supplementary information describing formal qualities, descriptive content, historical context, and possible interpretations of the painting were then provided. The participants were allowed to read this information at their own pace. Then, additional oral comments about *Olympia* were invited. Following additional remarks, the pre-service teachers were asked to suggest a lesson plan for their students based upon *Olympia* by Manet.

In Interviews II and III, each future teacher was allowed to select and discuss an artwork(s) of personal interest from among the group of ten color reproductions provided. The first group of ten reproductions was supplied for Interview II and the matched set of ten reproductions was provided in Interview III. No supplementary information was furnished in either of these interviews. Following the discussion of artwork(s) in each interview, prospective teachers were again asked to plan a lesson for young people based on their personal selection(s). The age group to be taught was not specified for either of these lessons by the researcher.

Lesson plans. In addition, a unit containing four lesson plans written for the Saturday art workshop was collected from each pre-service teacher participant. All lesson plans followed a two-part format. In part one of the lesson plan, future teachers described the focus and objectives of their lesson, evaluation criteria, supplies and materials to be used, clean-up procedures, resource materials, and vocabulary to be presented. In part two, the prospective teachers explained how lesson concepts would be introduced, how students would apply the new concepts, and how lesson content would be summarized for students in concluding activities. Lesson plans were completed independently by the participants over a period of five weeks.

Analysis of data. Data analysis was guided by the theoretical propositions on reductive bias suggested by the review of literature on advanced learners (Merriam, 1991; Strauss & Corbin, 1990; Yin, 1991). Awareness of reductive patterns in the thinking of advanced learners in other domains was then used to provide direction to the data analysis and assist in its interpretation (Strauss & Corbin, 1990).

An open coding process was used to identify and categorize informational units within the data for each case study (Strauss & Corbin, 1990). An informational unit has been defined as "the smallest piece of information ... that can stand by itself" (Lincoln & Guba, 1985, p. 345). Using the constant comparative method, units containing similar information were grouped together to form a category (Lincoln & Guba, 1985). Categories developed in this way were related to the formal, descriptive, historical or cultural, aesthetic, and critical dimensions of artworks.

Units of information within each dimensional category were then compared to like information found in the writings of domain experts. Comparisons revealed whether over-simplifications were present within the category data and if so, to what degree. Findings reflecting the presence or absence of over-simplification in each category were compared to similar findings in other categories to determine whether and to what degree over-simplification existed within the case study as a whole. Conclusions regarding reductive bias in each case study were then compared to similar conclusions in every other case study to determine whether replication was present (Yin, 1991). These comparisons revealed the existence of three different replicated patterns.

Replicated patterns of reductive bias reflective of pre-service art specialists' thinking and understanding were then compared to the patterns of reductive bias found in advanced learners from other domains as described in the review of literature. Comparisons were scrutinized for "literal" or "theoretical" replication (Yin, 1991, p. 112). Since neither literal nor theoretical replication was found, formulation of a modified theory of reductive bias appropriate to the thinking of pre-service specialists in the visual arts was necessary (Yin, 1991).

Findings and Discussion

Research evidence gathered on advanced learners in other domains suggests that over-simplifying tendencies characteristic of reductive bias are likely to exist among advanced learners in other fields of study such as visual art. Findings of the present study confirm this prediction. Almost all pre-service teacher participants displayed the over-simplified thinking characteristic of reductive bias in their understanding of artworks and lesson-planning activities. However, unlike findings reported on advanced learners in other fields of study, the degree of over-simplification varied widely among the participants.

Forms of Reductive Bias

When findings in the individual cases are compared, three distinct forms of reductive over-simplification are found. Reductive patterns can be distinguished by the number of dimensions the participants referenced in their comments about works of art. Pre-service teachers referencing a similar number of dimensions are grouped together. These groupings are then ordered from most reductive to least reductive as follows:

- **Most Reductive Group**—Pre-service teachers whose understanding of artworks was restricted to one dimension.
- **Moderately Reductive Group**—Pre-service teachers whose art understandings included two or three dimensions.
- **Least Reductive Group**—Pre-service teachers whose understanding of artworks incorporated four, five, or six dimensions.

While the participants within each group exhibit similar patterns of understanding when examining works of art, their approaches to lesson-planning sometimes vary. Variation in lesson-planning is particularly evident in the Most Reductive and Least Reductive Groups. In these two groups, lesson-planning does not reflect the participants' previously demonstrated ability to draw substantive connections to works of art. Instead, art lessons are either unrelated to the artwork(s) involved or exhibit a severely reduced version of the participants own connection-making ability. Only lesson-planning in the Moderately Reductive Group is reasonably consistent in reflecting the participants' art understandings as revealed in previous discussions about works of art.

One example of each reductive pattern is presented in the following discussion. In the interest of clarity and brevity, extracts are limited to those made by participants in Interview I where discussion and lesson-planning focused on Manet's *Olympia*.

Levels of Response to Olympia

As previously stated, future teachers in Interview I were given a color reproduction of *Olympia* and asked to discuss or describe the painting in as much detail as possible. Then, the participants read two pages of additional information about the painting and were encouraged to make additional remarks if they wished to do so. The interview concluded with each prospective teacher suggesting a lesson plan related to *Olympia*.

Every participant's initial discussion of *Olympia* was then examined to determine how many references were made to the painting's formal, descriptive, interpretive, historical, cultural, aesthetic, and critical dimensions. This analysis revealed that eight (44%) of the pre-service art specialists responded to Manet's painting in only one dimension (i.e., the Most Reductive Group). Five (28%) future art teachers made comments about *Olympia* in two or three dimensions (i.e., the Moderately Reductive Group). The remaining five (28%) prospective teachers explained Manet's painting in terms of four or more dimensions (i.e., the Least Reductive Group).

Most reductive responses. Further analysis of the participants' initial discussion of *Olympia* reveals that all eight art specialists in the Most Reductive Group limited their singular connection-making to either the formal or the descriptive dimension. Comments in either dimension were limited to the identification of isolated details. No participant in the Most Reductive Group attempted to find relationships between the details they mentioned or connect isolated details to *Olympia's* meanings. When supplementary pages containing information about other dimensions were presented and examined by future teachers in this group, they disregarded it. Consequently, any further discussion of *Olympia* and lesson-planning was based on their initial comments.

An example of understanding limited exclusively to the formal dimension of *Olympia* may be found in remarks by "Alice," a post-graduate student with a Bachelor of Fine Arts Degree in commercial illustration from a local four-year college. Alice's entire description of *Olympia* consisted of the following:

Appendix A-1

Its very high contrast is the first thing I noticed. It almost looks like it is cut out, you know, two-dimensional, flat. I think it's flat, the fore-figure is. This girl on the bed, her skin color bothers me, the yellow against the white *(formal qualities)*.

Alice then read the additional information on the painting's formal qualities, descriptive content, various interpretations, and historical context. However, she found the information neither meaningful nor useful and dismissed it with a single comment:

There's a lot in there, but I think I've about covered it.

Alice's singular focus on formal qualities was then transferred to lesson-planning for her students. Details enumerated in her initial discussion were abbreviated to become the basis of her lesson-plan:

[We'll talk about] his use of the dark and light. You know, in the foreground with the whites and the background all darks. Possibly having [students] do something where the foreground would be all white and the background all dark *(formal qualities)*.

In essence, Alice seems to recognize only formal qualities in works of art and is unaware that her singular focus limits what she is able to understand about *Olympia*. Alice's limited understanding is not expanded by additional information. She fails to acknowledge other dimensions of Manet's painting even when confronted with them. Both actions suggest a strong belief on the part of this future teacher that formal qualities alone can adequately represent the content and meaning of works of art, other considerations are irrelevant. In view of her Bachelor of Fine Arts Degree and post-graduate status, it is disturbing that Alice's over-simplification of *Olympia* to a single formal quality persisted even after reading supplementary information.

Moderately reductive responses. Five pre-service teachers understood *Olympia* in terms of two or three of its dimensions. Two-dimensional responses were generally confined to formal qualities and descriptive content. Three-dimensional responses commonly contained references to formal qualities and descriptive content as well as some interpretation.

An example of two-dimensional understanding can be found by examining "Kathy's" discussion of *Olympia* and related lesson plan. Kathy is an undergraduate senior majoring in art education. Her initial description of *Olympia* consisted of the following:

There are two female figures. One of them Caucasian, the other is of Black heritage. One of them is a female, nude, lying out on a bed *(descriptive content)*. And the background is very dark *(formal qualities)*. The foreground is very light. I guess it uses *chiaroscuro*, I believe *(formal qualities)*.

In contrast, "Nancy," a post-graduate student with a Bachelor of Fine Arts Degree in painting from a private local college, gave this three-dimensional response to *Olympia:*

Well, [this] reproduction shows a woman lying nude or reclining on a bed. Her back is propped up by pillows so her back is on a 45 degree angle. And, she has a tapestry or blanket draped underneath her. And, looking on, is what appears to be a servant or a maid. A black woman who's dressed in a white frock holding a bouquet of flowers, kind of with a gaze at [the other] woman *(descriptive content)* that seems to say "Where do you want me to put these flowers?" "Do you like them?" "Do you want them?" *(attempt to interpret).*

It's pretty balanced color-wise. There's a dark triangle in the lower left corner that balances out against the white, the stark, bright, white colors through the middle of the painting, versus the dark, dark background. Your eye gets led through it pretty well with the drape and the motion of the curves of the sheet. This big wide line right down the middle, kind of pulls you right down through the painting *(formal qualities).*

Both Kathy and Nancy respond to *Olympia* in terms of the painting's formal properties and descriptive content. However, Nancy's discussion contains more detail and includes some attempt to interpret meaning.

After reading additional information, both Kathy and Nancy become interested in the painting's historical background. Kathy is able to expand her understanding by adding historical information to the formal qualities and descriptive content she previously referenced:

I didn't know about the scandal it caused, I mean, following the other Italian artist, just changing his a bit [by] adding a few minor details to it, that turned the whole meaning of what he thought was a beautiful painting into something people were wanting to ruin.

Nancy adds historical and descriptive information to her previous understanding:

I think it's cool how it [*Olympia*] was based on another painting by Titian except that he [Manet] updated it to reflect the life of his times *(historical context)* and made the woman a prostitute *(descriptive content).* That was the most important thing I didn't know before.

In contrast to the Most Reductive Group, both of these Moderately Reductive pre-service teachers found supplementary information valuable in expanding their understanding.

Kathy and Nancy then incorporate their newly acquired historical information into an *Olympia*-based lesson plan. However, when Kathy adds historical information, she seems to abandon any previous interest in descriptive content.

Therefore, her resulting lesson plan is still limited to two dimensions although now they are historical context and formal qualities.

For one thing, [I'd] need something to compare it to. Maybe look at [Titian's *Venus of Urbino* (1538)] *(historical reference)* where more shading is done rather than just contouring and where it shows more depth versus how his just looks more like things are cut out and placed on *(formal qualities)*.

Nancy also decides to incorporate newly acquired historical information into her lesson plan on *Olympia*. However, unlike Kathy, she is still able to retain previous emphasis on formal qualities, descriptive content, and interpretation. In so doing, Nancy expands her own understanding to include four dimensions. With her newly expanded four-dimensional understanding, Nancy is then able to plan a four-dimensional lesson for students.

I'd get the *Venus of Urbino* and compare the two. What's different, what's the same? How's it different? Have them talk about stuff like color and position and people in the background *(formal qualities, descriptive content)*. Then ask them "When do you think these were painted?" I think I would tell them the story after, you know. Like which one was painted first, which one was painted after. And then, I would go ahead and say ... this painting is based on this painting. Manet was trying to show the reality of, you know, French life in the 19th century *(historical content)*. She's a prostitute. She's not idealized like the *Venus of Urbino* who's sort of dreaming off with all this hair ... *(descriptive content)*. And then we would have to talk about how she [*Venus of Urbino*] is really the "subject of the gaze" and how Manet tried to change all that. We'd talk about how women have been portrayed in art through time ... you know, traditionally *(historical context and interpretation)*.

Some pre-service teachers in the Moderately Reductive Group, like Kathy, were able to understand *Olympia* in terms of only two dimensions at a time. They acknowledged new information presented to them and incorporated the new information into a lesson plan for students. However, when new information was added, a previous area of interest was eliminated from thinking, presumably to maintain a two-dimensional focus. In contrast, future teachers in the Moderately Reductive Group like Nancy, who initially understood Manet's painting in terms of three dimensions, were able to maintain their three-dimensional views and expand understanding to four dimensions when provided with additional information.

The two- and three-dimensional understanding of pre-service art specialists in the Moderately Reductive Group appears to represent a pivotal point in the development of higher-order thinking, deeper understanding, and cognitive flexibility among aspiring art teachers. It seems that when initial understanding is increased from two-dimensional emphasis on surface qualities such as formal elements and descriptive content to include some interpretive awareness, understanding not only becomes deeper, but cognitive flexibility is increased allowing for the incorporation of new information into the learner's existing knowledge base. However, when initial understanding is restricted to two dimensions, new information appears to replace some portion of existing knowledge, and understanding remains as limited as before.

Least reductive responses. Five of the pre-service specialists in this study were classified as Least Reductive because they consistently demonstrated understanding of Mane's *Olympia* in four, five, or six dimensions. Formal elements, descriptive content, interpretation, and historical context were always included in the content of their interviews. Elements of criticism and aesthetic considerations were also referenced from time to time. In so doing, this group of future teachers approaches the comprehensive understanding and cognitive flexibility expected of advanced learners in visual art.

An example of least reductive responses is provided in an extract from "Mary's" initial description of *Olympia*. Mary is a post-graduate student with a Bachelor of Fine Arts Degree in Art Education who as an undergraduate chose a non-certification B.F.A. option. She begins her discussion by identifying *Olympia* by title and artist, then comments in a general way about meanings of the painting. Formal and descriptive information intertwined with historical references follow:

This is *Olympia* by Manet. I know he was attempting to copy the style of another artist *(historical context)*, but the [actual] subject matter was somewhat of a social comment on the bourgeoisie *(historical context and interpretation)*. [The subject] is lying on a white bed with two big pillows. In between her and the white bed is a tapestry-of-sorts, and it's an off-white color with roses or pink flowers on the trim and some gold threads *(descriptive content)*. I think there may be some connection with the [off-white] tapestry that's between her and the white bed. I don't know if the whiteness, the somewhat stark whiteness of the bed, represents purity of some sort. And this off-white tapestry that she's lying on may be a representation of the background of the subject *(descriptive content and interpretation)*. There is a woman standing next to her, possibly her maid or symbolizing a *servant (descriptive content and interpretation)*. She's a black woman and she is holding a bouquet of flowers up to the subject *(descriptive content)*. The main subject figure is contrasted with the other subject and with the background in the painting as far as light and dark [is concerned] *(descriptive content and formal qualities)*. [The contrast] brings [the main figure] to the forefront but yet at the same time, the way it is compositionally set up, it allows your eye to move more easily around the painting *(formal qualities)*.

Since Mary's initial comments were already inclusive, supplementary information added little to her previous understanding as expressed earlier in the interview:

It was interesting to see how [the figure of *Olympia*] was intentionally flat and there is no depth so you look at the picture instead of into the picture *(formal qualities)* ... It is a very interesting painting in many different ways.

Mary then transfers her own four-dimensional understanding into lesson-planning for students. However, in the process, she reorganizes her knowledge about the painting and adds elements from additional dimensions as well. This extract is taken from her proposed lesson plan on *Olympia*:

Starting out with the art historical reference and showing this piece, I would approach it saying this is Manet's intention and this is what was perceived. And what does this tell us about the time, what people were thinking of and how they thought ... their puritanical views ...

Then critically, you could describe the work and talk about Titian. O.K. In one sentence he is saying that his is only an updated version of this [Titian] masterpiece, yet the color he used, the composition, the manner in which it is set up ... that's saying something totally different ...

Aesthetically you could say well, what makes something a work of art. How do you judge a work of art? Do you base it on opinion, or do you base it on certain criteria that is set forth by art education, art historians, critics, so on and so forth, or the artist himself, or does the public decide?

And then, there's Manet's style of painting, his use of color and composition. It was innovative and it was important to the development of the modern movement. Discuss Manet's concern with formal qualities. Such things as looking at it instead of into it, contrast of light and dark enhances the central figure ...

I mean, over a period of lessons, you could examine so many issues pertaining not only to this time period, but how it touches all time periods from that point into contemporary art. You could compare it to other work from the same time period or even to works of art by Mapplethorpe, compare the public's reaction of Mapplethorpe with the public's reaction to *Olympia*, that type of thing. Teaching this would probably be better over a period of time, a few classes, an entire unit.

Mary appears to have considerable understanding of Manet's painting herself and suggests a means of developing deep understanding among students. Her lesson plan not only references the formal, descriptive, and interpretive dimensions, but considers historical, critical, and aesthetic dimensions as well. Connections are also provided to contemporary artists such as Mapplethorpe. When compared to discussion and lesson planning by pre-service teachers in the Most Reductive Group and Moderately Reductive Group, Mary demonstrates considerable cognitive flexibility and depth of understanding.

Mary's idea of a unit devoted exclusively to one painting may seem excessive. But, when pressed to limit lesson-planing to one or two lessons, she protested: No. I mean how could I? So you put up an example for example's sake and what does that tell you about the work of art? It has something to do with the value of [artworks.] If you see a work of art as valuable and rich in content and having the ability to create other avenues to teach from, you just can't show this to people, throw it up and say we'll do this, we'll do that, instantaneously. You have to make sure they understand everything that goes into every aspect of the work.

Mary's idea of exploring paintings in depth has a number of advantages. In-depth investigation encourages development of the learner's knowledge base and knowledge-seeking strategies similar to those used by experts in the field. In addition, learners obtain a greater appreciation of works of art and deeper understanding of domain knowledge. In contrast, one- and two-dimensional approaches to works of art by pre-service art specialists in the Most Reductive and Moderately Reductive groups contain underdeveloped understandings and misconceptions which are then passed on to students.

In Summary

To be effective art educators, aspiring teachers must possess in-depth understanding of the domain. In-depth domain understanding consists of: (a) substantial and accurate factual knowledge, comprehensive conceptual knowledge, and the cognitive flexibility to see numerous relationships between the two; as well as (b) strategies to select and transform relevant factual and conceptual knowledge in appropriate ways to fit diverse requirements of art viewing and lesson planning. Eleven (61%) of 18 future teachers participating in this study did not possess these abilities. Despite their advanced learning status and visual art specialization, the majority of pre-service teachers demonstrated overly simplistic thinking, shallow understandings, and superficial domain knowledge. Their instructional decision-making, as reflected in lesson plans, exhibited similar characteristics.

Extracts from Interview I presented here reveal that most future teachers did not comprehend the complexity of *Olympia*. The Most Reductive Group of pre-service teachers (44% of participants) limited their understanding of Manet's painting to formal properties such as line, shape and color, or to descriptive content detailing people and events. The group of Moderately Reductive participants whose understanding was limited to two dimensions (17% of participants) initially viewed *Olympia* as a cluster of formal elements containing a particular subject matter, nothing more. The approach of both groups (61%) reflects an underlying assumption that art objects do not consist of meaningful statements in visual form but simply embody a collection of miscellaneous components. These components are unrelated to one another, to the hand of their maker, and to time and circumstance. Such views do not denote higher-order thinking nor in-depth understanding on the part of future teachers specializing in the visual arts.

Research on pre-service specialists in other domains indicates satisfactory completion of university coursework does not guarantee domain understanding. Data collected in this study suggests similar difficulties exist among pre-service teachers specializing in the visual arts. Extracts detailed here represent patterns of understanding found across interviews and lesson-planning activities irrespective of the artworks involved. They are intended to offer a glimpse into what may prove to be a problematic area in the education of pre-service art teacher specialists.

This study was limited to case study research on 18 pre-service art specialists in a particular location. Further investigation of other future teachers specializing in the visual arts from a variety of locations is needed to gain additional insight into how future teachers think about and understand the domain, and why some future teachers obtain substantive domain understanding while others fail to do so.

References

Arditzoglou, S. Y., & Crawley, F. E. (1990, April). *A descriptive study of alternative life and physical science conceptions of pre-service elementary teachers.* Paper presented at the annual meeting of the National Association for Research in Science Teaching, Atlanta, GA.

Arnason, H. H. (1986). *History of modern art.* New Jersey: Prentice-Hall.

Ball, D. L. (1990). Prospective elementary and secondary teachers' understanding of division. *Journal for Research in Mathematics Education, 21*(2), 132-144.

Ball, D. L., & Feiman-Nemser, S. (1988). Using textbooks and teachers' guides: A dilemma for beginning teachers and teacher educators. *Curriculum Inquiry, 18,* 401-423.

Barrett, T. (1991). *Understanding photographs.* Mountain View, CA: Mayfield.

Barrett, T. (1994). *Criticizing art: Understanding the contemporary.* Mountain View, CA: Mayfield.

Bereiter, C., & Scardamalia, M. (1986). Educational relevance of the study of expertise. *Interchange, 17*(2), 10-19.

Carnegie Task Force on Teaching as a Profession. (1986). *A nation prepared: Teachers for the 21st century.* Washington, DC: Carnegie Forum on Education and the Economy.

Clark, T. J. (1984). Preliminaries to a possible treatment of *Olympia* in 1865. In F. Frascina & C. Harrison (Eds.), *Modern art and modernism: A critical anthology* (pp. 259-273). New York: Harper & Row.

Danto, A. C. (1981). *Transfiguration of the commonplace: A philosophy of art.* Cambridge, MA: Harvard University Press.

Efland, A. (1995). The spiral and the lattice: Changes in cognitive learning theory and their implications for teaching and learning in the arts. *Studies in Art Education, 36*(3), (this issue).

Efland, A. (1993). Teaching and learning in the arts. *Arts Education Policy Review, 94*(5), 26-29.

Feldman, E. B. (1987). *Varieties of visual experience* (3rd ed.). New York: Abrams.

Feltovich, P. J., Coulson, R. L., Spiro, R. J., & Dawson-Saunders, B. K. (1992). Knowledge application and transfer for complex tasks in ill-structured domains: Implications for instruction and testing in biomedicine. In D. Evans & V. Patel (Eds.), *Advanced models of cognition for medical training and practice* (pp. 213-244). New York: Springer-Verlag.

Feltovich, P. J., Spiro, R. J., & Coulson, R. L. (1988). *The nature of conceptual understanding of biomedicine: The deep structure of complex ideas and the development of misconceptions* (Tech. Rep. No. 440). Champaign: University of Illinois, Center for the Study of Reading.

Feltovich, P. J., Spiro, R. J., & Coulson, R. L. (1991). *Learning, teaching, and testing for complex conceptual understanding.* (Tech. Rep. No. 6). Springfield: Southern Illinois University School of Medicine.

Feltovich, P. J., Spiro, R. J., & Coulson, R. L. (1993). Learning, teaching and testing for complex conceptual understanding. In N. Frederiksen, R. Mislevy, & I. Bejar (Eds.), *Test theory for a new generation of tests* (pp. 181-217). Hillsdale, NJ: Erlbaum.

Fleury, S. C., & Bentley, M. L. (1991). Educating elementary science teachers: Alternative conceptions of the nature of science. *Teaching Education, 3*(2), 57-67.

George, A. L. (1979). Case studies and theory development: The method of structured focused comparison. In P. G. Laren (Ed.), *Diplomacy: New approaches in history, theory, and policy* (pp. 43-68). New York: Free Press.

Glaser, R. (1984). Education and thinking: The role of knowledge. *American Psychologist, 39*(2), 93-104.

Glaser, R., & Chi, M. T. H. (1988). Overview. In M. T. H. Chi, R. Glaser, & M. J. Farr (Eds.), *The nature of expertise* (pp. xv-xxxv). Hillsdale, NJ: Lawrence Erlbaum.

Goodman, N. (1984). *Of mind and other matters.* Cambridge, MA: Harvard University Press.

Gronberg, T. A. (Ed.). (1988). *Manet: A retrospective.* New York: Hugh, Lauter, Levin.

Grossman, P. M. (1990). *The making of a teacher: Teacher knowledge and teacher education.* New York: Teachers College Press.

Grossman, P. L., Wilson, S. M., & Shulman, L. S. (1989). Teachers of substance: Subject matter knowledge for teaching. In M. C. Reynolds (Ed.), *Knowledge base for the beginning teacher* (pp. 23-36). New York: Pergamon Press.

Holmes Group. (1986). *Tomorrow's Teachers: A Report of the Holmes Group.* East Lansing, MI: Author.

Koroscik, J. S. (1982). The effects of prior knowledge, presentation time, and task demands on visual art processing. *Studies in Art Education, 23*(3), 13-22.

Koroscik, J. S. (1992). Research on understanding works of art: Some considerations for structuring art viewing experiences for students. *The Finnish Journal of Education, Kasvatus, 23*(5), 549-477.

Lincoln, Y. S., & Guba, E. G. (1985). *Naturalistic inquiry.* London: Sage.

McDiarmid, G. W., Ball, D. L., & Anderson, C. W. (1989). Why staying one chapter ahead doesn't really work: Subject-specific pedagogy. In M. D. Reynolds (Ed.), *Knowledge base for the beginning teacher* (pp. 193-205). New York: Pergamon Press.

Merriam, S. B. (1991). *Case study research in education: A qualitative approach.* San Francisco: Jossey-Bass.

National Commission on Excellence in Education. (1983). *A nation at risk: The imperative for educational reform.* Washington, DC: U.S. Government Printing Office.

Nickerson, R. S. (1985). Understanding understanding. *American Journal of Education, 93,* 201-239.

O'Brien, D., & Stewart, R. (1990). Pre-service teacher perspectives on why every teacher is not a teacher of reading: A qualitative analysis. *Journal of Reading Behavior, 22*(2), 101-129.

Paget, G. (1989). History teachers are not historians! Theme: Why teach history? *History and Social Science Teacher, 24*(3), 132-134.

Prawat, R. S. (1989). Promoting access to knowledge, strategy and disposition in students: A research synthesis. *Review of Educational Research, 59*(1), 1-41.

Preziosi, D. (1989). *Rethinking art history.* London: Yale University Press.

Rey, R. (1986). *Manet.* New York: Crown Publishers.

Shulman, L. S. (1992). Toward a pedagogy of cases. In J. H. Shulman (Ed.), *Case Methods in Teacher Education* (pp. 1-30). New York: Teachers College Press.

Spiro, R. J., Coulson, R. L., Feltovich, P. J., and Anderson, D. K. (1988). *Cognitive flexibility theory: Advanced knowledge acquisition in ill-structured domains.* (Tech. Rep. No. 441). Champaign: University of Illinois at Urbana-Champaign, Center for the Study of Reading.

Spiro, R. J., Vispoel, W., Schmitz, J., Samarapungavan, A., & Boerger, A. (1987). Knowledge acquisition for application: Cognitive flexibility and transfer in complex content domains. In B. C. Britton (Ed.), *Executive control processes* (pp. 177-200). Hillsdale, NJ: Erlbaum.

Strauss, A., & Corbin, J. (1990). *Basics of qualitative research: Grounded theory procedures and techniques.* London: Sage Publications.

U.S. Department of Education. (1991). *America 2000. An educational strategy.* Washington, DC: Author.

U.S. Department of Education. (1994). *Goals 2000:Educate America Acts.* Washington, DC: Author.

Wolcott, A. G. (1994). Whose shoes are they anyway? *Art Education, 47*(5), 14-20.

Yin, R. K. (1991). *Case study research: Design and methods.* New York: Sage Publications.

Zutter, J. (Ed.). (1990). *Julian Schnabel: Works on paper.* Munich: Prestel.

APPENDIX A-2

Reprinted from *Studies in Art Education*, 33(3), 154-164.

Frameworks for Understanding Art: The Function of Comparative Art Contexts and Verbal Cues

Judith S. Koroscik, Georgianna Short, Carol Stavropoulos
The Ohio State University
and
Sylvie Fortin
University of Quebec at Montreal

> The purpose of this investigation was to study contextual variables that influence the understanding of works of art. A key artwork was introduced to college students with other works of art in three different comparative contexts (same-artist vs. same-theme vs. interdisciplinary). Verbal contextual conditions (cued vs. non-cued) were also manipulated to show whether students rely on explicit verbal prompts to find relationships among works of art. The results of a multiple-choice matching test and an open-ended writing task indicate both types of contextual variables can have a strong impact on what a student looks for and thinks about when examining a work of art. Verbal cues can prompt students to elaborate on possible art meanings. Comparative art contexts containing familiar ideas can reduce the occurrence of misunderstandings if those ideas are explicitly identified for students. These and other findings have a direct bearing on how educational interventions might be structured.

One of the most important characteristics of intelligence is the ability to transfer previously acquired knowledge to new learning situations (Bransford, Sherwood, Vye, & Rieser, 1986). In order for students to make use of their cognitive resources, they must find meaningful connections between their existing knowledge and whatever they are attempting to understand (Prawat, 1989). Research has shown that transfer is highly context-dependent because much of what a student understands is embedded in the original learning context (Perkins & Salomon, 1988). Studies in reading comprehension have shown that readers often determine meanings of texts by scrutinizing surrounding contexts for semantic cues (Bransford & Johnson, 1972; Carnine, Kameenui, & Boyle, 1984). Verbal contexts can provide meaningful cues for comprehending texts, and, conversely, the understanding of pictures can be influenced by verbal contextual cues (Warren & Horn, 1982). Verbalizations have been found to have particularly strong effects on the nature of understandings formed in art viewing experiences (Barrett, 1985; Koroscik, Garber, & Baxter, 1987, Koroscik, Osman, & DeSouza, 1988). What remains in question is how the presence of one artwork among other works of art affects viewers' understandings. The present investigation was conducted to help fill this gap in the research literature.

Comparative art contexts may provide implicit cues that guide the art viewer's search for meanings. If, for example, a painting is displayed with other works by the same artist, students might look for relationships they would not think to consider if the painting was shown alone. Comparing works of art may have particularly strong effects on the way students look at art because research on learning indicates novices tend to dwell on incidental similarities unless explicitly prompted to do otherwise (Bransford, Sherwood, Vye, & Rieser, 1986; Perkins, 1987; Perkins & Salomon, 1988). Experts can readily see past surface resemblances to find deeper analogies because their richer knowledge base provides alternative sources for comparison (Chi, Glaser, & Farr, 1988; Glaser, 1988).

Teachers must concern themselves with (a) helping students expand their knowledge base and (b) developing students' abilities to transfer existing knowledge when it is appropriate to do so. We were interested in studying both aspects of learning to better explain how contextual variables influence a student's choice of search strategies and construction of art understandings. We manipulated the comparative context in which a particular artwork was shown in order to determine if students seek out meanings in predictable ways. We questioned whether art contexts would guide students to look for common features and whether comparative relationships among artworks are comprehended without explicit prompting. Evidence was also gathered to reveal the usefulness of verbal cues in the comprehension of those comparative relationships. We speculated that verbal cues might facilitate transfer by helping students find connections between the artworks' characteristics and students' own prior knowledge.

Method

Design

Two between-subjects variables were factorially combined to form six experimental groups to which undergraduate student volunteers were randomly assigned. *Art Context* consisted of comparative conditions in which a particular work of art, i.e., the key artwork, was presented in three different ways: (a) with other paintings by the same artist, i.e., the *same-artist context;* (b) with paintings depicting the same theme, i.e., the *same-theme context;* or (c) with works in other art forms (a poem, a lithograph, and a dance) that have a direct relationship to the key artwork, i.e., the *interdisciplinary context*. A second, independent variable, *Verbal Cue*, consisted of two levels: (a) Cues were given relating the key artwork to its comparative context, i.e., the *cued condition*, or (b) cues were not given, i.e., the *non-cued condition*. Student understanding of the key artwork was assessed through use of a multiple-choice matching test and an open-ended writing task. The matching test included three levels of a within subject variable, i.e., *Dimension (formal, descriptive,* and *interpretive)*. A full description of how each variable was operationalized in the present investigation is included below in the Materials and Procedures sections of this report.

Participants

Undergraduate students (n = 120) attending a large public research university in midwestern United States served as subjects in the study. The participants were recruited on a volunteer basis from an introductory course on the role of contemporary arts in American society; instruction in this course was based on live, recorded, and filmed performances and exhibitions. The course attracts students from a wide range of undergraduate majors since it can be counted towards fulfilling the university's basic education requirements. In exchange for participating in the study, students received extra credit in the course. An equal number of volunteers *(n* = 20) were randomly assigned to each of the six experimental groups.

There were more sophomores (n = 53) who chose to participate in the study than students in any other class rank: freshmen (n = 26), juniors (n = 25), and seniors *(n* = 16). This general distribution pattern was consistent within each experimental group except in the same-artist context in which there were slightly more upperclass students in the non-cued condition. Only somewhat more women *(n* = 66) participated in the study than men *(n* = 54), although the ratio of males to females was approximately the same across all experimental groups.

Materials

Art stimuli. Marc Chagall's painting, *The Birthday,* 1915-1923, was chosen as the key artwork in the present investigation. This painting was selected because it is stylistically representative of Chagall's work, it depicts a common theme in art, it has strongly influenced work in other arts disciplines, and there is a sizeable body of published literature on the artist and this painting. Its subject matter is moderately recognizable (medium abstraction level), and its expressive content is relatively easy to interpret. The painting represents a warm, loving relationship between the artist and his wife (Compton, 1985; Makarius, 1988).

Students were shown slide reproductions of *The Birthday* along with other works of art in one of the following three comparative context conditions:

1. *Same-artist context.* In this context condition, students viewed color-slide reproductions of three other paintings by Marc Chagall from the same time period: *The Coachman*, 1911-1912; *I and the Village*, 1911-1912; and *The Fiddler*, 1912-1913.

2. *Same-theme context.* The artworks shown to students in this context condition consisted of paintings displaying the same dominant theme as *The Birthday*, i.e., they all depict relationships, either positive or negative, between men and women. The paintings chosen were: *Jawlensky and Werefkin in a Meadow*, 1908-1909, by Gabriele Munter (positive depiction); *Untitled #2*, 1962, by Richard Lindner (negative depiction); and *Dance of Life*, 1889-1900, by Edvard Munch (negative depiction). As in the same-artist context, all paintings were presented simultaneously with *The Birthday* (positive depiction) as projected color slides.

3. *Interdisciplinary context.* This context condition included other art forms that are documented as having been directly influenced by Chagall's artwork. They included a short poem (14 lines) by Paul Eluard, *To Marc Chagall*, 1911-1915 (Verdet, 1984); a lithograph by El Lissitsky, and *Came the Dog Ate the Cat*, 1919; and a 6.5 minute segment of a video-taped modern dance performance, *Chagall*, 1989, by the Canadian Dance Company O'Vertigo of Montreal. The dance's choreography by Ginette Laurin and musical score by Gaetan Lebeuf were inspired by a 1988 exhibition of Chagall's work at the Montreal Museum of Fine Arts.

Procedures

The experimental sessions were conducted in an art classroom that provided minimal distraction from extraneous stimuli. Not more than 13 and no less than 6 students participated in any one session at the same time. The participants were seated along a row of tables facing a wall onto which slides were projected and/or a VCR monitor was in view. The classroom offered adjustable lighting so students could clearly view all artworks simultaneously, and they were also able to see well enough to complete the assigned writing tasks.

The procedures we used were quite simple. First, we gave students a general idea about the purposes of the study and informed them that their participation would take about 30 minutes. Next, the artworks were introduced one at a time at one-minute-intervals in a randomized sequence that varied with each context. After all four artworks were simultaneously in view, students were asked to respond to the first part of an open-ended writing task corresponding to the verbal-cued or non-cued condition they were randomly assigned to receive. Three minutes later, the participants were instructed to stop writing. The second part of the cued or non-cued condition was then given, and the participants were instructed to continue writing.

Verbal cues. Those participants who received verbal cues were initially prompted to look for and write about common characteristics among the artworks shown. After three minutes the key artwork was identified, and a common characteristic among all the artworks was specified. In the same-artist context, students were told that "all of these works of art were painted by the same artist, Marc Chagall." In the same-theme context, it was explained that "all of these works of art have the same theme, in that they all depict relationships between men and women." And in the interdisciplinary context, a verbal cue was given informing students that all the works "were inspired by Marc Chagall's artwork."

Participants in the non-cued condition were not told to look for common characteristics nor were any such commonalities revealed to them during the study. Instead, non-cued students were first instructed to write down their thoughts about the artworks. After three minutes, they were merely told to continue writing for another couple of minutes (an additional three minutes were provided). Unlike the verbal-cued condition, no mention was made of the key artwork during either part of the writing task.

Matching test. A multiple-choice matching test was developed to assess the degree to which participants comprehended formal, descriptive, and interpretive dimensions of the key artwork, *The Birthday*. When referring to the visual characteristics of artworks, we used the operational term *formal dimension*. All references to subject matter content were labeled *descriptive dimension*. And all expressive meanings concerning an artwork's form and/or content were termed *interpretive dimension*. Although these dimensions of artworks are interrelated, we have found in earlier research that it is possible to differentiate the comprehension of one dimension from another (e.g., Koroscik, 1982; Koroscik, Garber, & Baxter, 1987).

The format of the matching test was similar to those used in our earlier investigations (cf. Koroscik, Garber, & Baxter, 1987). Test items were identified from a comprehensive literature review on Chagall and *The Birthday*. The items consisted of 30 words or phrases (10 items per dimension) of which half corresponded to the painting and half were plausible mismatches. In the formal dimension, matching test items included "multiple points of view" and "compressed space," whereas mismatches included "jagged brushstrokes" and "symmetrical balance." The descriptive items included such matches as "a bouquet of flowers" and "lovers suspended in the air," whereas mismatch items included "acrobats flying in the air" and "a couple on stage." In the interpretive dimension, matching items included "no suggestion of erotic desire" and "love has eliminated gravity," whereas mismatches included "an act of seduction" and "a feminist comment on male/female relationships."

Participants were instructed to take as much time as they needed to decide whether each test item matched or did not match *The Birthday*. The painting was in view throughout this entire portion of the study. After responding to each matching item, students were asked to rate their confidence in each response on a scale from 1 (not confident) to 5 (extremely confident). The confidence ratings were later used in scoring the matching test. When the matches and mismatches were correctly identified, positive numerical values of the corresponding confidence self-ratings were assigned. Incorrect responses received negative values of the corresponding confidence ratings. The values were then totaled for each level of the dimension variable (formal, descriptive, and interpretive) and compared in analysis of variance tests.

Results and Discussion

Matching Test Analyses

Data from the multiple-choice matching test were analyzed in a 3 (Comparative Art Context) x 2 (Verbal Cue) x 3 (Dimension) mixed analysis of variance. A summary of this analysis is presented in Table 1. The results did not

Table 1
ANOVA Summary Table of Matching Test Results as a Function of Comparative Art Context, Verbal Cue, and Dimension

Source	df	MS	F	p
Comparative Art Context (CAC)	2	163.53	1.14	NS
Error	114	143.63		
Verbal Cue (VC)	1	953.88	6.64	.0112
Error	114	143.63		
Dimension (D)	2	8282.53	78.73	.0001
Error	228	105.20		
CAC X VC	2	249.96	1.74	NS
Error	114	143.63		
CAC X D	4	44.13	.42	NS
Error	228	105.20		
VC X D	2	587.25	5.58	.0043
Error	228	105.20		
CAC X VC X D	4	84.57	.80	NS
Error	228	105.20		

show significant differences in performance among students in the three comparative context groups; however, differences were found for cue effects, Verbal Cue, $F(1, 114) = 6.64$, $p < .01$, $MS_e = 143.63$. Cuing students to make contextual comparisons led to higher scores on the matching test ($M = 15.16$) than those scores achieved by students who received no verbal cues (M = 11.91). Significant differences were also found for Dimension, $F(2, 228) = 78.73$, $p < .0001$, $MS_e = 105.20$, and for the Verbal Cue x Dimension interaction, $F(2, 228) = 5.58$, $p < .004$, $MS_e = 105.20$.

Further analysis of Dimension effects indicates students had greatest difficulty comprehending interpretive meanings of *The Birthday:* descriptive *(M* =18.83) = formal (*M* = 17.70) > interpretive (*M* = 3.97), p < .01. We expected to find lower scores for interpretive items because they require a deeper level of understanding (cf. Koroscik, Osman, & DeSouza, 1988).

Post hoc comparison of means in the Verbal Cue x Dimension interaction shows responses to interpretive items were most successful in all three art context conditions when students received explicit verbal cues linking *The Birthday* to other artworks (see Table 2). There was no evidence that cuing helped the participants make accurate responses to formal or descriptive items. These findings suggest that students possessed prior knowledge that was germane to understanding interpretive meanings of *The Birthday*, but they failed to access and apply this knowledge unless explicit cues were given. Even the brief verbal cues we provided led to significant differences in interpretive understandings.

Table 2

Matching Test Mean Scores as a Function of Verbal Cue and Dimension

Verbal Cue	Formal	Dimension Descriptive	Interpretive
Cued	17.72	19.65	8.12
Non-Cued	16.69	18.22	-.18

Writing Task Analyses

Responses to the two-part open-ended writing task were examined on several levels in order to gain a more complete picture of how students' understandings of *The Birthday* were affected by the comparative art contexts and verbal cues. We were particularly interested in determining whether the art contexts guided the students' choice of search strategies, i.e., whether the contexts provided any implicit cues about what to look for when examining the works of art. We then compared these implicit cue effects in relation to differences brought about by explicit cuing, i.e., the verbal-cued condition. Analyses were also performed to gauge how students' understandings may have been deficient. Although art educators do not often speak of misunderstandings, there are occasions when responses to artworks are clearly off-track (Koroscik, 1990a, 1990b). We wanted to determine the conditions in which misunderstandings were most likely to occur.

Searching for understandings. The participants' written responses were first examined for evidence as to what guided their searches for meaning. We expected to find contextual differences in orientation to the formal, descriptive, and interpretive dimensions of artworks. We predicted that students in the same-artist context would give greater attention to formal qualities because these constituted common characteristics among all the works. The connecting factor among artworks in the same-theme context was subject matter; therefore, we speculated that the context would prompt students to attend to descriptive content more than to the artworks' formal or interpretive dimensions. In the interdisciplinary context,

Table 3
Percent of Participants Who Made Some Reference to the Formal, Descriptive, or Interpretive Dimensions of Artwork in the Open-Ended Writing Task

Comparative Art Context	Writing Task Part 1			Writing Task Part 2		
	Formal	Descriptive	Interpretive	Formal	Descriptive	Interpretive
Same-Artist						
Cued	80	64	60	48	56	72
Non-Cued	85	73	46	62	65	50
Same-Theme						
Cued	60	83	69	14	37	77
Non-Cued	86	100	73	86	86	77
Interdisciplinary						
Cued	18	55	100	27	36	68
Non-Cued	33	33	92	50	58	83

all of the works were directly linked to Chagall's painting primarily by their expressive content, so we anticipated that this context would implicitly direct students to search for interpretive meanings.

Our predictions proved to be accurate for the first half of the writing task. There is evidence that when students first began writing, they paid some attention to all three dimensions (formal, descriptive, and interpretive) but concentrated their efforts on examining characteristics shared by all four artworks in a context. As shown in Table 3, formal attributes were written about by more participants in the same-artist context than descriptive or interpretive qualities. In the same-theme context, more students wrote about descriptive content than the other two dimensions. And in the interdisciplinary context, considerably more students wrote about interpretive qualities than any other dimension.

The results show that search strategies shifted during the second part of the writing task. In the cued condition, students were told how the artworks related to *The Birthday*. These students then continued examining all three dimensions of the artworks, but they gave most attention to writing about interpretive qualities. Not only did this pattern occur in the interdisciplinary context where it was expected, the same orientation was also adopted by students who received verbal cues in the same-artist context and the same-theme context. This explains, at least in part, why we found higher matching test scores for interpretive items among students who received verbal cues regardless of their art context group (refer to Table 2).

Participants in the non-cued conditions responded differently in part two of the writing tasks. As shown in Table 3, these students shifted emphasis away from writing about the artworks' shared characteristics and adopted a broader search strategy. Students in the non-cued condition may have assumed it was wise to diversify their search strategies for information after we announced there was only a short time remaining to write about the artworks. It seems they tried quickly to take in as much as possible just in case something significant was overlooked. This shift to a more diverse orientation probably occurred because non-cued students received no confirmation that their original search strategies were appropriate The non-cued students could only guess at what was important to look for and write about when viewing the artworks.

The occurrence of misunderstandings. Further analysis of the writing task results indicates that the understandings students formed were often mistaken. When understandings are wrong, it is common to refer to them as "misunderstandings" or "misconceptions" although these terms have perhaps limited usefulness in describing art-learning problems. Any single work of art can have multiple meanings, yet all understandings are not equal, and some are altogether inappropriate (Koroscik, 1990a). Even when students give sound reasons for their interpretations of an artwork, those interpretations may be off-track because students possess limited knowledge of fundamental contextual information about the artist and/or the work of art.

We judged the inappropriateness of all writing task responses on the basis of a literature review of each work of art. Multiple sources by art historians and other experts were used to obtain consensus, particularly with regard to an artwork's interpretive meanings. The following excerpts are representative of the misunderstandings we found:

1. A student in the non-cued, same-artist context wrote, "I think the center two [*The Birthday* and *The Coachman*] look like they were done by one artist and the outside two [*I and the Village* and *The Fiddler*] by another artist."

2. Another student in the same-artist context (non-cued condition) wrote that the artworks "seem dated c. 1600's."

3. A student in the cued, same-artist context remarked that "it [*The Birthday*] looks like something Salvador Dali might create."

4. A student in the cued, interdisciplinary context condition stated that "all of [the artworks] have a violent theme: a young couple in troubled times do not know how to release their aggression, so they take it out on each other."

5. Someone in the same-theme context (non-cued condition) described *The Birthday* as showing "a man desperately seeking to make up with his wife after they have had a confrontation. He is going out of his way to get to her."

Several patterns emerged from our analyses of written responses such as these. The first pattern concerns the syntactic nature of the individual's response. This is useful to consider because a person's thinking process is revealed to some extent by the manner in which he or she organizes and translates thoughts in writing. In our study, the syntax of written responses typically took the form of an itemized list or a paragraph and sometimes a combination of the two. The construction of lists suggests a "bits and pieces" approach to thinking, whereas paragraph writing (containing more-or-less complete sentences) suggests an attempt to synthesize material.

When the contents of lists and paragraphs were compared in our study, we found misunderstandings occurred more frequently when students wrote lists to convey their understandings of formal, descriptive, or interpretive characteristics. Of the students whose understandings were mistaken or inappropriate, 50% wrote lists, 38% wrote paragraphs, and 12% wrote both lists and paragraphs. We found that even the relatively simple task of describing such things as lines, colors, and shapes was not easy or obvious to the students we tested. This finding is noteworthy in light of the fact that our study involved college students. It is reasonable to conclude that younger and less experienced students would find this task even more difficult.

A second pattern to emerge from our syntactic analysis demonstrates another strong difference between the experimental groups who received verbal cues and those who did not. The verbal cues prompted more students to write paragraphs (72%) than lists (7%), although some chose to write in a combined format (21%). In the non-cued condition, we found that students (47%) were more inclined to list their thoughts. Fewer non-cued students wrote paragraphs (42%) or chose to combine formats (11 %). These findings suggest to us that the presence of verbal cues immediately enabled many participants to find commonalties or to synthesize their ideas across examples. When the same students were cued a second time, they elaborated on relationships among artworks on a deeper, interpretive level. In the absence of verbal cuing, students observed common characteristics, but they were less likely to elaborate on the nature of those connections.

Choosing to write in paragraphs did not guarantee the construction of accurate understandings. At times, comparative art contexts and verbal cues were inadequate for prompting students to access and transfer relevant prior knowledge, and at other times the students knowledge base was deficient in ways that could not be overridden by effective search strategies.

Table 4
Percent of Participants Who Expressed Some Misunderstanding of Artworks in the Open-Ended Writing Task

Comparative Art Context	Verbal Cue	
	Cued	Non-Cued
Same-Artist	44	58
Same-Theme	37	59
Interdisciplinary	73	75

A third pattern to emerge from the writing task analyses suggests that comparative art contexts and verbal cues helped students bridge gaps in their existing knowledge only when the contexts and cues called attention to familiar ideas. As Table 4 indicates, we found the occurrence of misunderstandings varied among the three comparative art contexts. The fewest misunderstandings were produced in the same-theme context when students were explicitly cued to look for connections regarding male/female relationships. It seems likely this comparison facilitated understanding by focusing the search for meanings on a theme that students could readily link to their prior knowledge of couples in daily life. When the nature of relationships among artworks was less consistent with the students knowledge base, i.e., the interdisciplinary context, understandings were more difficult to comprehend despite the use of appropriate search strategies. Of the three comparative contexts we provided, students were least successful when they were asked to compare *The Birthday* to the selected dance, poem, and lithograph. Even when we provided verbal contextual cues in the interdisciplinary context, misconceptions were prevalent (refer to Table 4). Almost three-fourths of the students who examined artworks in the interdisciplinary context produced misconceptions.

Conclusions

Works of art are seldom found in isolation. In classrooms and museums, for example, they are frequently displayed within the context of other artworks. The results of our investigation show that comparative contexts, such as those discussed in this report, can have a significant impact on the way students look at and think about a work of art. The art contexts we used implicitly prompted students to examine artworks in terms of shared characteristics. When artworks were grouped thematically, the students in our study concentrated most of their attention on examining subject matter. When we grouped works of art by another set of shared characteristics in the same-artist context and interdisciplinary context, students' choice of search strategies shifted accordingly to focus on those common characteristics instead.

It should he emphasized to teachers that comparative art contexts were most effective in our study when they were accompanied by explicit verbal cues about the artworks' shared characteristics. Although we introduced only brief verbal statements, these explicit verbal references helped students immediately synthesize their ideas across works of art. This resulted in the construction of more elaborate meanings and deeper understandings. The verbal cues we provided also helped reduce misunderstandings, although they did not eliminate such problems altogether. In the absence of explicit verbal cues, students elected to employ broader search strategies which proved to be far less effective. These findings suggest teachers should provide comparative contexts and explicit verbal cues when depth of understanding is preferred over breadth. It should not be taken for granted that students will find meaningful or accurate ideas about artworks on their own.

Art teachers routinely display art reproductions in their classrooms, but it is unlikely that teachers spend much time considering how such displays might dictate student thinking about a particular artwork. We recommend that art educators plan instructional interventions to capitalize on contextual effects. Since multiple comparisons are possible for any work of art, it is important for teachers first to decide on the key ideas they want students to learn (Perkins, 1987). Prawat (1989) insists that some ideas in a domain or discipline are more meaningful than others because they allow for a richer set of connections. Our findings suggest that it is wise to base art comparisons on key ideas that have some relationship to students' existing knowledge. We concur with Prawat that it is equally important for teachers to consider the structure of the discipline and the cognitive structure of expert learners in that particular discipline.

One thing that has become clear from expert-novice research is that the expert's knowledge base is organized around a more central set of understandings than the novice's. One way to promote accessibility, then, might be to provide students with the concepts and principles most likely to promote expert competence in the domain in question. This requires a good deal of thoughtful analysis on the part of educators. (Prawat, 1989, pp. 6-7)

Our findings also underscore the value of differentiating two components of learning: (a) the student's knowledge base and (b) the strategies used by the student to activate prior knowledge. We found that problems in understanding works of art can be a function of one component only or of both. If a student chooses a search strategy that is inappropriate, there is little chance relevant knowledge will be transferred even if the student possesses it. On the other hand, if effective search strategies are employed but the student's knowledge base is lacking, understanding will be impaired or misguided. In either instance, the remedies teachers use to overcome learning obstacles must correspond to the specific nature of the problem.

Researchers must provide teachers with valid diagnostic tools to assess the scope of a student's existing knowledge base. Researchers must also develop methods for assessing a student's ability to employ knowledge-seeking strategies at appropriate times. The results of our study suggest multiple-choice matching tests are only somewhat useful for this purpose. Open-ended writing tasks were found to be more useful, but analysis of them is extremely time intensive. This is yet another reason why it may be desirable for educators to focus learning objectives on a limited set of key ideas. Instead of assessing a full range of possible learning outcomes, teachers (and students) might restrict themselves to evaluating the depth to which key ideas have been learned.

References

Barrett, T. (1985). Photographs and contexts. *Journal of Aesthetic Education*, 19(3), 51-64.

Bransford, J. D., & Johnson, M. K. (1972). Contextual prerequisites for understanding: Some investigations of comprehension and recall. *Journal of Verbal Learning and Verbal Behavior*, 11, 717-726.

Bransford, J. D. Sherwood, R., Vye, N., & Rieser, J. (1986). Teaching thinking and problem solving: Research foundations. *American Psychologist* 41(10), 1078-1089.

Carnine, D., Kameenui, E. J., & Coyle, G. (1984). *Reading Research Quarterly*, 19(2), 188-204.

Chi, M. T. H., Glaser, R., & Farr, M. J. (Eds.). (1988). *The nature of expertise*. Hillsdale, NJ: Lawrence Erlbaum.

Compton, S. (1985). *Chagall*. New York: Harry N. Abrams.

Glaser, R. (1988). Cognitive science and education. *International Social Sciences Journals*, 115, 21-44.

Koroscik, J. S. (1982). The effects of prior knowledge, presentation time, and task demands on visual art processing. *Studies in Art Education*, 23(3), 13-22.

Koroscik, J. S. (1990a). The function of domain-specific knowledge in understanding works of art. *Inheriting the theory: New Voices and multiple perspectives on DBAE*. Los Angeles: J. Paul Getty Trust.

Koroscik. J. S. (1990b). Novice-expert differences in understanding and misunderstanding art and their implications for student assessment in art education. *Arts and Learning Research*, 8(1), 6-29.

Koroscik, J. S., Garber, E., & Baxter, L. R. (1987). Verbal mediation effects on comprehending works of art in a multi-cultural educational setting. *Journal of Multi-cultural and Cross-Cultural Research in Art Education*, 5(1) 39-56.

Koroscik, J. S., Osman, A. H., & DeSouza, I. (1988). The function of verbal mediation in comprehending works of art: A comparison of three cultures. *Studies in Art Education*, 29(2), 91102.

Makarius. M. (1988). *Chagall*. New York: Portland House.

Perkins, D. N. (1987). Art as an occasion of intelligence. *Educational Leadership*, 45(4), 36-43.

Perkins,D. N.,& Salomon,G.(1988).Teaching for transfer. *Educational Leadership*,46(l),22-32.

Prawat, R. S. (1989). Promoting access to knowledge, strategy, and disposition in students: A research synthesis. *Review of Educational Research*, 59(1), 1-41.

Verdet, A. (1984). *Chagall's world: Reflections from the Mediterranean*. New York: Dial.

Warren, L. R., & Horn J. W. (1982). What does naming a picture do? Effects of prior picture naming on recognition of identical and same-name alternatives. *Memory and Cognition*, 10(2), 167-175.

An Introduction: Standardized Testing and Authentic Assessment Research In Art Education

> One of the disadvantages in the public schools is that we assume and do things essentially without foundation in research....Some people say, "children's art should not be evaluated", "I do not believe in tests," "every child has a right to express what he or she wants," or that "children's art work should not be compared to other children's art work." [Standardized] testing obviously is on the other side of the spectrum. One group of people could say, "there are no tests in the future," the other group could say, "we need more tests in the future." (Gilbert Clark, in Clark, Zimmerman, & Zurmuehlen, 1987, p. 109)

Clark's statement above sets forth two extreme positions in respect to assessment research in art education. This chapter of *Research Methods in Art Education* consists of two parts. In Part I, Robert Sabol reflects on issues and products related to standardized testing in art education. He sets the stage for Enid Zimmerman's discussion in support of authentic assessment research in art education in Part II.

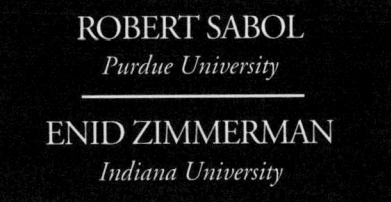

ROBERT SABOL
Purdue University

ENID ZIMMERMAN
Indiana University

PART I

Standardized Testing in Art Education

Robert Sabol
Purdue University

Calls for demonstrations of accountability through the use of standardized testing were made in the field of general education (*A Nation at Risk*, 1988; *America 2000: An Education Strategy*, 1991; *Goals 2000: Educate America Act*, 1994) and in visual arts education (Brandt, 1985; Clark, Day, & Greer, 1987; Hausman, 1988; Stiggins, 1985). Use of standardized tests has been ongoing in art education. Tests developed and used by Goodenough, Lewerenz, Meier, Lark-Horovitz, Horn, and Varnum have been used to measure student intelligence, aptitude, knowledge, and skills in art (Clark, Zimmerman, & Zurmuehlen, 1987). Tests developed by these researchers have not been incorporated with other standardized tests because art ability is still viewed by many as not related or indirectly related to general intelligence. Standardized tests currently used to measure art knowledge and skills include the National Assessment of Educational Progress (NAEP), the National Teacher Exam (NTE), Clark's Drawing Abilities Test (CDAT), and 26 visual arts achievement tests developed by ten state departments of education (Sabol, 1994). The NAEP is used to measure student knowledge and skills in visual arts at the 4th, 8th, and 12th grade in order to provide a baseline measurement of what students in American art education programs know and can do. The NTE is used by colleges and universities to measure knowledge and skills of pre-service teachers for the purpose of granting certification in teaching. The CDAT is used to identify students who are of high ability in the visual arts for the purpose of placement into programs designed for those who are gifted in the visual arts. State level visual arts achievement tests are used to measure effectiveness of visual arts programs and to identify student achievement levels related to state curricula in visual arts. Ongoing research about standardized testing in visual arts education is needed because standardized testing can provide valuable information for visual arts teachers who design testing programs for their school districts, for administrators at local, state, and national levels, and for the field of art education in general.

Defining Standardized Testing

It has been reported that more standardized testing is done in the United States than in any other country (Brandt, 1985; Haney, 1985; Higgins, 1989). Widespread use of standardized testing continues primarily because the public perceives test results as valid indicators of student progress and achievement. As long as this perception exists, teachers will continue to design and use standardized tests and administrators and others will continue to report test results. *Testing* may be thought of as a technique for obtaining information about specific topics and issues (Hopkins, Stanley, & Hopkins, 1990). *Standardized tests* are those that require common procedures, apparatus, and criteria for scoring so that "precisely the same test can be given at different times and places" (Cronbach, 1960, p. 22). Many types of standardized tests are used in education in order to measure such factors as intelligence, achievement, creativity, and aptitude. Results from standardized tests have been used by state departments of education to measure levels of student learning in relation to state curricula (Mamlin, 1986; Peterson, 1991; Sabol, 1994) and local curricula (Armstrong, 1994; Eisner, 1974, 1972). Analysis of test results also are used to identify curricular strengths and weaknesses (Armstrong, 1994; Eisner, 1972; Worthen & Sanders, 1987) and to provide degrees of legitimacy for the learning process by demonstrating the amount and quality of learning being achieved (Hausman, 1988). Standardized tests are a preferred assessment method because they impose controlled testing conditions that involve standard directions, time limits, and other controls that provide uniform testing conditions (Cronbach, 1970). Additionally, standardized tests are preferred because they permit uniform evaluations of students and permit comparisons of scores with those from other groups or with pre-established standards of performance. Summaries of pooled test scores from large populations provide a range of performances called *norms*. Tests that are designed to permit comparison of individual test scores to those of large populations are called *norm-referenced tests*. Scores on norm-referenced tests permit teachers to compare the score of an individual to mean scores from a large group of test takers. This enables a teacher to determine the relative performance of an individual to the larger group based on the range of scores found in the norms.

Frequently, visual arts teachers and researchers are interested in measuring student performance in relation to an established standard. This standard, such as a grade-point or performance rate, may be called a *criterion*. Tests designed for this purpose are called *criterion-referenced tests*. Unlike norm-referenced tests, scores from these types of tests are generally not compared to those of large populations of scores, but rather to a predetermined score or indicator. In this case a teacher is able to determine student achievement through comparison of a score to an established functional level rather than through comparison to scores from other test takers.

Validity and Reliability of Standardized Tests

Two factors that influence decisions to use standardized tests are validity and reliability. *Validity* is the most important consideration in test evaluation. Simply defined, validity is the measure of how well a test fulfills the function for which it is being used. Test scores lead to inferences about students' knowledge and skill levels. If tests have high degrees of validity, inferences about student achievement are validated because test content must be compatible with course content. Selection of tests and test items must represent the universe of knowledge, skills, and processes contained in course content. Test items represent a sampling of all possible types of learning that occur. The more closely a test or test items reflect total course content, the higher the validity rating of the test or the more accurately the test measures student achievement. Unless a test is proven to be valid, information it provides and inferences made from results are not considered to be useful.

Test validity is determined by the degree to which the total test and individual items match course content. Ebel (1983) defined *content validity* as the extent to which the test requires that the student demonstrate achievements which constitute the objectives of instruction in a specified area or areas. Tests with high content validity represent the topics, cognitive processes, and behaviors of a given course or unit. To determine content validity, a teacher must make professional judgments about the degree the test content is parallel to curricular content and processes, the degree the test and curricular emphasis are in proper balance, and the degree the test is free of prerequisites that are irrelevant or incidental to the measurement task (Hopkins, Stanley, & Hopkins, 1990). Benson (1981) suggested that the way items are written, such as item format, item reliability, and test instructions, influences the degree of content validity of standardized tests. It has been demonstrated that teacher ratings of content validity correlated highly with student performances on standardized tests (Hopkins, Stanley, & Hopkins, 1990). To assist teachers in determining the content validity of standardized tests, test publishers provide classifications of skills and content on tests. Examination of these breakdowns can assist teachers in the test selection process by determining the validity of a particular test. Unless careful examination of content validity is done, it is likely that the test will not measure what is being taught.

Visual arts teachers and researchers who are planning a study around a hypothesis must concern themselves with construct validity. *Construct validity* is the extent to which a particular test can be shown to measure a particular trait (Cronbach, 1970). For example, if a teacher is interested in measuring creativity in students, selecting a test that measures the trait of creativity is essential. Hopkins, Stanley, and Hopkins (1990) suggested a process for developing a measure for a construct and establishing its validity. They suggested the following: (1) development of a set of tasks or items based on a theory related to the construct; (2) formulation of testable predictions of student performance based on the relationship between the construct and the measures; (3) collection of data required to investigate the predicted relationships empirically; (4) elimination of items or tasks that operate contrary to the theory or modify the theory. A common mistake made in test selection is that a test may be selected on the basis of its name and reputation rather than its demonstrated construct validity.

Teachers and researchers who are interested in predicting student behaviors or some subsequent measure of performance must concern themselves with predictive validity of tests. *Predictive validity* or *criterion-related validity* is the measure of whether the test is a good indicator of some psychological trait or construct (Hopkins, Stanley, & Hopkins, 1990). A test's predictive validity is determined by how well predictions agree with subsequent behaviors. Accuracy of predictions is usually expressed by a correlation coefficient between test scores and one or more criteria.

Validity of tests cannot be established without a high degree of reliability. It is possible for a test to be reliable and not be valid, but tests that have proven to be valid generally will display significant degrees of reliability. *Reliability* is the extent to which test scores are consistent, dependable, and repeatable (Cronbach, 1970). To do a job well, tests must yield accurate results over a period of time and under a variety of conditions. This is one of the functions of reliability.

There are several methods for estimating reliability, most of which call for computing a correlation coefficient between two sets of similar measurements. The higher the coefficient the more reliable the measure. Reliability coefficients vary between values of .00 and +1.00, with +1.00 indicating perfect reliability, which is never attained in practice, and .00, indicating no reliability.

Reliability coefficients can be obtained by several different methods. The *coefficient of equivalence* is calculated when two parallel forms of a test are given to the same group and scores are correlated from the two forms. The *coefficient of stability* is calculated by correlating scores from a test that is given to the same group on two administrations. A problem in calculating this coefficient is determining the amount of time between administrations. Too little time or too much time between administrations may influence results positively or negatively. The *coefficient of internal consistency* may be determined in a single administration. The most widely used method to determine internal consistency is the split-half correlation. A test is administered to a sample. It is then split into halves (odd and even numbered items). Scores of these two subtests are calculated for each individual. The scores for the two subtests are then correlated. This correlation coefficient represents only half of the test. In order to calculate the reliability for the entire test the Spearman-Brown prophecy formula is used to complete the coefficient (Borg & Gall, 1989). Determining reliability of individual items on a test can be accomplished through use of the Kuder-Richardson formulas. These formulas require a single administration and yield a lower reliability coefficient than other methods because tests with low numbers of items permit individual items to contribute to the total score in greater proportion than items from tests with higher numbers of items. Discussion of specific applications of these formulas is beyond the scope of this discussion, but are considered to be basic statistical procedures for educational measurement. Each of the previously discussed methods have specific limitations and conditions under which they may be used effectively.

Implementing a Standardized Testing Program for Visual Arts Education

A decision to use standardized tests in visual arts education involves commitment of financial resources, time, knowledge of tests and test resources, training in test administration and in test taking, knowledge and skill with scoring procedures and techniques, ability for proper analysis of data, interpreting, and reporting of results, and administrative support. These and other concerns must be considered prior to implementing a testing program. What follows is a series of steps for implementing a standardized testing program for visual arts education.

1. **Establish a test program advisory group.** This group will provide input for the development of the program, do work needed to implement the program, and oversee its evaluation and continued development. Members of this group should include teachers, administrators, parents, and others who

have knowledge, expertise, and interest in testing. They will become a valuable resource for development and support for the program.

2. **Create a statement of purpose.** Beginning the testing process involves establishing a clearly defined set of reasons for including standardized testing in the visual arts program. Goals and objectives of the testing program must be clearly established and approved by decision-makers and by those who will be affected by the program.

3. **Establish test selection criteria.** Content from the statement of purpose should guide the creation of criteria against which available tests will be screened. Hopkins, Stanley, and Hopkins (1990) recommend that these criteria should include content validity, reliability, recency of norms, scoring representativeness of norms, availability of item-level norms, testing time required, ease of administration, types of converted scores available, articulation across grade levels, and costs and reporting aids and services.

4. **Establish procedures for test selections and make test selections.** Test selection requires careful examination of tests. Particular emphasis must be placed upon determining the validity and reliability of the tests in question. Determinations of how many, when, and by whom tests will be selected must be made. Tests are available from a variety of publishers and developers. *The Mental Measurements Yearbooks* (Mitchell, 1985) contains critical reviews of all current commercially available tests in the field of education. Tests are not supplied in this volume, but listings of publishers are identified. *Tests in Print* (Mitchell, 1983) contains comprehensive bibliographies of the construction, use, and validity of specific tests and descriptions of populations for which each test is intended. Keyser and Sweetland (1984-1988) include critical reviews of over 600 psychological and educational tests in *Test Critiques*. In *Tests: A Comprehensive Reference for Assessments in Psychology, Education, and Business* (Sweetland & Keyser, 1986), a listing of over 3,100 tests is found. Subsections of the listing identify tests for particular groups and purposes. Educational Testing Service, Addison Wesley Publishing Company, Bobbs Merrill Company, CTB/McGraw-Hill, and College Board are a few publishers who produce and publish standardized tests for educational use. Professional journals are another source of assistance in identifying tests and current research about educational testing and measurement. Among these are *The Journal of Educational Measurement, Educational and Psychological Measurement, Applied Psychological Measurement, The Journal of Experimental Education,* and

Educational Measurement: Issues and Practices. The American Educational Research Association published *Standards for Educational and Psychological Testing* (1985) in which standards for development, use, and selection of tests are presented.

5. **Establish training schedules for test administrators and for test takers.** Success of testing programs depends upon individuals who are trained in test administration and scoring. Training that permits test-givers to learn and develop test administration skills is vital to successful testing programs in order to maintain common procedures. Students must also be schooled in the processes of test taking. Improved test scores can result from instruction in test taking processes (Frederiksen & Collins, 1989).

6. **Establish methods for interpreting and reporting test results.** Test results often are reported in percentiles, stanines, standard deviations, and other technical jargon that may not be easily understood by the average person. An understanding of data analysis and establishing procedures through which results can be easily understood are necessary for reporting findings of testing programs. Reports of findings should be concise and explained in sufficient detail to permit adequate understanding among those who receive reports of findings.

7. **Establish review procedures and timelines to evaluate effectiveness of testing programs.** Periodic reviews of established testing programs and selected tests will provide opportunities to evaluate their effectiveness. Changes in programming, curriculum, funding, or state laws may necessitate revision of statements of purpose, testing schedules, or administration and reporting procedures.

Use of standardized tests to measure educational progress of students is on the increase in the United States (Peterson, 1991; Sabol, 1994). Sabol (1994) reported that twelve state departments of education had developed state level visual arts achievement tests and that nine additional states were at various stages of test development. Of states with tests, ten reported having a total of 26 tests that were most commonly given at the 5th, 8th, and 11th grade levels. These tests are used to measure students' art knowledge and skills at the end of various plateaus of public school education. Well-developed and organized testing programs provide a valuable resource to teachers, researchers, and administrators that enables them to measure more accurately student progress and to monitor student educational needs.

Development of Local Tests

Teachers regularly develop tests for their classroom or district use. Tests developed by teachers without training are usually of poor quality and provide inaccurate measures of student achievement. Because standardized tests generally focus on broad commonly accepted objectives and cover a wide range of curricular content, they are not always adequate for measuring specific objectives and course content. An adequate presentation of the test development process is beyond the scope of this discussion, but an outline of a few basic considerations may aid teachers interested in improving their test development skills.

A good test must be carefully planned and constructed. Consideration must be given to the topics and objectives that can be measured using paper-and-pencil tests. Tests should reflect both content and processes found in specific curriculum in proportion to their emphasis in that curriculum. Test items should cover the spectrum of knowledge, skills, and strategies needed in the visual arts domain. These tasks should address both the processes and products of visual arts and should include items that permit planning and reflection. Frederiksen and Collins (1989) recommend that a library of exemplars be created that reflect all levels of performance. A scale of exemplars would contain samples of actual student written, oral, or studio responses that are identified as typical performances of students for a given grade or developmental level. An example of exemplars in art education would be samples of student work commonly associated with the levels of child development in art. These exemplars show typical characteristics of children's art at the various stages of development in art. Exemplars of written or oral responses may contain quoted examples of student responses on individual test items. Exemplars should provide samples of high level performances and should include critiques of samples to demonstrate how the example was judged. These exemplars should be made available to students to enable them to improve their performances.

Test directions must be clear and concise. Incomplete or poorly worded directions will confuse test takers and negatively influence results. Use of standard administrative procedures is another important test development consideration. Student performance is increased if the testing procedures are familiar and based on previous testing experiences.

Creation of test items is an essential activity in test development. Higher numbers of items and items of good quality improve the reliability of tests. They must be written in clear concise language. Choice of language should reflect correct usage and grammar and reading level of the students who will be taking the test.

Tests should contain a number of items that students could reasonably complete in the given testing period. Test items should not permit widely varying interpretations of what is expected and they should include a range from easy to difficult. This will help distribute scores and eliminate clusters of scores at either end of the distribution so that a more accurate measurement of the range of student achievement results.

Various item types are recommended for use. In an examination of standardized state level visual arts achievement tests, Sabol (1994) reported that multiple choice items comprised 93 percent of all test item types analyzed, followed by essay (3%), true/false (2%), matching (1%), and completion items (.01%). Item types should be selected based on the type of knowledge being investigated.

Content of test items should reflect a range of mental processes. Test items that examine various levels of cognitive development will provide clear measurement of student achievement levels. Tests should consist of knowledge items that require factual recall of specific bits of knowledge; comprehension and application items that require translation and interpretation, and analysis, synthesis; and evaluation items that require breaking down of ideas, putting together elements or parts to make a whole, and making judgments about the value, purpose, or ideas contained in the items.

Writing good items is time consuming and requires continuous revision. Items should be written well in advance. A test hurriedly created is not likely to be valid or reliable.

Development of a scoring system is critical to successful evaluation of test responses. Identifying a scoring system and a range of possible responses to items will assist the test evaluator in evaluating individual responses. Making the scoring system available to test takers will help them internalize the criteria by which their responses are being judged and may lead to improved levels of performance.

Development of tests for local use requires an assessment of the validity and reliability of tests and test items. Revision of items and addition or removal of items that are not valid or reliable will help increase the efficiency and effectiveness of these tests. Revision of tests requires diligence and vigilance by reworking items in order to continue to improve measurement of student achievement.

Concerns About Standardized Testing

Questions about the appropriateness of standardized testing in visual arts programs have been raised. Standardized tests are restricted, by format and administration requirements, from measuring all types of learning that may occur in the visual arts classroom. Concerns about standardized testing include: (1) negative influences of test content on curriculum (Brandt, 1985; Hamblen, 1987); (2) over-emphasis on test results (Hamblen, 1987; Pipho, 1985); (3) essential learning reflected in judgment, analysis or high level skills needed for generating arguments and constructing solutions to problems are not reflected in test content (Frederiksen & Collins, 1989; Hamblen, 1987; Haney, 1985; Sabol, 1990; Stiggins, 1985; Zimmerman, 1992a); (4) questionable validity and reliability of current standardized visual arts tests (Clark, Zimmerman, & Zurmuehlen, 1987; Sabol, 1990); (5) use of inappropriate content in assessment items (Hamblen, 1988; Wilson, 1992); and (6) difficulty in evaluating subjectivity of art products and art content in responses (Sabol, 1990; Wolf, 1987).

When used to measure visual arts knowledge, tests are limited by certain factors. Most test items measure lower level thinking and are dependent upon recall of factual knowledge (Hamblen, 1988; Sabol, 1994). Traditional test items do not tend to explore creative problem solving abilities which are germane to visual arts programs. Solutions to art problems often require students to experiment and revise solutions as part of the problem solving process (Zimmerman, 1992a). Experiments and revisions can reveal important problem solving skills. Most test items do not permit students to demonstrate their abilities to revise and build responses.

Test items tend not to be representative of the wide span of various types of learning that occurs in visual arts classrooms (Haney, 1985; Hamblen, 1987; Sabol, 1990; Stiggins, 1985). Students come to testing situations with varied experiences and differences in learning environments, use of instructional resources and materials, and exposure to local curricular emphases that also may contribute to making findings of tests invalid and unreliable (Sabol, 1990). In addition students' familiarity with testing processes and forms, health, classroom environment, lighting, reading or writing abilities, and additional considerations may influence test results and prevent teachers and others from obtaining accurate measurement of student achievements.

Conclusion

Standardized tests are easy to administer and score, take a short amount of time to complete, and carry credibility for many audiences due to their popularity and long history of use (Archbald & Newmann, 1988). Use of standardized tests in a visual arts program, however, provides art teachers, administrators, parents, students, and other decision-makers with only a partial view of learning that occurs in art classrooms. Although criticisms of standardized testing abound, standardized tests, when incorporated with authentic assessments, can provide a complete picture of overall student achievement in visual arts programs.

PART II

Authentic Assessment Research in Art Education

Enid Zimmerman
Indiana University

Reform movements of the early 1990s have engendered interest in assessing the effectiveness and efficiency of educational institutions and their accountability to the public at local, state, and national levels. According to some educators, assessment has emerged as one of the dominant strategies for effecting educational change in this decade (Eisner, 1985; Hargraves, 1989). Interest in educational assessment is not limited to the United States, it is world-wide in its scope (Boughton, Eisner, & Ligtvoet, 1996). Definitions of the terms *evaluation* and *assessment* vary depending on where educational reform is taking place. Evaluation is a broader term than grading and testing (Eisner, 1985) and often refers to large-scale state and national endeavors, whereas assessment usually is related to local, site-specific settings. Sometimes, however, when accountability is mandated at the district or state level, assessments can be used to provide information about large numbers of students studying in a variety of contexts.

The terms *performance assessment, alternative assessment,* and *authentic assessment* often are used interchangeably. A number of researchers have offered explanations for differences between these terms. *Performance assessment* is a broad, umbrella term that refers to assessments where judgments are made about what students know and are able to do (Armstrong, 1994) and often encompasses both alternative and authentic assessments. Performance assessments usually require students to create and construct responses to problems and demonstrate, in a variety of contexts, processes by which they conducted their inquiries. Performance assessments occur over time and result in tangible products or observable performances with multiple paths to successful performance (Herman, Aschbacher, & Winters, 1992; Kirst, 1991; Marzano, Pickering, & McTighe, 1993). Classroom-based performance assessments have been contrasted and compared with large-scale standardized assessments which are generally formal, objective, time-efficient, cost-efficient, widely applicable, centrally processed, and single score-useful to policy makers. Local, classroom performance assessments usually are informal, teacher-mandated, adapted to local contexts, locally scored, sensitive to short term changes in student knowledge, meaningful to students, and able to provide immediate, detailed information (Shepard, 1989).

Alternative assessments refer to assessments that are non-traditional and differ from past standardized evaluations or classroom assessments. *Authentic assessments* are usually alternative assessments that are performance-based and require solutions to real world problems that include decisions similar to those made by professionals, such as art critics, art historians, and artists, that are applicable outside the classroom environment. Authentic assessment tasks are integrated, complex, and challenging; and students are encouraged to apply their previous knowledge and relevant skills to solve "realistic problems" when completing these tasks (Kirst 1991; Marzano et al., 1993; Rudner & Boston, 1994). Examples include participating in debates about proper places to display art works, keeping portfolios of in-process and completed art works that will be displayed in public arenas, and writing art criticisms for local newspapers.

Purposes of Assessment

There are diverse opinions about whether standardized tests, in respect to quantitative scoring, should be used as assessment measures in the field of art education. Boughton (1994) recommended that the visual arts require more reflective assessment measures than other disciplines and that standardized tests should not be used to determine degrees of learning in studio arts areas. This point of view can be contrasted with opinions of other art educators, such as Armstrong (1994) and Davis (1993), who advocate the use of quantitative and qualitative (standard and authentic) measures when conducting art assessments. Other educators also reflect differing opinions about the use of standardized and authentic measures of assessment. Marzano et al. (1993) were of the opinion that standardized response test formats such as multiple choice, true/false, and matching formats are too narrow in their focus and contended that authentic measures are better able to assess a broad array of academic and non-academic competencies. Brown (1989) explained that there is no reason to eliminate standardized tests, although he felt they should not be allowed to distort curricula or make school districts insensitive to a variety of diverse student needs.

Assessment involves *selection, collection,* and *interpretation of information* in respect to three kinds of accountability: program accountability, accountability of student learning, and teacher accountability (Davis, 1993; Rudner & Boston, 1994). Assessments can function in a number of different ways including: (1) gatekeeping procedures that involve placement of students and allowing them to enter certain programs and exit others; (2) making inferences about present and future success of students in terms of their progress and achievements; (3) determining how well goals of a program are being met; (4) providing feedback to teachers about various aspects of their teaching and instructional goals; and (5) deciding which elements of a curriculum should be added or maintained and which should be changed or eliminated (Armstrong, 1994; Boughton, 1994; Eisner, 1991; Rudner & Boston, 1994). To establish a valid authentic assessment program, a number of issues related to alternative assessment should be addressed, such as: (1) assuring that assessment goals are congruent with instructional goals; (2) examining processes as well as products of learning; (3) integrating assessment methodologies with instructional outcomes and curriculum content; (4) viewing student learning as active, holistic, and complex; (5) designing procedures that are directly related to the purposes of the assessment; (6) creating matches between tasks and intended student outcomes; (7) recognizing that criteria are critical in assessing student performance; (8) using multiple measures to develop tasks that do not have clear, single solutions, and require creativity, analysis, and integration of knowledge; and (9) including a broad range of competencies that require considerable student initiative (Archbald & Newmann, 1988; Herman et al., 1992).

What is Being Assessed?

What is being assessed and how it is being assessed depends on the philosophy underlying a program. Many authentic assessment programs in art education are based on curricular frameworks using goals and objectives that shape the form of assessments and the kinds of criteria, instruments, and tasks developed and implemented. For example, Armstrong (1994) stressed content and student behaviors, such as cognitive, motor, and affective skills and social responsibility, as the focus of her assessment program. She identified student art behaviors found in conceptual frameworks that were based on a behavioristic model applied to art education. In other models, assessment standards are linked to Marzano's five dimensions of learning (Marzano et al., 1993); Gardner's three categories of art learning that focus on arts production, perception, and reflection (Gardner, 1989); and the Getty Center for Education in the Arts' discipline-based art education initiatives that place emphasis on study of art history, art criticism, aesthetics, and art making (Greer & Hoepfner, 1986).

Procedures and Instruments

Procedures used in authentic assessments are open-ended and non-structured and can include observations, interviews, questionnaires, structured questions, oral self-evaluations, teacher log-books or journals, audio or video documentation, rating scales, student journals and sketchbooks, and portfolios. Once information is gathered informally and recorded in a standardized manner, instruments can be used, such as observation checklists, interview recording sheets, student and parent questionnaires, self-evaluation forms, behavior checklists, and rating scales. Profiles of student characteristics also can be used as instruments in authentic assessment to set forth, in a concise manner, teachers' ratings on scales of diverse competencies along with scores on more standard measures required in many school districts (Archbald & Newmann, 1988).

Types of Procedures and Instruments

In art classes, sources of evidence for developing understandings, skills, and techniques about studio art may include: (1) selected art pieces produced during a particular time period; (2) a portfolio of unfinished work and preliminary sketches containing written notes, diagrams, models, and final products or photocopies of slides, videos, and/or photographs of finished products; (3) peer critiques, student self-evaluations, student contracts, diary notes, and student journals that describe how the students developed their ideas, reflected on their art work, replied to teacher comments and questions, gathered sources for their ideas from magazine and newspaper articles, and notes on art work and artists from the past; (4) observation notes produced by the teacher in the form of checklists, anecdotal records, etc.; (5) interview notes compiled by the teacher from discussions with students about their art work; (6) work produced by students in response to specific tasks; (7) students "teaching back" newly learned skills and concepts to their peers; (8) checklists relating to technical processes; and (9) group presentations and performances that are public affirmations of art learning (Archbald & Newmann, 1988; Boughton, 1994; Rudner & Boston, 1994; Taylor, 1991; Zimmerman, 1992a).

In addition to studio art projects, evidence of learning in areas such as art criticism, art history, and aesthetics also can be assessed authentically through audio or video taped class sessions, debates about art issues, performance in class critiques, written reports from library searches, gallery visits, interviews, class and diary notes, essays, tests, quizzes, and written exams (Archbald & Newmann, 1988; Boughton, 1994). The role of "talk" in assessing student understandings of art content and at the same time developing relationships between teachers and students should not be minimized. Students can learn to discuss, debate, cross-question, present, and review ideas in public arenas and present their work to a variety of audiences. Such art learnings can be revealed through a wider range of abilities than assessment based only on written tasks (Ross, Radnor, Mitchell, & Bierton, 1993).

Portfolios can take the form of formative, in-process portfolios or summative, end-process portfolios, or a combination of both. They can allow student risk-taking, creativity, problem solving, and learning to make judgments by encouraging students to be partners in the process of their own assessments (Zimmerman, 1992a). *Assessment portfolios,* sometimes called *process portfolios,* are a rich source of evidence of art learning and also can enable students to: (1) evaluate their learning of course content and skills; (2) gain insights into their creative processes; (3) see growth and accomplishment over time; (4) increase their assessment skills by reflecting on their own work; (5) become active rather than passive learners; and (6) gain self-confidence by seeing themselves as successful learners (Taylor, 1991). Assessment portfolios also provide teachers with information about student progress and achievement by: (1) demonstrating evidence of student growth and suggesting areas for improvement; (2) promoting communication with students as they reflect on their work and teachers comment on those reflections; (3) enabling teachers to develop, assess, and revise course content; (4) helping teachers assess their successes in teaching course content; and (5) providing vehicles for helping parents, other teachers, and administrators understand students' growth in art over a wide range of tasks (Archbald & Newmann, 1988; Taylor, 1991; Zimmerman, 1992a).

Authentic assessment measures were employed in a painting class taught in a summer program Gilbert Clark and I coordinated for high ability arts students entering grades 8 to 11 the following Fall. Authentic assessment procedures and instruments were used to help select students for entrance into the program, provided feedback about teaching/learning processes, demonstrated to what extent students and teachers had meet their objectives, informed students and their parents about student progress and achievements and where improvements were needed, and encouraged changes in the program. My information was gathered by observing a painting class, interviewing the teacher and taping a number of teaching sessions, keeping classroom observation notes, taking slides of classroom activities and student portfolios, consulting journals kept by two art teachers who observed the class, and interpreting evaluation forms filled out by parents about their children's reactions to the class. In addition, focus group meetings and individual interviews with all students were held. Based on these authentic evaluation procedures, I determined most goals for the painting class were met and a number of changes were made based on the assessments I conducted (Zimmerman, in press).

How are Assessments Conducted?

Steps taken to conduct authentic assessment projects often include determining the purpose of the assessment, deciding on audiences for the assessment, and identifying resources (e.g. national standards, state frameworks, school restructuring efforts, and professional organizations such as the National Art Education Association) that would be helpful in contextualizing an assessment. Next, assessment tasks and instruments are selected that match intended instructional goals and objectives, educational philosophy, content and skills to be assessed, and student outcomes. Then, instruction is designed and implemented and tasks and scoring methods are constructed, along with criteria, to determine how the task will be assessed. Finally, student accomplishments on the tasks are assessed and reported to appropriate audiences (Herman et al., 1992) and follow-up steps taken to modify assessment procedures for future implementation (see Table 1).

How are Criteria Selected for Evaluations?

According to Wiggins (1989a), when conducting authentic assessment performances, a discipline should be represented faithfully so that learning experiences resemble those of adult professionals in a field, attention should be paid to criteria used for assessment, self-assessment should play an important role, and students should present their work and defend themselves orally and publicly to ensure that they have mastered the tasks at hand. One of the most important aspects of conducting authentic assessments is determining what criteria should be established to determine the progress and achievement of students, teachers, programs, and contexts in which art learning takes place. *Validity* and *reliability* of criteria and instruments should be taken into consideration during the development and implementation of authentic assessment projects. Validity refers to whether the assessment presents appropriate evidence, based on conclusions, that are relevant to the intended purposes for which the results are to be used; validity includes both *content validity* and *construct validity*. *Content validity* addresses whether instruments assess what they claim to assess and *construct validity* focuses on whether criteria accurately represent the concepts and ideas being assessed (Boughton, 1994).

Reliability refers to repeatability and stability of student performance so that generalizations can be made about the predictability of student performance from

Table 1
Processes That Can Be Used in Authenic Assessments

Step 1	Step 2	Step 3	Step 4
• Determine the purpose of the assessment • Decide on the audience for the assessment • Identify resources to enhance understanding of the context of the assessment	• Select assessment tasks based on instructional goals with objectives, educational philosophy, content, skills, and student outcomes that are to be assessed • Decide what procedures and instruments will be used to assess the selected tasks	• Design instruction and tasks • Implement instruction • Determine criteria as to how tasks will be assessed • Construct scoring or coding methods	• Assessments of student programs and achievements on specific tasks • Report outcomes to appropriate audiences • Conduct follow-up steps to modify curriculum and assessment procedures for future implementation

one occasion to another. Concerns about reliability focus on scores remaining consistent despite changes in the assessment situation, such as who is judging and when and where the judging takes place (Herman et al., 1992). When conducting assessments, it has been suggested that a balance needs to be established between utility and practicality on one hand and validity and reliability on the other (Rudner & Boston, 1994; Boughton, 1994).

What Criteria Are Used for Making Evaluations?

It has been suggested by a number of researchers that, when conducting authentic assessments, a variety of criteria be developed that use multiple strategies over a wide range of tasks so that a comprehensive view of student progress can be attained (Rudner & Boston, 1994; Zimmerman, 1992b). Linn, Baker, and Dunbar (1991), from the Center for Research on Evaluation, Standards, and Student Teaching (CRESST), offer the following suggestions for selecting criteria to judge the validity and reliability of performance-based assessment: (1) determine consequences of the assessments; (2) decide whether the test items used are fair; (3) judge whether skills in one area can transfer to another and what generalizations can be made from the results; (4) decide whether the assessment contains meaningful problems for students to solve; (5) consider whether the assessment requires students to use higher order thinking skills to analyze and solve issues rather than to memorize facts and solve structured, decontexturalized problems; (6) determine whether the assessment adequately covers the intended content and subject matter; and (7) estimate whether the data collection and scoring procedures are as efficient as possible. Additional criteria for authentic assessment include insuring that students exercise judgment in posing, clarifying, and solving problems, engage in-depth rather than breadth problems; locate and analyze information as well as draw conclusions; communicate results clearly; recognize that there are multiple solutions to problems; demonstrate skills of inquiry and expression; and use knowledge effectively and imaginatively in responding to a topic (Baron, 1991; Wiggins, 1989b). In addition, it has been suggested that authentic assessment tasks and measures employ concrete references and clear language that is understandable to students, parents, and other teachers. Tasks that are used should approximate attributes of disciplined inquiry and in-depth understanding of a problem. In addition, students should be encouraged to grasp relationships and integrate knowledge as well as produce new knowledge (Archbald & Newmann, 1988; Herman et al., 1992).

As an example of such tasks, Ursula Andrews (art teacher at Lowell High School, Lowell,. Indiana), divided a ten week unit she was teaching, *Boxes: Private/Public Spaces*, into three categories: regions of space, personal space, and space and movement. She described this unit as follows:

> The box—from embryo to coffin—serves as a metaphor to direct students to new paradigms for creating art. The juxtaposition of space, time, and energy provides an elastic framework for this unit. Students research psychology of space, survey the impact of space on sculpture, explore construction methods, and find solutions to atypical space and shape relationships. By participating in research activities, students trace objects to their sources, analyze and examine integral features, and determine the nature of the theme of Boxes. Students participate in group activities and produce art works that are displayed in juried shows. Most importantly, students are

challenged to link personal experiences to public art. The critical element is making students aware of how space/environment effects their lives. (Andrews, 1994, p.3)

Authentic assessment usually takes place over an extended period of time so that, in respect to their performances, students can become engaged in learning about, investigating, and exploring content, and in developing new insights. A decision needs to be made early in development of an assessment program as to whether the criteria used will be holistic or analytic; that is, will one overall score be given or will separate ratings of different aspects of the processes and products be used? Whatever the nature of the criteria, *rubrics* often are used to guide judgments made in authentic assessment procedures. A *scoring rubric* consists of a fixed scale and a list of characteristics describing performance for each of the points on the scale. Rubrics not only describe levels of performance, they also promote learning because they offer clear standards for students to attain (Baron, 1991).

Karen Chilman (art teacher at William H. English Middle School, Scottsburg, Indiana) gives rubric rating scales to her students before they do art work so that they are aware of what they are required to do to receive a specific grade. Students and teacher design the rubric rating scales and thereby become actively involved and interested in their own assessments. She wrote to me that a "rubric can be used in art criticism, art history, art production, portfolios, and every other kind of art activity. It is a lot of work, but well worth the effort. Rubrics take the guesswork out of assessing and students can look at the rubric and tell you about what they have learned." She uses many different kinds of rubrics; one she and her students designed to be used at the culmination of a unit on mask-making appears in Table 2.

Another example of a rubric, used as one of a group of measures to assess students at a summer institute, was used by Gilbert Clark and me in a program described previously in this chapter (see Table 3).

Both *on-demand* tasks, that set forth teacher expectations, as well as *open-ended tasks*, that are designed by students, can be used as sources of evidence. Linn et al. (1991) have suggested that sound assessment tasks (1) match important outcome goals; (2) are fair and free of bias, (3) are meaningful and challenging for students, (4) engage students in real world problems and situations with audiences, (5) are teachable, and (6) are flexible in implementing in terms of time, space, and resources.

Table 2
Rubric Grading Scale for Mask Unit

Circle an X for Each Category

	Not Evident	Emerging	Average	Competent	Outstanding
Mask:					
• construction in chosen media	X	X	X	X	X
• inspired by a culture	X	X	X	X	X
• authentic materials used	X	X	X	X	X
Museum Display:					
• background display that extends knowledge of a culture	X	X	X	X	X
• information tag that includes cultural inspiration, medium used, use of mask, why mask was made	X	X	X	X	X
• presentation of mask to a community audience	X	X	X	X	X
Portfolio:					
• table of contents	X	X	X	X	X
• sketches for mask and research notes	X	X	X	X	X
• research about a culture and references					
Column Total (add)	_____	_____	_____	_____	_____
Multiply By	0	1	2	3	4
Total Columns	_____	_____	_____	_____	_____
Grand Total					

A = 28-36 COMMENTS:
B = 19-27
C = 10-18
D = 1-9
F = 0

Table 3
Visual Arts Behavioral Assessment Form

Student_____
Teacher_____
School_____ Grade_____

	Seldom	Occasionally	Frequently	Always
Masters basic art making easily and quickly				
Works independently				
Concentrates on art projects for long periods of time				
Examines problems critically				
Completes art projects				
Spends a great amount of time doing art work				
Is critical of own work and that of others				
Uses different media effectively and confidently				
Shows interest and knowledge about works of art				
Demonstrates desire to improve own art work				
Column Total	_____	_____	_____	_____
Multiply x	0	1	2	3
Total Score				

Additional Comments:

Criteria for Portfolio Assessment

Much has been written in the past few years about criteria for portfolio assessment. Paulson, Paulson, and Meyer (1991) described a *portfolio* as a purposeful collection of student work that exhibits the student's efforts, progress, and achievements in one or more areas. They stressed that the collection should include student participation in selecting contents and judging criteria for merit, and demonstrate evidence of student self-reflection. When using portfolio assessment, it is suggested that the following criteria be applied: (1) the purpose of the assessment should be defined; (2) methods for deciding what should be placed in the portfolio, by whom, and when should be clarified; and (3) specific criteria for assessing either the entire contents or individual pieces should be set forth.

A number of issues related to portfolio criteria need to be addressed. How will progress be evaluated? How will different tasks, videos, art work, essays, journal entries, etc. be compared or weighted? How is conversation mediated between students and teachers? What is the role of student reflection? How should parents and others' input be included? What is the best balance between including process work and final products? How many judges are needed to make equitable assessments in large scale authentic assessments? How should new judges be selected, trained, and initiated? Should a whole years' work be submitted or just representative samples? (Arter & Spandel, 1992 ; Boughton, 1994; Wolf, 1989). There are also concerns teachers need to keep in mind when doing portfolio assessment; Is the work representative of student products? Is the work coached, done independently, and/or as part of a group? Do portfolio pieces match authentic tasks set by the teacher and student? Are portfolios reviewed consistently and criteria applied accurately and equitably? (Herman et al., 1992). All the above issues, and many more not included, could each be the germ of a research study that would contribute greatly to literature in the field of authentic assessment and art education.

Hausman (1993) described *portfolio critique* as a dialogue between teachers and students reflecting on what happened during the process of creating a portfolio. During such a critique, one work is compared with another in respect to quality of ideas, skill, and control in the use of media and tools, and suggestions are made for future art projects. The three most popular categories of criteria used by teachers to critique and assess student art work have been identified by MacGregor, Lemerise, Potts, and Roberts (1992) as: (1) the student's ability to develop and interpret a theme, (2) his or her level of technical expertise, and (3) the student's ability to achieve sensitive personal expression throughout the use of a variety of techniques and processes.

While many of the criteria contain global approaches and standards that could be useful in guiding authentic assessment research in art education, specific criteria have not yet been formulated due to a lack of research in this area. There are a few studies in subjects other than art that have drawn some conclusions about tasks that are used in authentic assessment. For example, Shavelson, Baxter, and Pine (1992) concluded that about ten tasks are needed to assess a student's understanding of a particular subject area. With fewer than ten tasks, inferences can only be made about the tasks the student actually performed. Problems of generalizability, therefore, can be addressed by increasing the number of tasks for all students and by restricting reliance on portfolio work to make judgments about a student's progress and achievements in art. Baker, Archbacher, Niemi, and Sato (1992) found that more tasks are needed in an assessment of student learning if the tasks are not carefully constructed or structured, or if the content area is broadly defined. Taylor (1991) found that teachers, who were conducting authentic assessments in a state level art program, indicated that the majority of their students at all grade levels, who participated in creating assessment portfolios, deepened their insights into how they created art, experienced personal growth in art learnings over time, increased their assessment skills, gained self-confidence, and showed clear evidence of progress and achievement in art when their portfolios were assessed. Ross et al. (1993) described different stages in their research that concerned a large-scale, authentic assessment in the visual arts, including how they constructed instruments, analyzed data, wrote results, and provided feedback to teachers. They concluded that students are capable of rich and sophisticated responses and understandings of their own art work and seem to be able to develop these responses and understandings in collaboration with their teachers.

Designing, Administering, Scoring, and Interpreting Results

There are many questions to ask when developing assessment programs. What are the roles of students and teachers in designing the plan? Is the teacher in control of the assessments? Does the teacher make decisions and the students concur? Do teachers and students have equal input into assessment criteria and scoring? Or are students in control of their own assessments? Answers to these questions will depend upon the educational philosophy of the teacher as well as local and state requirements for assessing student progress and achievement in art. Decisions must also be made early on about how to interpret results of assessments. Evidence of learning can be compared with a student's earlier performance (*self-referenced*), course criteria or outside standards (*criteria-referenced*), or other students' performances (*norm-referenced*) (Boughton, 1994; Hausman, 1994; Ross et al., 1993).

A number of suggestions have been made for those who are conducting large-scale assessments as well as those who doing assessments in their own classrooms. Not all work done by all students needs to be assessed at any one time. Systematic sampling of students' work over a period of time; random matrix sampling of schools, students and products (Popham, 1993); narrative summaries of portfolio assessment; and traditional test summaries all have been suggested as means to use samples of student work efficiently and effectively in authentic assessments. Also, achievements at each performance level, based on specific criteria, need to be made clear to raters or judges and students (Maeroff, 1991).

A specific recommendation for helping score assessment tasks is to gather a *library of exemplars* to be kept for administrative purposes so that scores can refer directly to models that demonstrate many ways for students to be successful. Such a library of student exemplars, with detailed descriptions of how each score was assigned, can be viewed as a set of case studies that: (1) demonstrate the nature of expert performance, (2) can be used to train scorers (3) help students in learning to assess their own work, and (4) develop a sense of standards and critical judgment (Frederiksen & Collins, 1989).

A number of researchers have offered hints for those who are beginning authentic assessments and wish to do research, often referred to as action research, in their own classrooms. They suggest that when starting: (1) a small number of students in a specific context should be included; (2) goals, objectives, and resources should be identified; (3) sample rubrics should be collected to adapt for specific purposes; (4) instruction, assessment tasks, and scoring methods should be designed and implemented; and (5) modifications and changes should be made, when necessary, based on how well instruction and assessments are matched (Herman et al., 1992; Rudner & Boston, 1994).

Who Is Being Assessed and For Whom?

When doing authentic assessments, it is important to consider a balance between students' own interests and those of teachers, parents and administrators (Hausman, 1994). Students, teachers, programming arrangements, curricular content, and educational settings can all be the focus of educational assessments. Audiences for authentic assessments can be comprised of art teachers, art educators conducting research, school administrators, local community members including parents and other interested citizens, and state and federal government officials.

Who is Doing the Assessment and Who is Getting Results?

Most of the discussion about new testing procedures has centered on large-scale testing programs. Most of the testing in the United States, ever, is done by individual teachers with tests they have constructed or selected to evaluate student progress in specific courses and for assigning grades. According to Nickerson (1989), the influence of this type of testing may be as great or greater than that of large-scale evaluation programs. Teachers need more education about how to construct their own assessment tasks and conduct systematic observations to inform their instruction. Although a few states are experimenting with authentic assessments, standardized tests receive the most media attention and are attended to by administrators and community members (Kirst, 1991). It is important, therefore, that parents and communities be sources of evidence for student progress and achievements and be involved in assessment procedures (Sletter & Grant, 1988) so that they can learn about how and why assessments are conducted and in turn become contributors to assessment programs in their schools and communities.

Age and Grade Appropriateness

It has been observed that authentic assessment, particularly portfolio assessment, is more appropriate for older students, although some imaginative researchers have developed ways to conduct authentic assessments with young learners. In developing criteria for judging written contributions, older students are more likely to be able to create criteria by which their work will be critiqued. Younger students may need more help in deciding what work to include in their portfolios. Older students also are better able to keep logs to report their progress and expand their portfolios to include photographs, peer review sessions, and performances and exhibits (Zimmerman, 1993).

Conclusion

Standardized test scores allow comparisons between students, schools, districts, and nations; they are expensive to develop but low in cost to administer and score. In contrast, more authentic approaches involve substantial scoring costs, but lower development costs (Archbald & Newmann, 1988). Authentic assessment places demands on teachers, students, and resources. For authentic assessments to be successful, teachers need extra time to plan, confer with others, develop materials and strategies, and meet with students. Such assessments also require extra space to store portfolios and equipment such as video cameras (Zimmerman, 1993).

There is a clear and present danger that, when authentic assessments are conducted, curricular statements may become behavioristic and not appropriate and sensitive to individual students' needs, the processes they experience, or products they produce (Boughton, 1994). Learning outcomes in the visual arts often are difficult to describe in behaviorist terms with simple predictable outcomes. With visual art standards being adopted as curricular guides in many states, it is especially important to be vigilant that authentic assessment's strengths of being integrated, meaningful, significant, challenging, and related to real life situations are not standardized and eroded away.

It is also important, when conducting authentic assessments, to take into consideration that learners differ in their interests, cognitive styles, rates of learning, patterns of developed abilities, motivations, work habits, temperaments, as well as ethnicity, sex, and social class. If authentic assessment measures are not sensitive to pluralistic issues, they may be used only to reinforce achievements of those students whose backgrounds reflect dominant Western culture and, at the same time, reinforce negative self-concepts and low self-esteem in students who come from diverse, non-Western backgrounds (Zimmerman, 1994). When planning authentic assessments, developers need to take into consideration the amount and kinds of resources available to students from different socioeconomic-economic groups and from either urban, rural, and suburban settings. Assessment developers also need to be aware of bias in assessment procedures as well as privacy issues related to student portfolios. They should be able to recognize that fewer students are viewed as deficient if a variety of assessment tasks and measures are used because the major thrust of assessment should focus on improving instruction not sorting students into groups (Sletter & Grant, 1988).

Whether assessments are wide-ranging or locally administered, they can help motivate students to learn, enable schools to support contemporary curricular concepts and skills, and make it possible for educational systems to account for what is taking place in classrooms in many different settings. By providing teachers with quality instructional tools and emphasizing teaching relevant skills, authentic assessments have great potential to improve teaching and learning at the classroom, district, state, and national levels (Rudner & Boston, 1994).

Although it is almost a decade since Clark (1987) speculated that either there might not be any standardized testing or there might be more support for standardized testing in art education's future, we are now in the future and there appears to be no resolution to this quandary. Just as there appears to be no way of reconciling universal and relative stances in education, the future is now and the healthy debate about standardized testing and authentic assessment continues.

References

Andrews, V. (1994). Unit-boxes: Private/spaces. In E. Zimmerman (Ed.), *Making a difference: Differentiated curriculum units by teachers in the 1993 Artistically Talented Program* (pp. 3-11). Indianapolis, IN: Indiana Department of Education, Office of Gifted and Talented Programs.

Archbald, D. A., & Newmann, F. M. (1988). *Beyond standardized testing: Assessing achievement in the secondary school.* Reston, VA: National Association of Secondary School Principals.

Armstrong, C. (1994). *Designing assessment in art.* Reston, VA: National Art Education Association.

Arter, J., & Spandel, V. (1992). Using portfolios of student work in instruction and assessment. *Educational Measurement: Issues and Practice, 11* (1), 36-44.

Baker, E. L., Archbacher, P. R., Niemi, D., & Sato, E. (1992). *CRESST performance assessment models: Assessing content and explanations.* Los Angeles, CA: University of California, Center for Research on Evaluation, Standards, and Student Testing.

Baron, J. B. (1991). Strategies for the development of effective performance exercises. *Applied Measurement in Education, 4,* 305-318.

Benson, J. (1981). A redefinition of content validity. *Educational and Psychological Measurement, 41* (4), 793-802.

Borg, W. R., & Gall, D. G. (1989). *Educational research.* (5th ed.). New York: Longman.

Boughton, D. (1994). *Evaluation and assessment in visual arts education.* Geelong, Victoria, Australia: Deakin University.

Boughton, D., Eisner, E.W., & Ligtvoet, J. (1996). *Evaluating and assessing the visual arts in education: Internatinal perspectives.* New York: Teachers College Press.

Brandt, R. (1985). Overview. *Educational Leadership, 43* (2), 3.

Brown, R. (1989). Testing and thoughtfulness. *Educational Leadership, 46* (7), 31-34.

Clark, G. (1987). Implications for future of inquiry research, and testing of children's art abilities. In G. Clark, E. Zimmerman, & M. Zurmuehlen (Eds.), *Understanding art testing* (pp. 98-109). Reston, VA: National Art Education Association.

Clark, G., Day, M., & Greer, W. D. (1987). Discipline-based art education: Becoming students of art. *Journal of Aesthetic Education, 21* (2), 129-193.

Clark, G., Zimmerman, E., & Zurmuehlen, M. (1987). *Understanding art testing: Past influences, Norman C. Meier's contributions, present concerns, and future possibilities.* Reston, VA: National Art Education Association.

Cronbach, L. J. (1960). *Essentials of psychological testing* (2nd ed.). New York: Harper & Row.

Cronbach, L. J. (1970). *Essentials of psychological testing* (3rd ed.). New York: Harper & Row.

Davis, D. J. (1993). Art education in the 1990s: Meeting the challenges of accountability. *Studies in Art Education, 34* (2), 82-90.

Ebel, R. L. (1983). The practical validation of tests of ability. *Educational Measurement Issues and Practice, 2,* 7-10.

Eisner, E. (1972). *Educating artistic vision.* New York: Macmillan.

Eisner, E. (1974). Toward a more adequate conception of evaluation in the arts. *Art Education, 27* (7), 2-5.

Eisner, E. W. (1985). *The art of educational evaluation: A personal view.* Philadelphia: Falmer Press.

Eisner, E. W. (1991). Should America have a national curriculum? *Educational Leadership, 44* (2), 76-81.

Frederiksen, J., & Collins, A. (1989). A systems approach to educational testing. *Educational Researcher, 18* (9), 27-32.

Gardner, H. (1989). Zero-based arts education: An introduction to ARTS PROPEL. *Studies in Art Education, 30* (21), 71-83.

Greer, W. D., & Hoepfner, R. (1986). Achievement testing in the visual arts. *Arts Education Policy Review, 88* (1), 43-47.

Haney, W. (1985). Making testing more educational. *Educational Leadership, 43* (2), 4-13.

Hamblen, K. A. (1987). What general education can tell us about evaluation in art. *Studies in Art Education, 28* (4), 246-250.

Hamblen, K. A. (1988). If it is to be tested, it will be taught: A rationale worthy of examination. *Art Education, 41* (5), 57-62.

Hargraves, A. (1989). *Curriculum and assessment reform.* Buckingham, UK: Open University Press.

Hausman, J. (1988). Back to the future: Reflections on present-day emphasis in curriculum and evaluation. *Art Education, 41* (2), 36-41.

Hausman, J. (Spring, 1993). Portfolio evaluation. *NAEA Advisory.* Reston, VA: National Art Education Association.

Hausman, J. (1994). Standards and assessment: New initiatives and continuing dilemmas. *Art Education, 47* (2), 9-13.

Herman, J. L., & Aschbacher, P. K., & Winters, L. (1992). *A practical guide to alternative assessment.* Alexandria, VA: Association for Supervision and Curriculum Development.

Higgins, R. E. (1989). *Approaches to evaluation in art education at the state level.* Paper commissioned by the Minnesota Department of Education.

Hopkins, K. D., Stanley, J. C., & Hopkins, B. R. (1990). *Educational and psychological measurement and evaluation.* Engelwood Cliffs, NJ: Prentice-Hall.

Keyser, D. J., & Sweetland, R. C. (Eds.). (1984-1988). *Test critiques.* Vols. 1-7. Kansas City, MO: Test Corporation of America.

Kirst, M. L. (1991). Interview on assessment issues: Lorrie Shepard. *Educational Researcher, 20* (2), 21-23.

Linn, R. L., Baker, E. L., & Dunbar, S. B. (1991). Complex, performance-based assessment: Expectations and validation criteria. *Educational Researcher, 20* (8), 15-21.

MacGregor, R. N., Lemerise, S., Potts, M., & Roberts, B. (1992). A short guide to alternative assessment practices. *Art Education, 45* (6), 34-38.

Maeroff, G. (1991). Assessing alternative assessment. *Phi Delta Kappan, 73* (4), 272-281.

Mamlin, H. R. (1986). Testing, testing, 1,2,3,.... *Design for Arts in Education, 88* (1), 24-26.

Marzano, R. J., Pickering, D., & McTighe, J. (1993). *Assessing student outcomes: Performance assessment using the dimensions of learning model.* Alexandria, VA: Association for Supervision and Curriculum Development.

Mitchell, J. V. (Ed.). (1983). *Tests in print III.* Lincoln, NE: University of Nebraska, Buros Institute for Mental Measurement.

Mitchell, J. V. (Ed.). (1985). *The ninth mental measurements yearbook.* Lincoln, NE: University of Nebraska, Buros Institute for Mental Measurement.

National Commission on Excellence in Education. (1983). *A nation at risk.* Washington, DC: U.S. Government Printing Office.

National Endowment for the Arts. (1988). *Toward civilization: Overview from the report on arts education.* Washington, DC: National Endowment for the Arts.

Nickerson, R. S. (1989). New directions in educational assessment. *Educational Researcher, 18* (9), 3-7.

Paulson, E. L., Paulson, P. R., & Meyer, C. A. (1991). What makes a portfolio a portfolio? *Educational Leadership, 48* (5), 61-63.

Peterson, J. (1991). *States assessment survey.* Paper commissioned by the California Department of Education.

Pipho, C. (1985, May 22). Tracking the reforms, part 5: Testing—can it measure the success of the reform movement? *Education Week.*

Popham, W. J. (1993). Circumventing the high costs of authentic assessment. *Phi Delta Kappan, 74* (6), 470-473.

Ross, M., Radnor, H., Mitchell, S., & Bierton, C. (1993). *Assessing achievement in the arts*. Buckingham, United Kingdom: Open University Press.

Rudner, L. M., & Boston, C. (1994). *A look at performance assessment for art education*. Reston, VA: National Art Education Association.

Sabol, F. R. (1990). Toward development of a visual arts diagnostic achievement test: Issues and concerns. In M. Zurmuehlen (Ed.), *Working papers in art education*, 1989-1990 (pp. 78-85). Iowa City, IA: The School of Art and Art History of the University of Iowa.

Sabol, F. R. (1994). A critical examination of visual arts achievement tests from state departments of education in the United States. *Dissertation Abstracts International*, 9518525, Vol. 56, Issue 2A. (University Microfilms No. 5602A)

Shavelson, R., Baxter, G., & Pine, J. (1992). Performance assessment: Political rhetoric and measurement reality. *Educational Researcher, 21* (4), 22-27.

Shepard, L. (1989). Why we need better assessments. *Educational Leadership, 46* (7), 4-8.

Sletter, C. E., & Grant, C. A. (1988). *Making choices for multicultural education: Five approaches to race, class, and gender*. Columbus, OH: Merrill.

Stiggins, R. J. (1985). Improving assessment where it means the most: In the classroom. *Educational Leadership, 43* (2), 69-74.

Sweetland, R. C., & Keyser, D. J. (Eds.). (1986). *Test: A comprehensive reference for assessments in psychology, education, and business* (2nd ed.). Kansas City, MO: Test Corporation of America.

Taylor, P. (1991). *In the process: A visual arts portfolio assessment pilot project*. Carmichael, CA: California Art Education Association.

U.S. Department of Education. (1991). *America 2000: An education strategy*. Washington, DC: U.S. Government Printing Office.

U.S. Department of Education. (1994). *Goals 2000: Education America act*. Washington, DC: U.S. Government Printing Office.

Wiggins, G. (1989a). Teaching to the (authentic) test. *Educational Leadership, 47* (2), 41-47.

Wiggins, G. (1989b). Toward more authentic and equitable assessment. *Phi Delta Kappan, 70* (9), 703-713.

Wilson, B. (1992). A primer on arts assessment and a plethora of problems. *Design for Arts in Education, 93* (3), 34-44.

Wolf, D. P. (1987). Opening up assessment. *Educational Leadership, 47* (7), 35-39.

Wolf, D. P. (1989). Portfolio assessment: Sampling student work. *Educational Leadership, 47*, 35-39.
Worthen, B. R. & Sanders, J. R. (1987). *Educational evaluation.* New York: Longman.
Zimmerman, E. (1992a). Assessing students' progress and achievement in art. *Art Education, 45* (6), 14-24.
Zimmerman, E. (1992b). How should students' progress and achievements be assessed?: A case for assessment that is responsive to diverse students' needs. *Visual Arts Research, 20* (1), 29-35.
Zimmerman, E. (1994). Authentic assessment does not always mean equitable assessment. *InSEA News, 1*, 3.
Zimmerman, E. (in press). Authentic assessment of a painting class: Sitting down and talking with students. In G. Phye (Ed.), *Handbook of classroom assessment: Learning, achievement, and adjustment.* New York: Academic Press.
Zimmerman, J. (1993). Student portfolios: Classroom uses. *Consumer Guide (OERI), 8*, 1-4.

Researching Paradigms in Art Education

The intent of this chapter is to introduce the art educator to the concept of paradigm research, the assumptions embedded in paradigm theory, and the methods associated with paradigm analysis. In the process, paradigm research will be related to questions and unsolved problems currently faced by the field of art education. This chapter also will explore particular merits of approaching problems of art education informed by an understanding of paradigms which govern theory and practice.

Paradigms, Paradigm Theory and Paradigm Analysis

A paradigm is a body of beliefs and values, laws, and practices which govern a community of practitioners. A paradigm is analogous to world view. Paradigm theory holds that the beliefs, values, laws, and practices of a community are embedded in its actions and documents. Paradigm analysis, as it provides a structure for research, requires determination of the character and structure of a professional community as well as an analysis of the substance of the paradigm.

References to paradigms began to appear in the literature following the publication in 1970 of Thomas Kuhn's second edition of *The Structure of Scientific Revolutions*. Paradigm analysis, according to Kuhn, provides a way of looking into practice so it can be of assistance in thinking about why things are the way they are. Widely cited as the primary reference for paradigm theory, Kuhn's notions of paradigm, paradigm change, and revolution have been applied to a number of fields outside science including art history (Clignet, 1985), education (Soltis,

KAREN LEE CARROLL
The Maryland Institute, College of Art

1971; Popp, 1975; Somolicz, 1974), and art education (Kuhn, 1984; Efland, 1992; Eisner, 1992; Pearse, 1983, 1992).

Some individuals have sensed the need for a new paradigm. For example, Kuhn (1984) saw an increase in interrelated arts programs uninformed by theory. She proposed that systems theory might provide a structure for a study of the nature of art. Such a study would look at the arts in a comprehensive manner and also honor their uniqueness, diversity, and individuality. Kuhn proposed that such a study would lead to establishment of a new paradigm which would restructure the future of art education curricula.

Some have sought to define one paradigm by positioning it in relationship to another paradigm. Clark, Day, and Greer (1989), for example, were commissioned to prepare a position paper on discipline-based art education (DBAE) for the Getty Center for Education in the Arts. DBAE was first aligned with "60s Discipline-Centered Reform" and then contrasted to a paradigm characterized as creative self-expression (pp. 133-134). Several categories were used to delineate how creative self-expression and discipline-based art education were composed of contrasting beliefs and values, laws, and practice. A number of categories were used to indicate how these two paradigms differed fundamentally in relationship to goals, content, curriculum, conception of learner, conception of teacher, creativity, implementation, works of art, and evaluation.

Some have explored the implications of paradigm changes in the world of art for the implications they might have for curriculum. Efland (1992), in this case, noted the waning of modernism, and speculated on the impact of postmodernist thought on art education. He began by identifying the attributes of modernism including: functions of art, the ideas of progress, cultural change and the avant-garde, abstraction, universalism, creative destruction, and denial of popular culture. Attributes he assigned to postmodernism included: rejection of the ideas of progress, conceptual conflict, dissonant beauty, pluralism and multiple readings, eclecticism, double coding, democratization, and concern for otherness. He concluded that the function of the arts continues to be "reality construction," and art should be taught to "widen and deepen our understanding of the cultural landscape we inhabit" (p. 118).

Some have suggested that values associated with the arts are beginning to emerge in paradigms of fields beyond art education. As an example, Eisner (1992), discussed the emergence of new paradigms for educational research and argued that there is a close relationship between what those who work in the arts value and newly accepted methodology. He suggested qualitative research methods place value on relationships, subtleties of practice, the uniqueness of outcomes, nuance, personal signature, the importance of voice and the creation of a sense of authorship, and aesthetic crafting of writing that fosters empathy, feeling and insight (p. 126).

Some have mused on the possibility that we have moved into an era which is postparadigmatic. Pearse (1992) raised questions about recent developments in art education and concluded that postmodernism is post-paradigmatic in that it pushes the boundaries of the notion of paradigm. For art education this means that we "have embarked on a postparadigmatic era, one in a constant state of flux, a kind of perpetual pluralism" (p. 250). Accordingly, Pearse argued, art teachers need to be versed in semiotics and methods for decoding sign systems as well as methods for deconstructing social meaning. For students in a postmodern era, the "challenge is not to produce novel forms but to produce work which meaningfully and critically interprets the potentially infinite array of cultural forms and interactions" (pp. 250-251).

It remains to be seen whether or not we have entered a post-paradigmatic era. Perhaps we have entered an era marked by the co-existence of multiple paradigms or the emergence of yet another paradigm. All these examples illustrate that we need ways of thinking about theory and practice in art education which encompass a wide range of concerns including values and beliefs, laws, and practices. To consider such factors is to think about belief systems, world views, and paradigms.

Paradigm Theory

The emergence of paradigm analysis as a promising area of research in education coincides with the increasing acceptance given qualitative research methods in the last decade. Certain assumptions underpin both these research areas and explain their appearance and significance in a post-modern era. Common to both is a sense that reality and truth are constructions that arise out of communities and must be seen contextually. Rather than making progress in a linear fashion towards absolute truth, Kuhn (1970) suggested that scientific communities, and other communities as well, structure the pursuit of truth. Paradigms develop which represent the universally recognized achievements that, for a time, model problems and solutions for a community of practitioners. The paradigm gains in strength as problems are solved, as the inherent theory becomes articulated, and as some ambiguities are resolved. The development of theory, codes, laws, and rules appears to be the hallmark of a mature paradigm.

Only when new information cannot be integrated into the existing paradigm or when problems persist which cannot be resolved, does a crisis arise. Here, the community engages in the process of seeking a new paradigm which appears to have greater promise. Kuhn's paradigm theory (1970), which is a theory about the process of revolutionary change, holds that a new paradigm is likely to replace another when the new one is thought to offer better solutions to problems and concerns than the previous one. For example, Clignet (1985) proposed that the history of art can be viewed as a series of artistic revolutions and paradigmatic shifts.

Paradigm Analysis

As a holistic approach to research, paradigm analysis offers more than a structure or framework for examining the status quo of a professional community. Paradigm theory concerns the structure of revolution and change and should therefore be helpful in projecting how change might occur. For example, the field of art education has its share of unsolved problems, the most persistent of which is the need to secure a position for the arts in the schools. As a long standing problem, it threatens the fate, mission and future of the field. Paradigm analysis may be of assistance in understanding why this is the case. Is this problem due to confusion or conflict or inconsistencies and contradictions within the governing paradigm of the field? Is it possibly related to the co-existence of several paradigms operating simultaneously within the larger governing paradigm? Is the problem related to powerful and competing paradigms held by others? Paradigm research offers ways of looking at such a problem. Research can be designed not only to help identify why things are the way they are but also to identify how ideas converge and where points of entry for a dialogue within or across community lines might be found.

Five examples of paradigm research (Baker, 1982; Dorn, 1994; Kerlavage, 1992; Carroll, 1987, 1993) will be used in this chapter to illustrate paradigm analysis. As a group, they represent a range of problems which can be explored through paradigm analysis. Further, they have been selected on the grounds that the researchers have explicitly referenced their search to Kuhn (1970), constructed research methods based on Kuhn's theory of paradigm, and their studies are characterized by a search to unravel and decode theory and practice in art education. This attempt to ferret out belief systems by engaging in paradigm research is different from describing one or more paradigms. In a sense, paradigm researchers deconstruct rather than construct theory and practice in order to reveal what belief and value systems are at work in a specific area of concern. Those who describe a paradigm, or contrast two or more paradigms, in an attempt to argue for their support or to explain their nature, are engaged with what might be called paradigm or theory construction rather than paradigm deconstruction.

Paradigms in Art Education

In defining a paradigm, Kuhn drew attention to the way in which a body of values, beliefs, laws, and practices bind a community together. Conversely, Kuhn held that any given community is also defined by its paradigms or the values and beliefs it holds to be true. One way to begin thinking about the meaning of paradigm is to ask: What is known about paradigms in art education?

The Search for a Governing Paradigm

Baker's (1982) thesis is that the field of art education is governed by a rather explicit body of beliefs, values, laws, and practice. His analysis of the literature, starting with Rousseau's *Emile* written in 1761, and subsequent developments in the field, led him to conclude that art educators own what he calls a Romantic Paradigm. He describes that paradigm as follows:

> It is child-centered, insisting that the child is a unique entity with particular needs and attitudes; it maintains that children reach maturity through predictable and sequential stages of growth and development; it stresses the critical importance of the senses and emotions as the primary means of learning. Furthermore, it places priority on the sense of sight; it advocates natural phenomena as a model for methodology; it is holistic, insisting that a proper education is well-balanced between the intellectual, sensory, physical and moral domains of human behavior; it is socialistic, being concerned with the child's assimilation into its culture and human relationships; it believes that art has value for *all* children at *all* ages and that it can be taught to *all* children; it views art instruction as primarily an instrumental function, although in a vague way it recognizes aesthetic functions; it believes that drawing is the primary mode of visual behavior; and it maintains that art has a basic structure which can be reduced to modes of instruction that move from simple to complex operations in a sequential manner (pp. 116-117).

Is Baker right in describing the paradigm that governs art education in this manner? Are these values and beliefs you hold to be true? Do these principles guide your everyday choices as you set about to make instructional decisions for your students? Do these beliefs and values somehow distinguish you from others in the school environment, perhaps those who would subscribe to a more academic paradigm where the preferred mode of thought would be scientific, the endorsed form of expression written and/or numerical, and the goal of education the transmission of a body of knowledge?

How does a community acquire a paradigm? The process begins rather intuitively with natural affinities and propensities which various individuals develop. For example, most art educators would probably describe themselves as having found tremendous pleasure in making things when they were children. They may think of themselves as highly sensitive and responsive to the visual world. In the elementary and secondary years, they might have demonstrated a preference for visual learning and sought visual ways to make their intelligence known. They may, as well, have shared a common educational history in which visual forms of intelligence, and art making in particular, were not highly prized.

Most of us pursued the study of art at the undergraduate level and some at the graduate level, as well, and in the process found mentors who encouraged us as we developed our expertise in studio art and/or art history. At some point, most of us discovered a desire to bring a love of art together with a love of people, coupled with a notion of wanting to use art to make a difference in the world of learners. What began, then, as a personal affinity developed over time through education and practice eventually becoming the basis for a career in the profession of teaching art.

Through the process of preservice education and internships, we learned the "laws" or essential concepts of art education and began to master the "practice" of teaching art. We were shaped by members of the art and art education community to see the world in a certain light, to think about the needs of learners in a special way, and to draw upon our knowledge of art in a particular fashion, translating it into curricula for our students. The paradigm we were introduced to came to us through our textbooks, the articles we read, the model art teachers we experienced along the way, and cooperating teachers under whom we apprenticed.

As professionals, we continue to experience our particular paradigm through in-service, interaction with our colleagues, community publications, reports from research, and curriculum development. Within our community, there are acknowledged pathways through service, scholarship, or advanced studies which lead to higher levels of authority, recognition, and reward. In turn, we encourage, nurture, and initiate another generation of members into the art education profession. What holds us together as a community is a constellation of beliefs and values, laws, and practices which Kuhn takes to constitute a paradigm. It follows that we also are defined, and seen as distinct from other communities, by the paradigm we share.

Shifting Paradigms

Does a paradigm change? Some would say that paradigms even "shift." Kuhn's (1970) study of scientific revolutions revealed patterns which can be seen in the field of art education as well. During what he calls "normal" periods, the work of the community builds and strengthens its governing paradigm. Practice develops and research is conducted to show that the paradigm helps the community solve its problems. Theory is articulated and the community itself may increase its numbers and a general sense that "we are on the right track" becomes evident.

There are times, however, when the community will experience some crisis related to its paradigm of beliefs and values, laws, and practice. Sometimes, a new idea emerges which cannot be accommodated into the existing paradigm. It doesn't seem to fit yet it commands attention. On the other hand, the community may discover that the existing paradigm is insufficient to solve problems it finds critical. In either case, a period of some uncertainty and even upheaval can develop. Some members may resist change while others embrace it. As new ideas are accommodated or adjustments are made so that problems can be better solved, the paradigm may be adjusted. In some cases, a radically new way of thinking emerges and such would constitute a paradigm shift.

Clark, Day and Greer (1989) proposed, for example, that the Getty initiated a paradigm shift with the introduction of discipline-based art education (DBAE). This paradigm shift was motivated, in part, by a sense that the old paradigm, characterized as creative self-expression, was insufficient to solve the most critical problem faced by the field of art education, i.e., the need to establish secure grounding for the arts in the schools. To consider whether or not DBAE produced a radically new way of thinking about art education, one would have to ask: In what ways did DBAE fundamentally change the way teachers think about children and the role of the arts in the schools? Has practice shifted from one form to another, from a child-centered approach to a subject matter-centered approach? Or have there been some adjustments in the governing paradigm? Perhaps it will take some time to sort out these questions. Kuhn (1970) would hold that only in retrospect can one really determine whether a community has experienced a "paradigm shift."

Unraveling the Co-existence of Multiple Operating Paradigms

The co-existence of multiple paradigms operating simultaneously within a larger, governing paradigm is another possibility worth investigation. Dorn's (1994) thesis identifies three dominant paradigms in contemporary art education which he traces to sources in art, art history, criticism, aesthetics, and education. Dorn has titled them to capture a sense of the operating ideas embedded in each. The *Art as Schema-Motif Paradigm* borrows the term schema from Gombrich's *Art as Illusion* (1972) and recognizes that pictures come from other pictures" (Dorn, 1994, p. 73). The *Art as Form-Gestalt Paradigm* found its beginning in Clive Bell's notion of significant form and is critically referred to as formalism although the concept is broader. The *Linguistic-Metaphorical Paradigm* holds that art is a concept and a sign linked to social behavior or ritual. In Dorn's assessment, identifiable sets of artists, art works, and pedagogical traditions have developed around these different conceptions of art. The possibility that multiple paradigms co-exist in an unexamined, even subliminal way, raises even more questions about the nature and coherency of practice. This may explain some of the confusion and even conflict felt by teachers confronted by a wide range of pedagogical options and choices.

Both Baker (1982) and Dorn (1994) assert that the field may be operating 'blind" without a full and conscious notion of what it believes and values or how some beliefs and values, laws and practices, may exist in conflict with each other. Even if a community, or an individual within a community, has not examined or articulated the beliefs and values which govern its everyday actions, a paradigm still may be strongly felt. As such, the paradigm works in a subliminal way governing decisions which seem to be made intuitively, instinctively, or simply out of habit.

Detecting Conflict within a Paradigm

The possibility of conflict within a paradigm is entertained in a study by Kerlavage (1992). Applying paradigm analysis to the historical development of art appreciation within the context of early childhood education, Kerlavage identified the nature of the conflict as well as a cyclical pattern in the reappearance and disappearance of art appreciation practices as child-centered approaches receded or gained in prominence over the past century. The problem, Kerlavage concluded, is a failure to fully resolve beliefs and values which govern art in early childhood education so that art appreciation models for practice can be evaluated and applied within the context of children's individual developmental needs.

Unraveling Conflict Between Communities with Different Paradigms

The conflict of paradigms, particularly as they set communities apart, also has been the focus of two research studies I conducted (Carroll, 1987, 1993). In the first of the studies, paradigm analysis was used to ascertain how differently practitioners and scholars in the fields of gifted education and art education viewed matters ranging from the identification of exceptionalities to instruction. These two communities within the field of education, with apparent mutual concerns regarding special behaviors and creativity, were found to be governed by dramatically opposed paradigms. Deeply profound differences in values and belief systems exist between those who honor artistic modes of thought and expression and those who honor academic modes. Given the significance assigned unsolved problems in paradigm theory, this study revealed that both art education and gifted education communities own similar unsolved problems which are not unrelated to each other's fates and missions. The analysis also identified points of convergence between the two fields which suggest how an inter-community dialogue might be developed.

In my subsequent study (Carroll, 1993), the manner in which a paradigm antithetical to the arts has been set into place by the texts and practices in the larger field of teacher preparation was identified. Here the unsolved problem of one community, art education, can be seen in context of the beliefs and values of another community, teacher preparation. Once again, art education's beliefs, values, laws, and practices are seen as competing with powerful and very different world views. What becomes clear here is the manner in which the roots of these world views are shaped very early on in the initiation of professionals new to the field of teaching. This study suggests that the ways colleagues in the larger profession of teaching are prepared by those in teacher preparation to think, or not think, about the arts affects the future of the field of art education in profound ways. Certain ideas, theories, and theorists central to art education were found to be missing, or presented as dismissible, in literature of the fields of educational psychology and the history of education. Such exclusions and omissions included recognition and significance of visual learning styles, the nature of visual intelligence, and the utility of drawing behaviors and art-like activities in the curriculum. This study suggested that the larger field of education might better solve some of its own problems if it were to embrace many of the values, beliefs, and practices central to art education. It was concluded that success of the larger field of education is directly tied to the status of the arts in the schools and that both communities have much to gain from opening these paradigms to critical inspection, inter-community dialogue, and revision.

The Utility of Paradigm Analysis and Research in Art Education

Broad questions such as those dealing with the interface of paradigms of large communities or sub-communities within a profession can be served well by paradigm analysis. In addition, paradigm analysis can be used to examine more subtle differences within a field. For example, how beliefs about art, teacher characteristics, or preparation affect everyday instructional decisions or student learning in art is a territory ripe for paradigm analysis. As an illustration, an exploratory study was initiated to consider the relationship between high levels of studio expertise among novice art teachers and the manner in which such expertise translated into their teaching practice (Carroll, 1994). Preliminary findings suggested these novice teachers plumbed their special areas of studio expertise for teaching ideas and placed great value on constructing experiences with sensuous materials and processes. In these experiences, the construction of personal meaning was facilitated by processes for thinking and making integrated with critical discussions and references to the world of art. In what ways does such an inquiry reflect paradigmatic concerns? It does so in the search for connections between the values and practice of the artist with the values and practices embedded in teaching.

Even more finite forms of paradigm analysis can be imagined wherein the relationship between a given teacher's belief system and the ideas and work generated by his or her students is examined. In some ways, it becomes difficult to imagine any meaningful research without some attention to the paradigms in operation within a specific context or contexts being studied.

Choosing to Use Paradigm Analysis in Art Education

Since the first question in paradigm analysis usually asks what is known about the community under study, it seems appropriate to begin by asking what characterizes those who engage in this form of research and how it became their method of choice. Taken as a group, researchers Baker, Dorn, Kerlavage and I all share the advantage of having worked at a number of different levels in the art education profession. We have taught in the public schools and held various administrative posts with responsibilities for curriculum development and professional preparation. Baker and Dorn have held leadership positions in the National Art Education Association. In these various roles, all of us have had to look at the "bigger picture" and in doing so, developed an awareness of how art education interfaces with other sub-communities within the larger field of education, parent audiences, the political arena, and the public at large. All have had to argue for the arts in the schools and know what it is to encounter resistance to notions and beliefs art educators take as common sense and good practice.

An Interest in Unsolved Problems

As researchers, these same individuals also share a sense that the art education profession owns serious unsolved problems and, further, that any resolution of these problems will require a close examination of the belief systems and practices which shape the field. Baker and I are particularly interested in the way in which problems in art education are profoundly intertwined with the belief systems held by others. Common to all these researchers is the hope of engaging others within art education and the larger field of education in dialogue across philosophical and community lines.

Our research often begins with some baseline observation or hunch that beliefs and values are operating in a powerful yet unarticulated manner. Baker's (1982) historical study began with observations about the beliefs and practices of the profession. During his tenure as editor of *School Arts*, this magazine conducted a survey which provided baseline data. Baker combined the results with insights from his decade in the classroom and another decade in administration. Introduced to Kuhn's paradigm theory and Collingwood's (1977) theory of history, he began to trace formative ideas in the field as they moved from one practitioner to another, and from Europe to America. His goal was to trace the historical ascendancy of the "romantic paradigm" in art education.

Dorn's (1994) search for the substance of multiple operating paradigms developed as he reflected on more than forty years of teaching and administering programs in art coupled with a life-long interest in philosophical issues. Moved by the notion that teachers teach what they believe to have value and questioning whether or not discipline-based art education constituted a viable paradigm upon which to base art education, he turned to his philosophic interests searching for conceptions of art upon which to base theory and practice. Dorn seemed motivated, in part, to undertake such an endeavor by his belief that the field of art education would be served well if it owned alternative or multiple paradigms which could provide philosophically coherent models resulting in integration and mutual reinforcement, rather than contradiction, among areas including studio, art history, and aesthetics.

Kerlavage's study (1992) was initiated as a way of thinking about the inconsistencies she felt as a practitioner and curriculum developer. Having started her career as a head start teacher and subsequently focusing her teaching on young children, she was troubled by the appearances of practices which required young children to approach works of art cognitively. She conducted an initial research study regarding children's preferences for imagery but still her questions where not answered. Ultimately, she chose to do a paradigm study which traced picture study and the use of art images from the 1880s, when art appreciation programs first entered the schools as a handmaiden to industrial drawing programs, to the 1990s and discipline-based art education. Her hope was to bring some resolution to questions concerning the appropriate use of art images with children that would be consistent with child-centered approaches to teaching art.

My own research (Carroll, 1987, 1993) was motivated by a growing awareness of how the arts were omitted, misrepresented, and diminished by our colleagues in the larger field of education. Having been a teacher and director of programs for the gifted in the arts, I became increasingly involved with practitioners and scholars in gifted education. My first paradigm study was sparked by interactions with this community. The field seemed to have a gravitational pull towards the arts which was contradicted by confusing terminology, a lack of commitment, and strangely naive and uninformed notions about the nature of creativity. I wanted to know more about how two fields, seemingly united around issues of exceptionality and creativity, could be at such odds. I discovered that there are rich possibilities for dialogue and that both art education and gifted education communities stand to gain by inter-community discourse. My second study (Carroll, 1993) was motivated by a desire to understand more about the way in which teachers, in general, were prepared to think, or as it turns out, not to think, about the arts. This study produced recommendations for improving the status of the arts in the schools through inter-community dialogue at the higher education level with colleagues in teacher preparation, educational psychology, and the history of education.

A Structure for Research Ideally Suited to Art Educators

Thus, paradigm research becomes an appropriate strategy for those who are interested in viewing issues, questions, and unsolved problems contextually. It is a structure for inquiring why things are the way they are and what the options and avenues for change might entail. In some ways, paradigm research seems ideally suited for visual thinkers. Common to all the studies described was a sense that something was "wrong with the big picture," that underneath appearances, contradictions and discrepancies were at work. Questions arose as a kind of visceral response akin to "If this sounds so good, why doesn't it make me feel good?" Visual thinkers and artists often have sensibilities for such discrepancies due, perhaps, to their willingness to look at the whole gestalt and then consider how the parts function within that context. Those who have developed skills in description, analysis, interpretation, and evaluation of art will find themselves well prepared to engage with processes related to conducting paradigm research. With its emphasis on identifying characteristics, patterns, contrasts, coherences, inconsistencies, conflicts, and the "reading" of visual as well as verbal evidence, models, symbols, and exemplars, art educators should find themselves able paradigm researchers.

The Art Education Research Agenda: Ripe with Opportunities for Paradigm Analysis

Research questions arise out of practice, out of a sense that unsolved problems, unresolved conflicts, and contradictions in beliefs and actions in some way block us from being better at what we do. The National Art Education Association has identified several arenas for research in art education (1996). Decoding belief systems and values, as well as the history of ideas which shape contemporary practice, seems critical if we are to better understand teacher preparation, conceptual issues, contexts, curriculum, instruction, student learning, and assessment.

Solving Methodological Challenges of Paradigm Research

Researchers in the field of art education, like those in many other fields, are just beginning to realize the potential of paradigm analysis and the critical role it might play in addressing the art education community's most profound and complex problems. As a relatively new structure for research analysis, methodology is still in a formative stage. Yet it is possible to report on how some of the problems of paradigm research have been solved and how the process works. Some procedures have been developed which help illuminate both sources and substance of single, contrasting, or co-existing paradigms. Usually, the overall process is not complete until patterns have been identified and interpreted, significance has been assigned to unsolved problems, and points of entry for dialogue about change have been identified.

Aspects Significant to the Analysis of One or More Paradigms

The initial tasks of paradigm research usually involve an analysis of the character and structure of a given community and, subsequently, an analysis of the substance of governing and/or operating paradigms. While Kuhn (1970) directs attention to the documents of a community, data can also include analysis of observations from practice. Paradigm research also may call upon and embrace various methods of research such as case studies, ethnographic studies, demographic surveys, and educational criticism. The following discussion covers a number of aspects which, depending on the exact nature of a study, may prove significant to the analysis of one or more paradigms. These include:

- analyzing the character and structure of a given community,

- delimiting choices by selecting documents and actions for analysis,

- employing issues to focus the search for paradigm substance,

- decoding meaning embedded in words, images, symbols, and metaphors,

- identifying patterns in the paradigm and making connections,

- identifying unsolved problems,

- analyzing paradigm interface, and

- anticipating the convergence of ideas and points of entry for a dialogue about change.

The five examples of paradigm research focused on in this chapter model different emphases. Two studies (Baker, 1982; Kerlavage, 1992) focused on the historical development of a single paradigm. One study (Dorn, 1994) focused on unraveling the historical development and contemporary manifestation of three coexisting paradigms. My two studies (Carroll, 1987, 1993) involved a comparative inquiry into paradigms within a contemporary time frame. The design and justification of research methods tailored to a given question are, as in all forms of research, important first steps. In assembling the following review of possible research problems, the assumption is made that each study may require its own special methods.

Analyzing the Character and Structure of a Given Community. Establishing the character and structure of a given community is usually an essential part of paradigm studies. Whether the community being studied is a community of one, an entire field such as art education, or an interdisciplinary community sharing common interests, it will be necessary to develop a profile of the characteristics of that community. Some of this information can be gathered through interviews or surveys. Sometimes, it is possible to use surveys conducted by others. Baker (1982) began with some global descriptors of art educators drawn from surveys. My comparative study of two different educational communities (Carroll, 1987) drew on existing surveys and accounts of the profession to establish: (1) preprofessional training and employment patterns; (2) avenues for professional development; (3) the history and theory of the field as characterized in primary texts; and (4) avenues for professional advancement and research, opportunities to publish in the field's journals, and the manner in which certain members become authorities in the field.

Delimiting Choices By Selecting Documents and Actions for Analysis. Since it is not possible to analyze everything nor does everything deserve analysis, it is necessary to delimit choices on defensible grounds. For example, texts for which multiple editions have been published are generally accepted as holding more authority in a field than those texts which only exist in the first edition. Multiple editions, then, are taken as a sign that the ideas and authors have a sustained impact on a field, and it follows that those with the greatest number of multiple editions can be assigned higher levels of authority. Journals can be evaluated relative to their distribution and also in regard to the different audiences in the field which they serve. Some journals are juried, have small distributions, and focus on reporting research and inquiry in a particular field. Others are broadly read by practitioners, often feature practitioners as authors, are more practical in their application of ideas, and thus serve as an excellent source of prescribed models and examples of practice.

Another way of selecting documents for analysis is to consider a variety of documents and sources wherein important information about the paradigm might reside. For Baker (1982), important information was found in the writing of early educationists in Europe and America and, later, in writings by American art educators. In Dorn's (1994) study, essential information was found in the writings of Western philosophers and critics, artists, and art educators. Kerlavage (1992) found significant information not only in the writings of art educators but in curriculum guides, school textbooks, and visual resource materials.

In my study of the gifted and art education communities, the following sources provided a structure and sequence for analysis: (1) reports from practice including program models, content, and instructional strategies; (2) reports from research; (3) curriculum documents; (4) theoretical conceptions as presented in texts and references; (5) exemplars or models used to illustrate theoretical conceptions; (6) illustrations translating theory into practice; (7) instructional strategies suggested in texts and references; (8) statements regarding educational responsibility; and (9) interpretations of broader questions and issues.

Similar problems exist in setting criteria for the identification of authorities recognized in a field. Here criteria such as having responsibility for the training of new members, holding national offices in field-based organizations, editing the field's journals, and recognition outside the field are useful indicators. Citations are another way to identify those who bear influence in, or outside, a field. Citations or references are of particular importance to historical studies in which the ascendancy of or movement of ideas is an important aspect of the research.

Employing Issues to Focus the Search for Paradigm Substance. Just as it is not possible to analyze everything, it is not possible or even useful to attempt a broad, unfocused analysis. Rather, the use of particular issues which seem central to the research question serve to sharpen the search for substance in the paradigm. In Baker's (1982) study, a focus on drawing methodology centered the inquiry. In Dorn's (1994) study, major philosophic traditions and conceptions of art were employed to guide the search. In Kerlavage's (1992) study, definitions of art appreciation, the rationale for using art works with children, the reasons for selecting art exemplars, and the types of exemplars chosen provided a thematic focus. In my study comparing the gifted education community and the art education community (Carroll, 1987), issues of exceptionality and instruction were used as a dual focus. These studies suggest that paradigms can be viewed through particular aspects and that conclusions can be drawn about the whole of the paradigm from a sharply delineated and focused analysis.

Decoding the Meaning Embedded in Words, Symbols. Images. and Metaphors. Careful analysis of examples seems to be very useful in clarifying what is really meant by a theoretical position. Examples meant to illustrate often make visible the real intent, limitations, or parameters of an idea, theory, or assumption which cannot be known otherwise. The task here is to be alert for inconsistencies and contradictions wherein an example alters or compromises the ideas expressed in theory. Equally significant is the use of visual evidence and in particular photographs and art work meant to illustrate ideas. It is not uncommon, for example, to find that ideas presented, reinforced, or implied by images are simultaneously denied in words or by silences. For example, one text on gifted education made prominent use of students engaged in the arts on the cover yet, within the text, made no serious attempt to address the needs of artistically gifted students or to define the role of the arts in the education of academically gifted students.

As well, word choice and definitions bear careful attention. For example, the dual and sometimes inter-changeable terms of "gifted" and "talented" were found to mask important meanings and imply hierarchical order. Also, the gifted education community often referred to academic behaviors as intelligent, thus leaving artistic behaviors, by inference, outside or beyond intelligence. A careful analysis of word use often reveals biases and misconceptions so subtle that they go unrecognized, and unchallenged, in their normal use.

Metaphors and analogies also can have a powerful influence. Consider the manner in which organic and nurturing metaphors are associated with a child-centered philosophy or the way in which children's minds are compared to computers processing information in subject-matter centered orientations. With an increased interest in metaphors from science and nature, educators will no doubt test new metaphors as ways of presenting conceptions about the mind, human behavior, schools, and relationships. As terms loaded with values and beliefs, assumptions and biases, they are well worth noting and decoding.

Identifying Patterns in the Paradigm and Making Connections. An analysis of patterns across categories should begin to yield a sense of the beliefs and values, laws, and practices of the paradigm. An important key here is to look for relationships among different aspects of the paradigm by cross-referencing, for example, beliefs with recommended practices, values with models for practice, and "laws" with beliefs. Before proceeding on to subsequent levels of analysis and interpretation, it may prove useful to draw some conclusions about the relationship between the character of the community and the substance of the paradigm.

Identifying Unsolved Problems. The role of problems left unsolved by a paradigm should not be underestimated. If a paradigm has failed to solve problems central to the fate or mission of a field, the paradigm is vulnerable for adjustment or even revolutionary change. Some paradigm studies begin with the sense that some problems remain unsolved and the task is to take a more in-depth look at the sources, manifestations, and subtleties of the unsolved problem. For Dorn (1994), the unsolved problem was the sense that the field needed alternative and philosophically coherent paradigms for practice which offer ways to match teachers' philosophies with a system of beliefs they can support. Sometimes, the unsolved problem is the presence of conflict within the paradigm (Kerlavage, 1992). My own studies (Carroll, 1987, 1993) have attempted to unravel the forces that keep the arts from gaining a stronger foothold in the schools. The resolution of problems seems, in many cases, to depend ultimately on greater paradigm awareness and consciousness among a community as well as a willingness to address inconsistencies and conflicts. Some problems are related to competing paradigms and unsolved problems of others.

Analyzing Paradigm Interface. It has been suggested here that the unsolved problems of one community may be in some ways related to the unsolved problems of another community. A close analysis of these unsolved problems can reveal ways in which they cohere or interrelate. It also is possible that a kind of collusion may be detected wherein neither community realizes how they reinforce or contribute to the perpetuation of each other's misconceptions. As I found in one study (Carroll, 1987), two communities were unaware of the coherence between their unsolved problems. In my second study (Carroll, 1993), unsolved problems of the art education community were shown to be deeply affected by biased visions and theoretical omissions embedded in general education teacher preparation textbooks. In this example, specific biases and omissions left the larger educational community in the dark without a meaningful way to think about the role of the arts in education. Discoveries of less obvious yet significant findings also may emerge from such analyses. In this case, it was the realization that the unsolved problems of the larger educational community are likely to remain so until more of the art education paradigm is integrated into the broader fields of educational psychology, the history of education, and the field of general education.

Anticipating the Convergence of Ideas and Points of Entry for Dialogue. How can paradigm research help in directing intra- and inter-community dialogue? Two keys to that dialogue can emerge from a thorough analysis of both practice and theory: (1) the identification of the everyday language of a community and (2) the convergence of ideas. The everyday language of a community provides clues as to what holds the attention of the field. For example, the field of art education talks of "schemas" and "symbolic language." The everyday language of the gifted community, for example, is likewise concerned with "symbolic language" and the use of "symbols" (Carroll, 1987). The discovery that each field has its own way of talking about certain phenomena, and that two fields have some shared interest in a given phenomena, suggests what Kuhn (1970) calls "points of entry for discourse." Here it becomes possible to open a dialogue around mutual interests and to begin an exchange of terms and meanings, references and interpretations. Such a discourse allows fields with seemingly competing paradigms to talk to one another and to forge more holistic notions of compelling phenomena. Likewise, identification of ideas which exist in separate fields, but converge in certain ways, offers yet another avenue for discourse and intercommunity dialogue.

If it becomes clear that the fate and mission of one community is bound up with the fate and mission of another, intercommunity dialogue and discourse may become critical for the survival of both. Knowing how to communicate with each other and where to find values and interests of mutual concern and support seem to be an important key to this process of problem-solving and paradigm evolution.

Evaluating Paradigm Research and Analysis

While a given paradigm analysis can be critiqued for how carefully and thoroughly it has been executed and how well it has ferreted out unsolved problems, contradictions, and convergences, the real test of paradigm research is the value it ultimately holds for a particular community. Specifically, does a paradigm study help members of a community think about unsolved problems in a new light? Does it make a community more conscious of ways in which perceptions and practices have been shaped and molded? Does it awaken a community to the presence of contradictions that need to be resolved? Does it not only identify conflict and differences in points of view but lead, as well, to points of entry for a dialogue with others, within or beyond, an immediate community?

Given the range and complexity of problems facing education, it would seem that the entire education community would be well served by dialogues which integrate its best thinking from a number of informed points of view. Built into the notion of paradigm theory is the prospect of change and evolution. If we, as art educators, are to further develop our ideas and work together for the good of all learners, it would seem initiating a dialogue about paradigms which govern and operate in our own field might give us the practice and experience we need to open a dialogue with the rest of our colleagues in education. We might even discover we are curious to know how and why others think the way they do. Then we will really begin to learn from our colleagues and know better how to help them learn from us.

Seeing Oneself As a Member of A Community With A Paradigm

In the interest of a more conscious and informed practice in art education, and with a sense that many interesting conversations and potential research questions lie ahead, I encourage you to take the first step and generate for yourself a self portrait or profile of your development as a member of this community. Then make a working draft or visual image of your values, beliefs, and the models for practice you employ. As you move in and out of the classroom, begin to think about the sources of the paradigm to which you ascribe. Track down some of those sources and take a fresh look. Find a colleague, inside or outside the field of art education, who sees the world a little differently. Start sharing perceptions, look for connections, and see what can be discovered by looking through a different lens. Admitting what is troublesome about the practice with which one is engaged, is often the first step in paradigm research. Opening that practice and belief system to inspection is a beginning stage in engaging in paradigm analysis.

Summary

In a postmodern world where the significance of interrelationships have become more obvious and where beliefs and values, however conscious or subliminal, operate in powerful ways, it seems that any research study which does not, in some way, attend to the paradigms at work, will ultimately be diminished. Paradigm analysis offers a way of looking at the beliefs and values, laws and practices that govern communities such as education and art education. Paradigm analysis, based on the theories of Kuhn (1970) involves analysis of the character of a community as well as the substance of its paradigm(s). Paradigm analysis can accommodate a wide range of questions. At one extreme, the relationship between an individual teacher's belief system and what a student learns can be studied. At the other extreme, "meta" questions that ultimately influence the fate and mission of the profession as a whole can be explored. Underpinning the interest in paradigm research is the hope that a fuller consciousness of our beliefs and values might help us do our jobs more efficiently and effectively. As a profession, we suffer from not examining the paradigms that underpin our theory and practice. We have too little consciousness of the beliefs and values which may be served, or compromised, by the practice we extol. Yet, the profession of art education is funded by worthwhile values, strong beliefs, and astute insights; it has substantial pedagogical traditions and is funded by a conceptually rich discipline. In commenting on the importance of paradigm consciousness, Baker (1982) concluded:

> If the art education community is ambivalent towards its history and the beliefs and values and practices embedded in it, then the field is destined to repeat mistakes, weaken its successes by instructional stagnation, and expend its energies and resources on irrelevant curricular questions and instructional efforts. Of all this study suggests, it is that a community pays a dear price for "blind" practices. (p. 333)

Perhaps the real promise of paradigm analysis may lie in the manner in which it can help position art educators for intra- and inter-community dialogue. The paradigm research discussed in this chapter makes it clear that art education owns its own contradictions and, as well, competes with powerful and seemingly oppositional paradigms. Yet, there is some evidence that bridges can be built among communities with different world views. Much stands to be gained by being able to share perceptions with colleagues within and across disciplinary lines. We have much to learn from our colleagues, and we, in turn, have much to offer. This is the real test and promise of paradigm analysis.

References

Baker, D. W. (1982). Rousseau's children: An historical analysis of the romantic paradigm in art education. *Dissertation Abstracts International*, 4310A. (University Microfilms No. 8305613).

Carroll, K. L. (1987). Towards a fuller conception of giftedness: Art in gifted education and the gifted in art education. *Dissertation Abstracts International*, 4807A. (University Microfilms No. 8721089).

Carroll, K. L. (1993). Taking responsibility: Higher education's opportunity to affect the future of the arts in the schools. *Arts Education Policy Review*, 95(1),17-22.

Carroll, K. L. (1994, April). *Translating studio expertise into the classroom*. Paper presented at the meeting of the National Art Education Association Convention, Baltimore, MD.

Clark, G., Day, M. & Greer, D. (1989). Becoming students of art. In R. Smith (Ed.), *Disciplined-based art education*, (pp. 129-193). Urbana, IL: University of Illinois.

Collingwood, R. G. (1977). *The idea of history*. New York: Oxford University.

Clignet, R. (1985). *The structure of artistic revolutions*. Philadelphia: University of Pennsylvania Press.

Dorn, C. M. (1994). *Thinking in art: A philosophical approach to art education*. Reston, VA: The National Art Education Association.

Efland, A. (1992). Art education and postmodernism: Curriculum problems at century's end. In L. Piironen (Ed.), *Power of images* (pp. 114-120) Finland: INSEA Finland and the Association of Art Teachers in Finland.

Eisner, E. (1992). The emergence of new paradigms for educational research. In L. Piironen (Ed.), *Power of images* (pp. 122-128). Finland: INSEA Finland and the Association of Art Teachers in Finland.

Gombrich, E. (1972) *Art as illusion*. Princeton, NJ: Princeton University.

Kerlavage, M. (1992). Art works and young children: An historical analysis of the paradigm governing the use of art appreciation in early childhood. *Dissertation Abstracts International*, 5306A. (University Microfilms No. 9229580)

Kuhn, M. (1984). Restructuring the future of art education curricula. *Studies in Art Education*, 25(4) 271-275.

Kuhn, T. S. (1970). *The structure of scientific revolutions.* (2nd ed.) Chicago: University of Chicago.

NAEA Commission on Research in Education, E. Zimmerman, Chair. (1996). *NAEA Research Agenda Briefing Papers.* Reston, VA: National Art Education

Pearse, H. (1983). Brother, can you spare a paradigm? The theory beneath the practice. *Studies in Art Education,* 24(3),158-163.

Pearse, H. (1992). Beyond paradigms: Art education theory and practice in a postparadigmatic world. *Studies in Art Education, 33*(4), 244-252.

Popp, J. (1975). Paradigms in educational inquiry. *Educational Philosophy, 25,* 28-39.

Soltis, J. (1971). Analysis and anomalies in philosophy of education. Philosophy of Education Society: *Proceedings, 27,* 28-46.

Somolicz, J. (1974). Kuhn revisited: Science, education and values. *Organon,* 45-59.

Feminist Research: Themes, Issues, and Applications in Art Education

During the "first wave" of the women's movement in the United States, women struggled for, among other things, their right to be educated (Reinharz, 1992). During what has been called the "second wave" or the contemporary women's movement, women have claimed "the right to criticize the accepted body of knowledge" as well as "the right to create knowledge" (p. 11)—in other words, the right to do scholarly research. Having experienced the early phase of the contemporary women's movement, we vividly recall that in the 1970s, it was radical to insist that women pursuing their own interests could be serious critics and creators of knowledge as well as serious subjects for study, and that "a person might call her method 'feminist' merely by virtue of the fact that she was studying women" (p. 11). Given the nature of feminist research at that time (p. 21)[1], it is easy to understand why we and others were initially inclined to describe it as research conducted *by* women, *on* women, and *for* women.

After more sharply focused reading, criticism, and discussion, however, we quickly realized that our initial "by-on-for" definition of feminist research was far too facile and perhaps even misleading. For example, although debate continues about whether males are or are not qualified to do feminist research (Mills, 1984),

---

[1] Stanley & Wise (1990) further describe feminist research during the early phase of the contemporary women's movement as not only typically on, by, and for women, but often embracing qualitative methods and rejecting quantitative methods (as 'male'), and as being "overtly political in its purpose and committed to changing women's lives" (p.21). They also note that there was "little attention to problematising the research process for feminists.....the view was that 'they' had 'bias' while we feminists did not" (p. 21).

GEORGIA COLLINS
University of Kentucky

RENEE SANDELL
Maryland Institute College of Art

men identifying themselves as feminist or pro-feminist have engaged in inquiries that they and others are willing to call "feminist" (Jardine & Smith, 1987). Although some feminist researchers fear that any shift away from a simple focus on women would be a drastic political mistake (Nicholson, 1990, p. 6), most of us have enlarged our concern about women to include a more general concern about gender issues (O'Barr, 1988). Some, refusing to "privilege" the category of gender (Dill, 1994, pp. 53-54), include a more general concern about "virtually all forms of domination," recognizing that "women fill the ranks of every category of oppressed people" (Alcoff & Potter, 1993, p 4).

Although the notion of feminist research as simply research by, on, and for women has some relevance when reviewing the historical developments of feminist activity in academia, it is clearly not capable of suggesting either the full range or the underlying continuities of recent feminist scholarship in terms of its themes, issues, and applications. In our search for a more inclusive working definition, we consulted other, more sophisticated descriptions and prescriptions for doing feminist research.[2] Wanting to avoid biased, dogmatic, narrow, and/or exclusionary definitions of feminist research, we have settled on one developed by Reinharz (1992, p. 6) in connection with her comprehensive review, *Feminist Methods in Social Research*. Stated here in our own words and as a basic assumption for the following discussion, we take feminist research to be research done by people who are willing to call themselves and their research "feminist" and who have a stake in developing the positive significance of this appellation through their inquiry. This inclusive definition should allow us the most latitude in our following efforts to identify and review the why, the what, and the how of feminist research, the major issues and themes that have surrounded this research, and the practical concerns of those of us who do or would like to do feminist research in art education.

The Why of Feminist Research: Purpose and Incentives

In spite of the fact that women's studies programs in higher education have encouraged and allowed academic feminists to take interdisciplinary points of view in research, the majority of us who are feminist researchers still belong to departments closely identified with particular disciplines. We share with other members of our respective professions traditional motivations for doing research,

---

[2] See for examples, Alcoff & Potter, 1993; Fonow & Cook, 1991; Gergen, 1988; Hartman & Messer-Davidow, 1991; Hekman, 1990; Lather, 1991; Stanley & Wise, 1983, 1990, 1991.

Feminist Research: Themes, Issues, and Applications in Art Education

namely to test and extend knowledge in our particular fields, and to attain and secure our individual positions, ranks, salaries, and scholarly reputations. In some instances, particularly early in the second wave of the women's movement, these traditional research incentives, while encouraging research, discouraged *feminist* research. For example, both of us were told at one time or another that if we wanted to "make it" at the higher education level of art education, we should not become too closely identified with research that was overtly feminist—especially before obtaining tenure. The incentives for doing feminist research, however, were so compelling and support from other feminists so enabling that many of us were willing to take our chances. Although some academic careers undoubtedly suffered and perhaps still suffer because of close identification with the women's movement, at this point in time, feminist research is well-established as a legitimate, scholarly enterprise at most major American universities.

In addition to being motivated as well as restrained by traditional reasons for engaging in scholarly inquiry, feminist research is animated by political commitment. Those who do feminist research want to help bring about positive changes in the treatment and position of women in our society (Reinharz, 1992). They often decide to use their academic training, skills—their interests and delight in discovering new knowledge—for the liberation and betterment of women. This decision is based on and shaped by what is called a "raised feminist consciousness." According to Lerner (1986):

> Feminist consciousness consists (1) of the awareness of women that they belong to a subordinate group and that, as members of such a group, they have suffered wrongs; (2) the recognition that their condition of subordination is not natural, but societally determined; (3) the development of a sense of sisterhood; (4) the autonomous definition by women of their goals and strategies for changing their condition; and (5) the development of an alternate vision of the future. (p. 274)

Although not all feminists do research and not all feminist researchers do feminist research, a major motivation of those who do is their feminist political commitment. One indication of this commitment is a researcher's efforts to bring about improvements for women in a particular field of study by exposing and eliminating the sexism found in its androcentricity (i.e. the ignoring or deploring of females), its overgeneralization of male experience, its use of sexist language, its gender insensitivity, and its sex-related double standards (Eichler, 1988).

The political optimism that encourages feminist research often is challenged both by feminist activists and by non-feminist academics. For example, some feminist activists are skeptical that feminist, theoretical research can help liberate women because it will inevitably be co-opted by male dominated institutions with inherently elitist traditions of esoteric research (hooks, 1984; Wolff, 1990). On the other hand, the notion that political commitment can inspire creditable inquiry and contribute to knowledge within (or beyond) the various disciplines is challenged by those academics who subscribe to certain modernist world views that claim knowledge can and should be "objective" and that politics and scholarship don't mix (Nicholson, 1990). Feminist researchers are aware of these challenging criticisms. We argue, however, that research shedding light on women's situations can at the very least help raise consciousness and increase pressure for positive change. We also argue that only those in power can afford to ignore the degree to which their own political interests or those of others are being served by their research. Also, only those in power can assume that methodologies developed under conditions of social privilege and bias somehow allow them to transcend their own place in time and space, their own subjectivity.

At a personal level, the rewards of doing feminist research encourage ongoing activity in this area. Feminist researchers question the privileging of the public over the private sphere[3], the separation of the political from the personal, and the presumption that Western masculine values are generic human values, noting these principles have had negative effects on women and other "minorities." Feminism suggests that the personal is the political, that the problems of women in the private as well as the public spheres are worth our studious concern, and that some female-identified values might productively be subscribed to in public enterprises such as scholarly research. For these reasons, feminist researchers often choose research problems that concern them in their "actual," everyday lives and take innovative approaches to inquiry which allow them to experience a fusing of the personal and the political (Fonow & Cook, 1991). The result is a feeling of self-empowerment and legitimation, a de-trivialization of our own experiences by asserting they are worthy of political and scholarly concern (Stanley & Wise, 1983).

Feminist research often seeks a fusion of the personal, the professional, and the political, of lived experience with academic theory. This synthesis is perhaps the

---

[3] For a clarifying discussion on the differences between and significance of the public and private spheres, see Chapter 2, "The Culture of Separate Spheres: The Role of Culture in Nineteenth-Century Public and Private Life" in Wolff (1990), *Feminine Sentences*, pp. 12-33.

most salient motivation of all for doing feminist research for women (and men) who wish to explore alternative values of collaboration, intuition, and connection, who only recently have demanded equality in the public sphere, who are resisting the pressure to play by "men's rules," and who are reluctant to give up their involvements in the so-called private sphere. In addition to traditional academic and political incentives, then, many individuals are inspired to do feminist research because it is life-enhancing, productive, and energizing. In redefining research, enlarging its boundaries, and exploring a diverse range of possibilities in research incentives, topics, and methods, feminists experience personal, political, and professional renewal as a response to the challenges, as well as the rewards, of feminist research.

The What of Feminist Research: Themes and Topics

In general, subjects under scrutiny in feminist research have typically been that of women, gender, or complex patterns of oppression related to these categories. The specific topics selected by feminist researchers often are suggested by prevailing theories and traditional content of the particular discipline with which the researcher is associated (Wolff, 1990, p. 105). Thus, a feminist in art education is more likely than a feminist in sociology to select gender differences in children's art as a research topic—although interdisciplinary perspectives in women's studies encourage exceptions to this rule (for example, see Reeves & Boyette, 1983).

In addition to the influence of one's academic discipline, patterns in topic selection often are shaped by the particular political orientation of the feminist researcher. Although political orientations within the women's movement are neither static nor entirely separable, the kinds of topics chosen for study in feminist research have not only evolved with the political history of the women's movement, but they have continued to form discernible patterns or clusters, depending on researchers' attitudes toward *difference* and *change* (Collins, 1981). One way of organizing these clusters of topics for review is to group them under the now familiar rubric of *liberal feminism, cultural feminism,* and *poststructuralist feminism* (Alcoff, 1988).

Liberal feminists have attended to differences in the treatment and opportunities of women within past and current Western societies and institutions. They have focused their research on documenting the existence and effects of sex roles, sex bias, and sex inequities in our society and its institutions. Their research in art, for example, has "discovered" and documented differences in the education, numbers, visibility, critical reception, and historical treatment of women artists, as well as analyzing stereotypical images of women in art. To bring about change, liberal feminists have proposed, implemented, and researched results of various sex-equity strategies including integration, affirmative action, assertiveness training, and female networking in professional and public spheres.

Cultural feminists have attended to differences between men's and women's cultures as well as criticizing male definitions and devaluations of the feminine. They balk at the notion that male values are generic human values and that women must become aggressive and competitive like many men in order to be treated as equals (Alcoff, 1988). They note that the integrationism of liberal feminism, while bringing about many positive reforms for women in our society, has had negative side effects on women including sex-role conflicts, the "superwoman syndrome," and the further de-valuation of women-associated activities in the so-called "private sphere." To bring about change, cultural feminists have challenged positivistic approaches to research and have focused their inquiries on structural or institutional gender bias, the self-definition and pride of women, discovery of women's voices, various ways of knowing, and an ethics of care (Hicks & King, 1996). Their research in art, for example, has explored such things as women-identified art traditions, the hierarchy of Western art forms, masculine bias in the notions of creativity and genius, collaborative art forms, art and ecology, and feminist approaches to teaching, creating, and showing art.

Poststructuralist feminists have focused their research on differences between women and between groups of women, identity politics, and the deconstruction of terminology, narratives, and perspectives that often mask difference in naive feminist efforts to speak for others or assert unity. They find cultural feminism's tendency toward essentialism, or the assumption of a "homogeneous, unproblematized, and ahistorical conception of woman" (Alcoff, 1988, p. 413) at best misguided, and at worst, morally and intellectually reprehensible. Poststructuralist feminist research in art, for example, is likely to analyze shortcomings of earlier feminist art theory and practice, to explore postmodernist forms of art and inquiry, and to trace the implications of postmodern epistemology(ies). Liberal and cultural feminists who regard research as a form of or basis for political activism, fear poststructuralist research will de-politicize academic feminism, undermine the solidarity of the women's movement, and result in feminist practice taking a back seat to theory extension and construction (Hekman, 1990; Wolff, 1990).

Although these three political orientations have evolved historically in the order presented, none has yet achieved hegemony within the feminist research community. As a result, the full range of research topics suggested by each and all of these orientations continues to be viable, and the development of a healthy intra-feminist critique (such as the discussion above) sheds new light on issues related to these topics. A similar range of issues and mutual critiques can be found within the developing methodologies of feminist research.

The How of Feminist Research: Is There a Feminist Research Methodology?

Very few feminists would argue for either the development or adoption of one correct or "official" way of doing feminist research. Feminists are "not interested in telling feminists what methods to use" (Reinharz, 1992, p. 5). Reluctance in this regard is consistent with the origins of feminism itself. Stanley and Wise (1991) stated it this way:

> Feminism directly confronts the idea that one person or set of people have the right to impose definitions of reality on others. Feminist research and researchers should [therefore] attempt to avoid doing the same thing in research situations. (p. 281)

Most feminists claim for themselves and others the right to choose from a full range of extant theories, methodologies, and methods[4] associated with scholarly research and the opportunity to critique and modify these to accommodate feminist intentions and sensitivities (Jayaratne & Stewart, 1991). Reinharz (1992) suggests that feminists have in certain instances created their own ways of doing research (e.g., consciousness raising, nonauthoritative research voice, stream of consciousness narratives, conversations, and so forth); others (Stanley, 1991) discern the outlines of what might be called a de facto feminist methodology emerging from the modifications feminists make when appropriating androcentric theories and methods (e.g., rejecting the subjective/objective dichotomy, disclosing personal and political interests, focusing on previously trivialized concerns of

---

[4] Although informal references to "theory" might simply mean a "speculative idea or plan as to how something ought to be done" (V. Neufeldt [Ed.] [1988]. *Webster's New World Dictionary of American English*, 3rd College Edition. New York: Simon & Schuster, p.1387), in the context of this paper we take its meaning to be "a formulation of apparent relationships or underlying principles of certain observed phenomena which has been verified to some degree" (p. 1387). Following the lead of Stanley & Wise (1990), we distinguish between methodology and method in the following manner, seeing "'method' as 'techniques' or specific sets of research practices, such as surveys, interviews, ethnography and the like....[and seeing 'methodology' as] a 'perspective' or very broad theoretically informed framework...which may or may not specify its own particular 'appropriate' research method/s or technique/s" (p.26).

women, and so on) ; and still others worry that any appropriation of "the master's tools" (Holland, 1990; Lorde, 1981) will inevitably reproduce the sexism, racism, classism, and other systems of dominance inherent in their historical development and use (Shotter & Logan, 1988). Although potentially divisive, such differences can be the source of energy and pride among feminists. According to Reinharz (1992):

> Feminists are creatively stretching the boundaries of what constitutes research. We are versatile, many of us having engaged in numerous methods....And, most important, we are not uniform. Some of us choose to use a personal voice, but formats are being developed for those who choose not to do so. Some of us see feminist research as self-reflexive, collaborative, attuned to process, oriented to social change, and designed to be *for* women rather than only *of* women. Some of us are concerned with racism and heterosexism (very few with ageism), some express feminist distrust, some begin with their own experience, some incorporate a critique of androcentrism, and some are concerned primarily with the empowerment of women. (pp. 268-269)

These and other variations in opinion create tensions, as well as healthy debate, when it comes to considering how feminists ought to do research. Although an analysis of these controversies is beyond the scope of this chapter, we believe it is important to keep them in mind as we attempt to make some descriptive statements about how many, but not all, feminists have done research. Our review of related literature (see the Extended Reference List) suggests, as noted above, that feminist approaches to doing research have included critique, appropriation, and modification of pre-existing theories, methodologies, and methods. We also find in this literature a growing awareness among feminist academics that our evolving, inclusive, open-ended research tradition has in practice often exhibited characteristics, principles, or themes not usually identified with non-feminist research. We think it helpful to consider some of these observed commonalties.

Although feminist researchers are more likely than some academics to pursue interdisciplinary approaches to their scholarship, most have been schooled in particular academic disciplines. These disciplines are often strongly (but certainly not exclusively) associated with particular types of theory: for example, psychology/Freudianism, education/critical theory, sociology/Marxism, literary criticism/post-structuralism, and so on. One is not surprised, then, to discover that feminist researchers schooled in Western universities have adopted, adapted, or appropriated a wide variety of pre-existing theories historically developed by males (Donovan,1985; Nye, 1988). These theories suggest to the individual researcher not only what to look for and where to look for it, but how to look for it (and how to assure others that one has probably found it). For feminist researchers, armed only with raised consciousness of women's historical oppression and the conviction that women's experience and concerns must no longer be trivialized (Collins, 1993), these theories have provided intellectual traditions, theoretical platforms, and specialized languages for exploring, describing, explaining, and changing women's situations. A suspicion that these pre-existing, male-developed methodologies contain built-in world views that are inherently sexist has inevitably led some feminists to question whether scholarly research can be an effective tool for women's liberation (Daly, 1978). This same suspicion has led others to make major modifications in pre-existing theories and methodologies in an effort to reduce the possibility of reproducing oppressive values and practices. The revelation of the shortcomings in this regard has constituted an ongoing *feminist critique*, itself a form of feminist research.

If those who do feminist research have been schooled in both theories and research methodologies associated with their particular academic discipline, they have not subscribed blindly to one type of research. On the contrary, as Biklen and Shakeshaft (1985) points out:

> Feminist researchers will always call upon a variety of research methods to accomplish their goals, particularly because we are concerned that the problem shape the method, and not the reverse....Whatever method we choose, however, we must ....place tremendous importance on the process of discovering the questions that will get to the heart of women's experiences....We will need to depend on a variety of research styles and methods to reach this goal. The new emphasis on letting women speak in their own voices has heightened interest in qualitative methods, since these approaches provide participants an opportunity to construct their social realities. (pp. 50-51)

Although feminist research has often been associated with qualitative methodologies, feminists have used a variety of methods such as empirical, historical, and philosophical, as well as case studies, interviews, collaborations with research "subjects," and action research.

In spite of the fact that most feminists would argue that the methods chosen should suit, rather than determine the problem studied, the particular expertise and training of an individual, as well as her or his theoretical orientation, also will influence the methodology chosen. Fonow and Cook (1991) noted that other factors may influence the type of methods selected by feminists; for example, methods requiring high tech, money, and institutional support often have not been available to female feminists as a direct or indirect result of gender bias.

Although there are many factors that contribute to a feminist researcher's theoretical orientation and choice of methodology, viewed collectively, feminists have tended to make certain modifications to these hand-me-down sets of tools. Often, these modifications are presented in the reviews of feminist research as lists of principles, themes, strategies, or characteristics that in effect sketch out a de facto feminist research methodology. We present our own version of these descriptive summaries here and acknowledge the contributing published sources, referring interested readers to them for more detailed discussion. The sources upon which we base our characterization of feminist research include Eichler (1988), Fonow and Cook (1991), Jayaratne and Stewart (1991), Reinharz(1992), and Stanley (1991).

How Do Feminists Do Research?

What themes, principles, strategies, and ideals have tended to characterize feminist research? How do feminists *do* feminist research? We have found that many feminist researchers:

- identify or are willing to identify themselves and their research project as "feminist" or "womanist."

- take a feminist perspective and explicate feminist theory at critical junctures of their research.

- intend that their research help women by raising consciousness and changing their situations in positive directions.

- choose pre-existing, combine, and/or create new qualitative or quantitative methods that promise to answer their research questions in the most effective and credible manner.

- critique problems associated not only with non-feminist scholarship but with their own choices and uses of theories and methodologies, attempting to acknowledge and modify these to be consistent with and advance their feminist intentions.

- question epistemologies, methodologies, and methods that claim to be free of values, politics, and personal intentions.

- take responsibility for doing careful, excellent research, making the results widely available, and following up on the implications for changes in theory, law, policy, and so forth.

- are alert to, reflect on, and report personal, political, professional, procedural, privileging, affective, and other critical aspects of the research problem, process, and context.

- check, change, or avoid "voice," terminology, methodology, and presentations of research that involve slurs, stereotyping, condescension, objectification, and bias in regard to gender, race, age, ableness, "level" of expertise, sexual orientation, class, ethnicity, and other types of human differences.

- select research topics and methods that address problems in their own and other women's personal experiences within the immediately at-hand, everyday environment.

- attend to and value interpersonal relationships with collaborators, research "subjects," authors of the research literature, readers, and students.

- strive to recognize and respect diversity, attempting to "converse with" rather than "speak for" others, including other women and other feminists.

- attend to previously silenced, invisible, trivialized, marginalized persons and issues.

In spite of disclaimers to the contrary, there is always a temptation to regard a list of how something has been done as a set of rules for how it should be done. No one would argue that feminists are immune to the temptations of methodological "correctness" when it comes to criticizing the research of other feminists who prefer to use different methodologies. Martin (1994) reviewed the major criticisms feminists have leveled against one another in this regard, listing among them accusations of essentialism, ahistoricism, and over-generalization. She points out that these postmodern criticisms have merit because: (a) essentialist definitions of "women" marginalize, abnormalize, or silence women who do not fit the definition; (b) ahistoric accounts of women's oppression ignore temporal context, suggesting women's oppression is fixed, uniform, and "natural," and ignoring the degree to which notions of gender, gender difference, and even oppression are socially constructed; and (c) false generalizations mask diversity by taking an unrepresentative sample. In the latter case, for example, diversity is masked by using experiences of Western, white, heterosexual, able, young, middle-class, academic women and presenting them as holding true for the whole population of women.

Acknowledging the value of self critique, Martin (1994) nevertheless warns feminists against disempowering ourselves by overcorrecting for the methodological "sins" of essentialism, ahistoricism, and overgeneralization. From her point of view, this overcorrection would involve (a) falling silent because the use of language and "naming" masks differences; (b) denying a priori the possible existence of similarities between women; and (c) privileging an historical context over other contexts of knowledge and inquiry. Beyond the potential negative effects of essentialism, ahistoricism, and overgeneralization on the one hand, and overcorrection for them on the other, Martin worried most that fearfulness of being accused by other feminists of "methodological incorrectness" or "overcorrection" could have a dampening effect on feminist research itself. She reminds us of the following:

> Where intellectual inquiry is concerned, fear often produces timidity and self-censorship. If in the world of the coeducational college classroom this too frequently translates into a woman's inability to speak up, her increased disposition toward self-doubt, and even a tendency to drop out academically, we can expect it to have analogous consequences in the realm of feminist research. (p. 650)

Like Martin (1994) and others, we envision as the ideal, a mutually supportive, non-destructive, self-correcting system of feminist research, a "collective enterprise" conducted in "a research community governed by an open welcoming spirit, one that is as inclusionary on the methodological level as on the personal" (p. 654).

Applications: Feminist Research in Art Education

Thus far we have presented a working definition of feminist research, permitting us to consider a wide spectrum of feminist scholarly inquiry for the purpose of sorting out the why, the what, and the how of this activity. Relating this working definition to the field of art includes but extends beyond feminist research findings dramatically presented to the general public by the Guerilla Girls (1995). For the concluding sections of this chapter, we have decided to narrow our focus by attending to feminist research done by art educators or responses to that research by art educators. Rather than present the "findings" of this research, we will suggest the range and scope of topics, themes, and issues addressed, augmenting this loosely categorized overview with a larger list of readings found in the Extended Reference Section at the end of this chapter. It is our hope that this method of presenting topics and titles will entice readers who have a potential interest in feminist research in art education to search out and read the original works.

Following the topical review, we will draw on our own experience and that of other feminist researchers in an attempt to "demystify" the research process from a feminist point of view. Our chapter will conclude by suggesting possibilities that might be considered and steps that might be taken in the process of doing one's own feminist research.

Some Topics That Have Been Addressed by Feminist Research in Art Education

Sometimes prior, often during, and certainly following the identification of a research "problem," feminists, like other researchers, review the related literature to determine what has been discovered, theorized, debated, or perhaps distorted or ignored. Due to the nature of art education as well as women's studies, reviews of literature by feminists in art education seem inevitably to carry us into interdisciplinary waters (Koroscik, 1994). Drawing on research literature in other fields, seeing what feminists in art history, education, psychology, and other disciplines have been doing or saying gives a connected quality or healthy dimensionality to feminist research in art education. Sometimes, however, our attention to feminist research in other disciplines threatens to replace rather than augment our understanding of feminist research within the field of art education. We have noted a slight tendency in both feminist and nonfeminist research in our field—including our own work—to cite theory and research from other fields more often than from our own field of art education. From a feminist point of view, a failure to take seriously, cite, and criticize the research literature developed by colleagues in our own field is behavior not altogether different from that of women who avoid identification with other women or are too "modest" to mention their own accomplishments. If the research traditions in these other fields are more advanced, powerful, or prestigious than our own, we can learn from them through emulation and identification to enhance the credibility of our own individual research. This does not mean we should ignore our need for mutual support and critique or that we should reinforce the trivialization of those who share our immediate concerns, unique perspectives, and special skills as women and as art educators. This is one reason we decided to call attention to the contributions feminist art educators have made and are making to a feminist knowledge base in art education. A second reason is that for a comprehensive search of the literature, this is a good place to start. Indeed, it will not take long to discover those "out of field" works of feminist scholarship that might be highly relevant to art education. We need only survey the reference lists at the end of each published piece of feminist research in art education, including this one, to discover relevant research that may not fall under the rubric of art education inquiry.

What follows is a casual, assorted list of topics treated by feminist research in art education with a few examples listed in each category. We remind the reader that, although the list is alphabetized, it is neither exhaustive nor prioritized. We present it here as a place to start rather than a place to stop. Some listed references could be put into more than one category; other categories could be added; and articles other than those listed might turn out to be better examples of a particular category (see the Extended Reference List at the end of this chapter.) Topics addressed by feminist research (or responses to feminist research) in art education include:

- *Art history, criticism, and aesthetics* (Chalmers, 1977; Congdon, 1991, 1996; Garber, 1990, 1992a, 1992b,1996; Hagaman, 1990; Hicks, 1992; Hilson, 1991; McRorie, 1996; Sandell, 1980).

- *Art museums and collections* (Blandy & Congdon, 1991; Springer, 1996).

- *Children's drawings* (Feinburg, 1977; Flannery & Watson, 1995; Grauer & Trilling, 1985).

- *Creativity* (Snyder-Ott, 1974).

- *Critiques and Reviews of Research* (Korzenik, 1990; La Pierre, 1993; Sacca, 1989).

- *Curriculum and pedagogy* (Ament, 1996; Attenborough, 1996; Calvert, 1996; Dossor, 1990; Ettinger & Hoffman, 1990; Sandell, 1991; Sandell, Collins, Sherman, 1985).

- *Discipline-Based Art Education* (Collins & Sandell, 1988; Davenport, 1990; Huber, 1987).

- *Early childhood education* (Colbert, 1996).

- *Environment* (Avery, 1995; Hicks & King, 1996).

- *Gender differences in the art classroom* (Zimmerman, 1993/1994)

- *History of art education* (Chalmers, 1995; Efland, 1985; Soucy, 1989; Smith, 1988; Stankiewicz, 1982a; Zimmerman, 1989, 1991).

- *Images, stereotypes, and censorship* (Barrett, 1994; Blandy, 1996; Congdon & Blandy 1990; Freedman, 1994; Helgadottir, 1993; Klein, 1993; Lang, 1993; Tarlow-Calder, 1993).

- *Leadership and empowerment* (Hicks, 1990; Irwin, 1993; Michael, 1977; Thurber & Zimmerman, 1996).

- *Male/female ratios, salaries, rank, status, professional behavior* (Glenn & Sherman, 1983; Lovano-Kerr, 1981; Lovano-Kerr, Semler, & Zimmerman, 1977; Rush, 1987).

- *Men in feminism* (Congdon & Blandy, 1990; jagodzinski, 1990; Marantz, 1990; Pariser & Zimmerman, 1990b; Snider, 1990)

- *Multiculturalism* (Dufrene, 1993; Finley-Stansbury, 1993; Garber & Gaudelius, 1992; Hicks, 1991; Zastrow, 1982).

- *Overviews—Books, anthologies, and bibliographies* (Collins & Sandell 1984, 1996; Loeb, 1979; Snyder-Ott, 1978; Soucy, 1991a, 1991b).

- *Personal accounts* (Collins, 1995b; McFee, 1975; Packard, 1974b)

- *Publications* (Helgadottir 1991; Sacca 1989; Turner 1990, 1996).

- *Social activism* (Wyrick, 1996).

- *Theory, critique, and opinion* (Blaikie, 1992; Collins, 1977, 1978, 1987; Daniel, 1996; Hausman, 1992; Helgadottir, 1991).

- *Women art educator's achievements & biographies* (Congdon & Zimmerman, 1993; Smith, 1990; Stankiewicz, 1983, 1985; Stankiewicz & Zimmerman, 1984, 1985; Zimmerman & Stankiewicz, 1982).

- *Women's art movement and organizations* (Packard, 1974a; Sandell 1979, 1980).

- *Women art students* (Park, 1996; Whitesel 1975a, 1975b, 1977; Zimmerman, 1991).

- *Women artists* (Anderson, 1992; LaDuke, 1992; Mullen, 1989).

The listing above covers a wide range of topics. As Pariser and Zimmerman (1990b) noted with regard to the special issues of *Studies in Art Education* devoted to women's concerns and gender issues, published in 1977 and 1990, most feminist research in art education has been in the realms of theory, history, and issues, reviewing the literature and drawing implications for practice in art education. Very little has been done by way of traditional qualitative or quantitative studies on gender differences in the art classroom. There may well be practical or ideological reasons for this as noted above, but the pattern of feminist research in general education suggests otherwise. In a survey of feminist research on gender differences having educational significance, Grossman and Grossman (1994) reviewed numerous reported differences in general education that may or may not be relevant to the art classroom. The list of observable and testable gender differences is long and detailed and might provide a good starting place for feminist research in art education that is more empirical in nature. Among those reported are gender differences in "interpersonal relationships, moral development, communication styles, learning styles, enrollment in academic and vocational courses, participation in extracurricular activities, academic achievement, and behavior problems" (pp. 31-32).

Specific gender differences that might entice art educators to design follow-up studies in the art classroom include those that have been discovered in career aspirations, motivations to avoid success, sensitivity to nonverbal cues, performance on visual spatial tasks, bias in curricular materials, teaching styles, computer literacy, as well as interactions of gender, ethnic, and socioeconomic differences. In any case, for those feminists who want to support their arguments for change based on results of empirical research, the field is wide open and precedents in education research might suggest a place to begin.

Feminist Research: Themes, Issues, and Applications in Art Education

Selecting and Developing an Appropriate Methodology

Given their political commitments, feminists often identify a problem and then select or develop a methodology that promises to shed the most light on the problem. Subscribing to the feminist belief that women should build self-confidence and view their personal lives and problems as relevant and important, feminist researchers also tend to factor in their "discipline," present skills, and interests when choosing a methodology (Reinharz, 1992, p. 243). Those of us who have completed graduate study and have maintained an interest in scholarly research, have been told that traditional approaches to research include such methods as empirical, historical, philosophical as well as qualitative field and case studies, and action research. No matter how eager we are to search for new and significant knowledge, the research traditions behind these forms of research, the terminology and methods prescriptively associated with them, and the worldviews they imply can be intimidating. For this reason, we share here our suggestions for how to demystify ourselves with regard to conducting research and drawing conclusions for the field of art education.

Demystifying Research Methodology

Research involves looking into, keeping track of, thinking about, evaluating, explaining, sharing (publishing) what one discovers (or does not discover) about what was, is, could be, or should be. The ways, method(s), or how-to's one uses to discover things about the past, present, possible, or ideal have traditionally been somewhat different from each other. The following methodological groupings are based on those suggested in *Creating a Visual Arts Research Agenda* (NAEA Commission on Research in Art Education, 1993, see p.5).

1. *To discover what was:* Try historical research, that is, look for and gather public and private documents, eye witness accounts, oral histories, and patterns of and relationship between events. Compare different "official" accounts and interpretations of the same event or series of events. Ask: The history of *what?* What has been left out? Example: Stankiewicz's (1982), "The Creative Sister: An Historical Look at Women, Art, and Higher Education."

2. *To discover what is:* Try predicting, observing, manipulating, controlling, and interacting with present situations and events. The following types of research (some are regarded as subcategories of others) associated with such efforts are: empirical, descriptive, survey, correlation, qualitative, ethnographic, case study, experimental, quasi-experimental, participant observa-

tion, and action research. Ask: What difference would it make to discover the "what" of "is"? What do I expect to find? What might I tend to ignore? Example: Lita Whitesel's (1975a), "Scale Construction for the Measurement of Women Art Student's Career Commitments."

3. *To discover what is possible:* Try explaining, predicting, theorizing, hypothesizing, and checking for coherence of your ideas and their correspondence with experience and existing knowledge or theory. This is sometimes called theoretical research or philosophical inquiry. It is often found in combination with numbers 1, 2, and 4 of these groupings. Ask: Is the purpose of this research to provide rationales for practice and policy or directions for other types of research? Does it make certain assumptions or ignore certain perspectives? Example: Enid Zimmerman's (1990), "Issues Related to Teaching Art from a Feminist Point of View."

4. *To discover what is desirable:* Try describing or analyzing the meaning or significance of a concept, event, tradition, practice, or theory in terms of its ethical, aesthetic, cultural, epistemological, ontological, political, and/or personal value(s). Ask: Who and where am I? What are my purposes? What and whom might I be ignoring or oppressing by this activity? Example: Doug Blandy and Kristin Congdon's (1990), "Pornography in the Classroom: Another Challenge for the Art Educator."

In all four categories, what we decide to look for, or are most likely to notice and therefore "discover," is influenced by a great number of things including one's life experiences, disabilities, historical situation, class, ethnic identification, age, sexual orientation, as well as what theory we subscribe to or are testing. It therefore is helpful to acknowledge these contextual filters.

Seeking and Finding Support and Challenge in Feminist Research Endeavors

Feminist research in art education has challenged sexist bias and androcentric values in the form, content, and practice of traditional art education. It has discovered and reported missing information and misinformation about women in art. It has developed models of criticism and proposals for change. Above all, it has been informed by the explicit political purpose of improving the situation and status of women in art and reevaluating feminine-identified art activities in our society. Perhaps unaware of how traditional research has served and preserved their inherited political privileges (Alcoff & Potter, 1993, p. 13), members of the academic community who subscribe to the rules and procedures of disinterested objectivity in scholarly inquiry tend to take a dim view of research conducted for overt political purposes. It is not easy for individuals interested in doing feminist research to challenge these and other established conventions and sets of values, especially when (or if) these have been internalized, subsequently undermining, disallowing, or trivializing one's personal experiences, consciousness of injustice, and political point of view. To do so has taken a great deal of collaboration and support. These many forms of support include professional networking, letters of encouragement and critique from and for others doing feminist research, proposing panel discussions, sharing bibliographies, responding to calls for papers, encouraging the publication of special issues of journals, joining the NAEA Women's Caucus and participating in its programs, and engaging in collaborative research including cross-disciplinary research, co-authoring, research and research presentations with students, and co-inquiry between university educators and classroom teachers.

Feminist researchers in art education are encouraged by the NAEA Commission on Research in Art Education's (1993) recognition of the value of feminist inquiry on gender issues in a report suggesting that these and other issues in art education are in need of study and in line for funding (pp. 2, 3). Beyond this level of encouragement, those engaged in feminist research, "those of us who want our intellectual engagement to matter in the struggle toward social justice" (Lather, 1991, p. 164) can find challenge, inspiration, and direction in Martin's (1994) vision of an effective feminist research community as a "collective enterprise" powered by

> people who hold up high standards for themselves and each other but do not demand perfection....scholars from different backgrounds and with quite different kinds of training who are expert enough to see the mistaken assumptions and the gaps in other women's research, generous enough to give constructive criticism and to recognize the positive contributions contained in the work of others, and wise enough to know that their way of doing research is not the only right way....(p. 654)

Extended Reference List

[This reference section contains readings cited in the text of the chapter and other readings related to feminist research done by art educators or responses to that research by art educators.]

Acuff, B., & Packard, S. (1974). Women's views. *Art Education, 27* (9), 24-25.
Alcoff, L. (1988). Cultural feminism versus post-structuralism: The identity crisis in feminist theory. *Signs, 13*(3), 405-436.
Alcoff, L., & Potter, E. (1993). Introduction: When feminisms intersect epistemology. In L. Alcoff & E. Potter (Eds.), *Feminist epistemologies* (pp. 1-14). New York: Routledge.
Ament, E. (1996). Strategies for teaching art based on feminist aesthetics. In G. Collins & R. Sandell (Eds.), *Gender issues in art education* (pp. 104-115). Reston, VA: National Art Education Association.
Anderson, H. (1992). Making women artists visible. *Art Education, 45* (2), 14 22.
Attenborough, D. (1996). Feminist interventions in teaching art history. In G. Collins & R. Sandell (Eds.), *Gender issues in art education* (pp. 116-125). Reston, VA: National Art Education Association.
Avery, H. H. (1995). The integration of feminist discourse in built environment education. *Canadian Review of Art Education, 21*(2), 85-90.
Barrett, T. (1994). Culture wars. *Studies in Art Education, 36*(1), 3-7.
Bastian, L. (1975). Women as artists and teachers. *Art Education, 28*(7), 12-15.
Biklen, S. K., & Shakeshaft, C. (1985). The new scholarship on women. In S. Klein (Ed.), *Handbook for achieving sex equity through education* (pp. 44-52). Baltimore: John Hopkins University Press.
Blaikie, F. (1992). Thoughts concerning a feminist emphasis in art education. *Art Education, 45*(2), 49-52.
Blaikie, F. (1993). Visibility and invisibility in art and craft. *The Journal of Social Theory in Art Education, 13 ,* 131-142.
Blandy, D. (1996). Gender reconstruction disability images and art education. In G. Collins and R. Sandell (Eds.), *Gender issues in art education* (pp. 70-77). Reston, VA: National Art Education Association.
Blandy, D., & Congdon, K. G. (1990). Pornography in the classroom: Another challenge for the art educator. *Studies in Art Education , 32*(1), 6-16.
Blandy, D., & Congdon, K. G. (1991). Art and culture collections in art education: A critical analysis. *Journal of Multicultural and Cross-Cultural Research in Art Education, 9,* 27-41.
Calvert, A. E. (1996). An art curriculum model for gender equity. In G. Collins & R. Sandell (Eds.), *Gender issues in art education* (pp. 154-164). Reston, VA: National Art Education Association.
Chalmers, F. G. (1977). Women as art viewers: Sex differences and aesthetic preferences. *Studies in Art Education, 18*(2), 49-53.
Chalmers, F. G. (1995). Fanny McIan and London's Female School of Design, 1842-57. *Woman's Art Journal, 16*(2).

Colbert, C. (1996). Issues of gender in the visual arts education of young children. In G. Collins & R. Sandell (Eds.), *Gender issues in art education* (pp. 60-69). Reston, VA: National Art Education Association.

Collins, G. (1977). Considering an androgynous model for art education. *Studies in Art Education, 18*(2), 54-62.

Collins, G. (1978). Reflections on the head of Medusa. *Studies in Art Education, 19*(2), 10-18.

Collins, G. (1979). Women and art: The problem of status. *Studies in Art Education, 21*(1), 57-64.

Collins, G. (1981). Feminist approaches to art education. *The Journal of Aesthetic Education, 15* (2), 83-94.

Collins, G. (1987). Masculine bias and the relationship between art and democracy. In D. Blandy and K. Congdon (Eds.), *Art in a democracy* (pp. 26-43). New York: Teachers College Press.

Collins, G. (1990). The not so mysterious ways of mystification. *The Journal of Social Theory in Art Education, 10,* 130-132.

Collins, G. (1993, April). *Stone soup: A paper in progress (On making feminist theory in art education).* Unpublished manuscript of a paper presented to the Graduate Seminar, The Program of Art Education, Pennsylvania State University.

Collins, G. (1995a). Art Education as a negative example of gender enriching the curriculum. In J. Gaskell & J. Willinsky (Eds.), *Gender in/forms curriculum* (pp. 43-58). New York: Teachers College Press.

Collins, G. (1995b) Explanations owed my sister. *Studies in Art Education, 36* (2), 69-83.

Collins, G., & Sandell, R. (1984). *Women, art, and education.* Reston, VA: National Art Education Association.

Collins, G., & Sandell, R. (1987). Women's achievements in art: An issues approach for the classroom, *Art Education, 40* (3), 12- 21.

Collins, G., & Sandell, R. (1988). Informing the promise of DBAE: Remember the women, children, and other folk. *Journal of Multicultural and Cross-Cultural Research in Art Education, 6* (1), 55-63.

Collins, G., & Sandell, R., (Eds.). (1996). *Gender issues in art education.* Reston, VA: National Art Education Association.

Congdon, K. (1991). Feminist approaches to art criticism. In D. Blandy & K. G. Congdon (Eds.), *Pluralistic approaches to art criticism,* (pp. 15-23). Bowling Green, OH: Popular Press.

Congdon, K. (1996). Art history, traditional art, and artistic practices. In G. Collins & R. Sandell (Eds.), *Gender issues in art education* (pp. 10-19). Reston, VA: National Art Education Association.

Congdon, K. G., & Blandy, D. (1990). Introduction(s) to men in feminism. *The Journal of Social Theory in Art Education, 10,* 117-120.

Congdon, K., & Zimmerman, E. (1993). *Women art educators III.* Bloomington, IN: Mary Rouse Memorial Fund at Indiana University and the Women's Caucus of the National Art Education Association.

Daly, M. (1978). *Gyn/Ecology: The metaethics of radical feminism.* Boston: Beacon Press.

Daniel, V. A. H. (1996). Womanist influences on curricular ecology. In G. Collins & R. Sandell (Eds.), *Gender issues in art education* (pp. 78-89). Reston, VA: National Art Education Association.

Davenport, M. G. (1990). Discipline-based art education: Issues from the feminist perspective. *Art Papers, 14* (5), 7-11.

Davis, H. E. (1993). The temptations and limitations of a feminist deaesthetic. *The Journal of Aesthetic Education, 27* (2), 99-105.

Dill, B. T. (1994). Race, class, and gender: Prospects for an all- inclusive sisterhood. In L. Stone (Ed.), *The education feminism reader* (pp. 42-56). New York: Routledge.

Dobbs, S. (1975). Women in the arts: An optimistic forecast. *Art Education, 28* (7), 24-26.

Donovan, J. (1985). *Feminist theory: The intellectual traditions of American feminism.* New York: Frederick Ungar.

Dossor, D. (1990). Gender issues in tertiary art education. *Journal of Art and Design Education, 9* (2), 163-169.

Dufrene, P. (1993). Reaching in and taking out: American women artists in a different feminism. In K. Congdon and E. Zimmerman (Eds.), *Women art educators III* (pp. 127-138). Bloomington, IN: Mary Rouse Memorial Fund at Indiana University and the Women's Caucus of the National Art Education Association.

Efland, A. (1985). Art and education for women in 19th century Boston. *Studies in Art Education, 26* (3), 133-140.

Eichler, M. (1988). *Nonsexist research methods: A practical guide.* Boston: Allen & Unwin.

Ettinger, L. F., & Hoffman, E. (1990). Quilt making in art education: Toward a participatory curriculum metaphor. *Art Education, 43* (4), 41-47.

Feinburg, S. G. (1977). Conceptual content and spatial characteristics in boys' and girls' drawings of fighting and helping. *Studies in Art Education, 18* (2), 63-72.

Feminism and Censorship in Art Education: Four Perspectives (1993). *The Journal of Social Theory in Art Education, 13,* 113-116.

Finley-Stansbury, K. (1992-1993). Art work and social work: Transition in the teens, *Arts and Learning SIG Proceedings Journal, 10* (1), 69-80.

Finley-Stansbury, K. (1993). Airing wounds and healing arts: Feminism and multicultural education. In K. Congdon & E. Zimmerman (Eds.), *Women art educators III* (pp. 115-126). Bloomington, IN: Mary Rouse Memorial Fund at Indiana University and the Women's Caucus of the National Art Education Association.

Flannery, K. A., & Watson, M. W.(1995). Sex differences and gender- role differences in children's drawings. *Studies in Art Education, 36* (2), 114-122.

Fonow, M. M., & Cook, J. A. (1991). Back to the future: A look at the second wave of feminist epistemology and methodology. In M. M. Fonow & J. A. Cook (Eds.), *Beyond methodology: Feminist scholarship as lived research* (1-15). Bloomington, IN: Indiana University Press.

Freedman, K. (1994). Interpreting gender and visual culture in art classrooms. *Studies in Art Education, 35* (3), 157-170.

Garber, E. (1990). Implications of feminist art criticism for art education. *Studies in Art Education, 32* (1), 17-26.

Garber, E. (1992a) Art critics on Frida Kahlo: A comparison of feminist and non-feminist voices. *Art Education, 45* (2), 42-48.

Garber, E. (1992b). Feminism, aesthetics, and art education. *Studies in Art Education, 33* (4), 210-125.

Garber, E. (1992-1993). The women's movement in art education, 1880-1930: Response to symposium papers. *Arts and Learning SIG Proceedings Journal, 10* (1), 81-87.

Garber, E. (1996). Art criticism from a feminist point of view: An approach for teachers. In G. Collins & R. Sandell (Eds.), *Gender issues in art education* (pp. 20-29). Reston, VA: National Art Education Association.

Garber, E., & Gaudelius, Y. (1992). Object into subject: Feminism, art, education, and the construction of the self. *Canadian Review of Art Education, 19* (1),12-33.

Gergen, M. (Ed.) (1988). *Feminist thought and the structure of knowledge.* New York: New York University Press.

Glenn, D. D., & Sherman, A. (1983). The status of women art education faculty in higher education. *Studies in Art Education, 24* (3), 184-186.

Grauer, K., & Trilling, D. (1985). Sex bound distinctions in conceptual content and spatial characteristics in adolescents' and children's drawings. *Canadian Review of Art Education, 12,* 59-67.

Grossman, H., & Grossman, S. H. (1994). *Gender issues in education.* Boston: Allyn and Bacon.

Guerilla Girls (1995). *Confessions of the Guerrilla Girls.* New York: HarperCollins.
Hagaman, S. (1990). Feminist inquiry in art history, art criticism, and aesthetics: An overview for art education. *Studies in Art Education, 32* (1), 27-35.
Hamblen, K. (1990). A modernity-postmodernity dialectic on men in feminism. *The Journal of Social Theory in Art Education, 10,* 121-124.
Hausman, J. (1992). From gender competition to creative independence—an editorial. *Art Education, 45*(20), 4-5.
Hartman, J. E., & Messer-Davidow, E. (1991). *(En)Gendering knowledge: Feminists in academe.* Knoxville, TN: The University of Tennessee Press.
Hekman, S. J. (1990). *Gender and knowledge: Elements of a postmodern feminism.* Boston: Northeastern University Press.
Helgadottir, G. (1991). Commentary: Gender issues in art education. *Studies in Art Education, 32*(4), 248-250.
Helgadottir, G. (1993) Feminism and feminisms: The prospect of censorship. *The Journal of Social Theory in Art Education, 13,* 124-130.
Hicks, L. E. (1990). A feminist analysis of empowerment and community in art education. *Studies in Art Education, 32*(1), 36-46.
Hicks, L. E. (1991). The politics of difference in feminism and multicultural art education. *Journal of Multicultural and Cross-Cultural Research in Art Education, 9,* 11-26.
Hicks, L. E. (1992). The construction of meaning: Feminist criticism. *Art Education, 45*(2), 23-32.
Hicks, L. E., & King, R. J. H. (1996). Ecofeminism, care, and the environment: Towards a greening of art education. In G. Collins & R. Sandell (Eds.), *Gender issues in art education* (pp. 90- 101). Reston, VA: National Art Education Association.
Hilson, M. (1991). Neolithic art and the art history class. *Studies in Art Education, 32*(4), 230-238.
Holland, N. J. (1990). *Is women's philosophy possible?* Savage, MD: Rowman & Littlefield.
hooks, b. (1984). *Feminist theory: From margin to center.* Boston: South End Press.
Huber, B. W. (1987). What does feminism have to offer DBAE? or so what if Little Red Riding Hood puts aside her crayons to deliver groceries for her mother? *Art Education, 40*(3), 36- 41.
Irwin, R. L. (1993). Charismatic and transformational leadership within a community of women arts educators. *Canadian Review of Art Education, 20*(2), 80-98.

jagodzinski, j. (1990). On the impossibility of men *in* feminism: Taking a hesitant step through the minefield of pheminism in art and education. *The Journal of Social Theory in Art Education, 10,* 133-137.

Jardine, A., & Smith, P. (Eds.). (1987). *Men in feminism.* New York: Methuen.

Jayaratne, T. E., & Stewart, A. J. (1991). Quantitative and qualitative methods in the social sciences: Current feminist issues and practical strategies. In M. M. Fonow & J. A. Cook (Eds.), *Beyond methodology: Feminist scholarship as lived research* (pp. 85-106). Bloomington, IN: Indiana University Press.

Klein, Sheri (1993). Breaking the mold with humor: Images of women in the visual media. *Art Education, 46* (5), 60-65.

Koroscik, J. S. (1994). Blurring the line between teaching and research: Some future challenges for arts education policymakers. *Arts Education Policy Review, 96* (1), 2-10.

Korzenik, D. (1990). Women doing historical research. *Studies in Art Education, 32* (1), 47-54.

LaDuke, B. (1992). Inji Efflatoun: Art, feminism, and politics in Egypt. *Art Education, 45* (2), 33-41.

Lang, K. (1993). Freedom of speech and censorship. *The Journal of Social Theory in Art Education, 13,* 116-124.

La Pierre, S. (1993). Issues of gender in spatial reasoning. Paper. Chicago, IL: National Art Education Association Convention. [ERIC Reproduction Service, No. ED 358 016].

Lather, P. (1991). *Getting smart: Feminist research and pedagogy with/in the postmodern.* New York: Routledge.

Lerner, G. (1986). *The creation of feminist consciousness: From the middle ages to eighteen-seventy.* New York: Oxford University Press.

Lewis, H. P. (1987). Women as artists and teachers [Editorial]. *Art Education, 40* (3), 5.

Loeb, J. (1975). Our women artist/teachers need our help: On changing language, finding cultural heritage, and building self- image. *Art Education, 28* (7), 9-11.

Loeb, J. (Ed.). (1979). *Feminist collage—educating women in the visual arts.* New York: Teachers College Press.

Lorde, A. (1981). The master's tools will never dismantle the master's house. In C. Moraga & G. Anzaldua (Eds.), *This bridge called my back* (pp. 99-101). Watertown, MA: Persephone.

Lovano-Kerr, J. (1981). A review of the historical and current contextual factors affecting the status of women art educators in administration. *Studies in Art Education, 22* (3), 49-58.

Lovano-Kerr, J., Semler, V., & Zimmerman, E. (1977). A profile of art educators in higher education: Male/female comparative data. *Studies in Art Education*, *18* (2), 21-37.

Marantz, K. (1990) 'Queen-of-the-Mountain': A game I can play. *The Journal of Social Theory in Art Education*, *10*, 128-129.

Martin, J. R. (1994). Methodological essentialism, false difference, and other dangerous traps. *Signs*, *19* (3), 630-657.

McFee, J. K. (1975). Society and identity—a personal perspective. *Art Education*, *28* (7), 5-8.

McRorie (Hagaman), S. (1996). On teaching and learning aesthetics: Gender and related issues. In G. Collins & R. Sandell (Eds.), *Gender issues in art education* (pp. 30-38). Reston, VA: National Art Education Association.

Michael, J. A. (1977). Women/men in leadership roles in art education. *Studies in Art Education*, *18* (2), 7-20.

Mills, C. (1994). Multiculturalism and cultural authenticity. *Report from the Institute for Philosophy and Public Policy* (pp. 1-5). College Park, MD: School of Public Affairs, University of Maryland.

Morbey, M. L. (1992-1993). *Arts and Learning SIG Proceedings Journal*, *10* (1), 88-100.

Mullen, C. A. (1989). The artistic world of seven housewives. *Journal of Multicultural and Cross-Cultural Research in Art Education*, *7* (1), 56-68.

NAEA Commission on Research in Art Education (1993). *Creating a visual arts research agenda toward the 21st century*. Reston, VA: National Art Education Association.

Nicholson, L. J. (Ed.). (1990). *Feminism/postmodernism*. New York: Routledge.

Nye, A. (1988). *Feminist theory and the philosophies of man*. New York: Croom Helm.

O'Barr, J. F. (1988). Editorial. *Signs*, *13* (3), 399-402.

Packard, S. (1974a). Finally! A women's caucus in art education. *The Feminist Art Journal*, *3* (3), 15.

Packard, S. (1974b). A personal statement on discrimination. *Art Education*, *27* (9), 25.

Packard, S. (1977). An analysis of current statistics and trends as they influence the status and future for women in the art academe. *Studies in Art Education*, *18* (2), 38-48.

Packard, S., & Zimmerman, E. (Eds.). (1977). *Sex differences as they relate to art and art education [Special issue]*. *Studies in Art Education*, *18* (2).

Pariser, D., & Zimmerman, E. (Eds.) (1990a). *Gender issues in art education.* [Special issue] *Studies in Art Education, 32* (1).
Pariser, D., & Zimmerman, E. (1990b). Gender issues in art education [Editorial]. *Studies in Art Education, 32* (1), 3-5.
Park, C. S. (1996). Learning from what women learn in the studio class. In G. Collins & R. Sandell (Eds.), *Gender issues in art education* (pp. 2-9). Reston, VA: National Art Education Association.
Reeves, J. B., & Boyette, N. (1983). What does children's art work tell us about gender? *Qualitative Sociology, 6* (4), 322-333.
Reinharz, S. (1992). *Feminist methods in social research.* New York: Oxford University Press.
Rush, J. C. (1987, May). Male and female: Patterns of professional behavior in the university. *Art Education, 40* (3), 22-24, 33- 35.
Sacca, E. J. (1989). Commentary: Invisible women: Questioning recognition and status in art education. *Studies in Art Education, 30* (2), 122-127.
Sacca, E. J. (1996). Women's full participation in art teaching and research: A proposal. In G. Collins & R. Sandell (Eds.), *Gender issues in art education* (pp. 52-59). Reston, VA: National Art Education Association.
Salkind, L. (1985). Maud Ellsworth: Art educator and master teacher. In M. A. Stankiewicz, & E. Zimmerman (Ed.), *Women art educators II* (pp. 114-130). Bloomington, IN: Mary Rouse Memorial Fund at Indiana University and the Women's Caucus of the National Art Education Association.
Sandell, R. (1979). Feminist art education: An analysis of the women's art movement as an education force. *Studies in Art Education, 20* (2), 18-28.
Sandell, R. (1980). Female aesthetics: The women's art movement and its aesthetic split. *The Journal of Aesthetic Education, 14* (4), 106-111.
Sandell, R. (1991). The liberating relevance of feminist pedagogy. *Studies in Art Education , 32* (3), 178-187.
Sandell, R., Collins, G., & Sherman, A. (1985). Sex-equity in visual arts education. In S. Klein (Ed.), *Handbook for achieving sex equity through education* (pp. 298-318). Baltimore: John Hopkins University Press.
Saunders, R. J. (1987, May). 'American Gothic' and the division of labor. *Art Education, 40* (3), 6-11.
Sherman, A. (1984). Sex differences and research relevant to art education. In G. Collins & R. Sandell (Eds.), *Women, Art, and Education* (pp. 143-161). Reston, VA: National Art Education Association.
Shotter, J., & Logan, J. (1988). The pervasiveness of patriarchy: On finding a different voice. In M. M. Gergen (Ed.), *Feminist thought and the structure of knowledge* (pp. 69-86). New York: New York University Press.

Smith, P. (1988) The role of gender in the history of art education: Questioning some explanations. *Studies in Art Education, 29* (4), 232-240.

Smith, P. (1990) An art educator for all seasons: The many roles of Euginia Eckford Rhoads. *Studies in Art Education, 31* (3), 174- 183.

Smith, R. (Ed.). (1994). *Journal of Aesthetic Education 28* (4). [Series of articles on the display of Goya's *Maja Desnuda* in a university classroom against a professor's wishes.]

Snider, A. B. (1990). Feminism as metaphor. *The Journal of Social Theory in Art Education, 10*,125-127.

Snyder-Orr, J. (1974). The female experience and artistic creativity. *Art Education, 27* (6), 15-18.

Snyder-Ott, J. (1978). *Women and creativity*. Milbrae, CA: Les Femmes Publishing.

Soucy, D. (1989). More than a polite pursuit: Art college education for women in Nova Scotia. *Art Education, 42 (*2), 23-24, 37-40.

Soucy, D. (1991a, June). *Feminist theory: An annotated bibliography of book and articles*. Unpublished bibliography.

Soucy, D. (1991b, June). *Women & art: An annotated bibliography of books and articles*. Unpublished bibliography.

Soucy, D. (1992-1993). Art education and suffrage: Campaigns of similar priority for Nova Scotia's clubwomen. *Arts and Learning SIG Proceedings Journal, 10* (1), 58-87.

Springer, J. (1996). Deconstructing the art museum: Gender, power, and educational reform. In G. Collins & R. Sandell (Eds.), *Gender issues in art education* (pp. 40-51). Reston, VA: National Art Education Association.

Stankiewicz, M. A. (1982a). 'The creative sister': An historical look at women, the arts, and higher education. *Studies in Art Education, 24* (1), 48-56.

Stankiewicz, M. A. (1982b). Woman, artist, art educator: Professional image among women art educators. In E. Zimmerman & M. A. Stankiewicz (Eds.,) *Women art educators* (pp. 30-48). Bloomington, IN: Mary Rouse Memorial Fund at Indiana University and the Women's Caucus of the National Art Education Association.

Stankiewicz, M. A. (1983) Rilla Jackman, pioneer at Syracuse. *Art Education, 36* (1), 13-15.

Stankiewicz, M. A. (1992-1993). Women's clubs, art, and society. *Arts and Learning SIG Proceedings Journal, 10* (1), 48-57.

Stankiewicz, M. A. (1985). Mary Dana Hicks Prang: A pioneer in American art education. In M. A. Stankiewicz & E. Zimmerman (Eds.), *Women art educators II* (pp. 22-38). Bloomington, IN: Mary Rouse Memorial

Fund at Indiana University and the Women's Caucus of the National Art Education Association.

Stankiewicz, M. A., & Zimmerman, E. (1984). Women's achievements in art education. In G. Collins & R. Sandell, *Women, art, and education* (pp. 112-140). Reston, VA: National Art Education Association.

Stankiewicz, M. A. & Zimmerman, E. (Eds.). (1985). *Women art educators II*. Bloomington, IN: Mary Rouse Memorial Fund at Indiana University and the Women's Caucus of the National Art Education Association.

Stanley, L. (1991). Feminist auto/biography and feminist epistemology. In J. Aaron & S. Walby (Eds.), *Out of the margins: Women's studies in the nineties* (pp. 204-219). New York: Falmer Press.

Stanley, L., & Wise, S. (1983). 'Back to the personal' or: Our attempt to construct 'feminist research.' In G. Bowles & R. D. Klein (Eds.), *Theories of women's studies* (pp. 192-209). Boston: Routledge & Kegan Paul.

Stanley, L., & Wise, S. (1990). Method, methodology and epistemology in feminist research processes. In L. Stanley (Ed.), *Feminist praxis: Research, theory and epistemology in feminist sociology* (pp. 20-60). New York: Routledge.

Stanley, L., & Wise, S. (1991). Feminist research, feminist consciousness, and experiences of sexism. In M. M. Fonow & J. A. Cook (Eds.), *Beyond methodology: Feminist scholarship as lived research* (pp. 265-283). Bloomington, IN: Indiana University Press.

Tarlow-Calder, P. (1993). Censored by omission: Imagery that is excluded from the art education classroom. *The Journal of Social Theory in Art Education, 13*, 142-156

Thurber, F., & Zimmerman, E. (1996). Empower not in power: Gender and leadership roles in art teacher education. In G. Collins & R. Sandell (Eds.), *Gender issues in art education* (pp. 144-153). Reston, VA: National Art Education Association.

Turner, R. M. (1990). Gender-related considerations for developing the text of art instructional materials. *Studies in Art Education, 32* (1), 55-66.

Turner, R. M. (1991a). *Georgia O'Keeffe: Portraits of women artists for children*. Boston: Little, Brown and Company.

Turner, R. M. (1991b). *Rosa Bonheur: Portraits of women artists for children*. Boston: Little, Brown and Company.

Turner, R. M. (1992). *Mary Cassatt: Portraits of women artists for children*. Boston: Little, Brown and Company.

Turner, R. M. (1996). The development and use of instructional resources for gender balance. In G. Collins & R. Sandell (Eds.), *Gender issues in art education* (pp. 134-143). Reston, VA:National Art Education Association.

Whitesel, L. S. (1975a). Scale construction for the measurement of women art students' career commitments. *Studies in Art Education, 17* (1), 47-53.

Whitesel, L. S. (1975b). Women as art students, teachers and artists. *Art Education, 28* (3), 21-26.

Whitesel, L. S. (1977). Attitudes of women art students. *Art Education, 30* (1), 25-27.

Wolff, J. (1990). *Feminine sentences: Essays on women and culture.* Berkeley: University of California Press.

Wyrick, M. (1996). Teaching feminist art and social activism. In G. Collins & R. Sandell (Eds.), *Gender issues in art education* (pp. 126-133). Reston, VA: National Art Education Association.

Zastrow, L. M. (1982). American Indian women as art educators. In E. Zimmerman & M. A. Stankiewicz (Eds.), *Women art educators (*pp. 88-95). Bloomington, IN: Mary Rouse Memorial Fund at Indiana University and the Women's Caucus of the National Art Education Association.

Zimmerman, E. (1985). To test all things: The life and work of Leta Stetter Hollingworth. In M. A. Stankiewicz & E. Zimmerman (Eds.), *Women art educators II* (pp. 64-81). Bloomington, IN:Mary Rouse Memorial Fund at Indiana University and the Women's Caucus of the National Art Education Association.

Zimmerman, E. (1989). The mirror of Marie Bashkirtseff: Reflections about the education of women art students in the nineteenth century. *Studies in Art Education, 30* (3),164-175.

Zimmerman, E. (1990). Issues related to teaching art from a feminist point of view. *Visual Arts Research, 16* (2), 1-8.

Zimmerman, E. (1991). Art education for women in England from 1890-1910 as reflected in the Victorian periodical press and current feminist theories of art education. *Studies in Art Education, 32* (2), 105-116.

Zimmerman, E. (1993/1994). "A lot of girls don't realize their talents": Factors influencing the art education of artistically talented girls. *The Journal of Secondary Gifted Education, 6*(2), 103-112.

Zimmerman, E., & Stankiewicz, M. A. (Eds.). (1982). *Women art educators.* Bloomington, IN: Mary Rouse Memorial Fund at Indiana University and the Women's Caucus of the National Art Education Association.

Zimmerman, E. & Stankiewicz, M. A. (1985). Introduction. In M. A. Stankiewicz & E. Zimmerman (Eds.), *Women art educators II* (pp. 1-8). Bloomington, IN: Mary Rouse Memorial Fund at Indiana University and the Women's Caucus of the National Art Education Association.

ACTION RESEARCH

Part 1

Reprinted from *Studies in Art Education, 34*(2), 114-126.

"Teachers-as-Researchers" or Action Research: What Is It, and What Good Is It for Art Education?

Wanda T. May
Michigan State University

Conceptions of "teacher-as-researcher" or action research are examined in epistemological, professional, sociopolitical, and historical contexts. Using examples, the author presents six assumptions underlying action research: (a) teachers theorize and develop theories-in-practice, (b) action research involves more than technical problem solving, (c) a practitioner of any professional field and at any level can engage in action research, (d) research methods matter and are usually interpretive or qualitative, (e) action research can be collaborative, and (f) such inquiry can purposefully address social inequities and issues of power. Questions are raised that action research proponents themselves have not addressed to any great extent but which should be discussed by art educators who are interested in action research.

Learning to teach is a lifelong endeavor. Were we to know all there is to know about art, teaching, students, and ourselves upon initial certification, the remainder of our life's work would be incredibly predictable, unresponsive, and boring. Fortunately, neither life nor any profession is like this, and learning things that matter to us is never predictable or boring. Thus, I am operating on the

assumption that most of us are not "burned out" or cynical about teaching and that teaching art matters to us a great deal.

Also, I am assuming that our collective work in art education is guided by a strong commitment to enhancing teaching and learning in art, whether or not we would identify ourselves as "teacher educators." Through our individual perspectives, diverse professional activities, and shared understandings, we educate ourselves and others about what it means to experience art. In this sense, we are all art teachers and teacher educators, no matter our perceived role or job title.

Learning to teach well requires being conscientious students of our own practice (Dewey, 1904). It requires an orientation of thoughtfulness and authenticity toward the subjects we teach, ourselves, our students, and an area of human experience and expression such as the arts which we believe is significantly worth our attention, time, and experiencing. Enhancing our practice is informed by much more than experience narrowly described as on-the-job, trial-and-error, sink-or-swim, problem solving, hard knocks, or personally trying to incorporate content or formulaic teaching strategies externally recommended for all. These are features of practice that can describe any occupation, particularly those jobs where the primary subjects of that work are not persons, but objects and products.

What Is Action Research?

In short, action research is the study and enhancement of one's own practice. The view that teachers can and should be "researchers" or critical inquirers of their own practice enjoys a long tradition, in theory, at least, e.g., Dewey, 1904. However, only in the last decade has this view of teaching and research been rather visibly promoted and articulated in practice in the United States.[1] I qualify this by saying, action research has been explored in only a few teacher education programs, single university courses, or funded research projects. Even less attention has been given to practice-centered inquiry in public school settings and staff development programs.

Terms used somewhat interchangeably for this orientation to inquiry besides action research are reflective teaching, teacher-as-researcher, teaching as inquiry, and critical praxis. No matter the different labels and orientations to this form of research, there are some common underlying assumptions. These assumptions reflect particular epistemological, professional, and sociopolitical interests which

---

[1] For an overview of action research and sample case studies in edited volumes, see Boud, Keogh and Walker (1985); Clift, Houston, and Pugach (1990); Goswami and Stillman (19X7); Hustler, Cassidy, and Cuff (1986); Oberg and McCutcheon (1990); Schon (1991); and Sleeter (1991).

are not isolated categories with distinct boundaries. They are more like figure-ground. For the sake of clarity, however, I present these overlapping interests separately.

A Framework of Interests Represented in All Research

By epistemological interests, I mean one's view of knowledge and how it is constituted or acquired. This refers not only to one's view of the nature of knowledge in general but of art knowledge in particular. Epistemological interests relate to how one might be concerned about such things as reliability, validity, objectivity, or what counts as evidence or truth claims. It suggests one's preferences for how knowledge is best communicated, e.g., discursively and/or nondiscursively, as in argumentative, narrative, poetic, or visual forms. It also refers to how one then perceives theory, practice, and research and the relationships and purposes of these human activities. For example, a popular assumption not held by proponents of action research is that researchers theorize and teachers teach. This assumption perpetuates an artificial dichotomy between theory and practice. Finally, how one views knowledge and the nature of humans obviously will influence what one believes constitutes the nature of teaching and learning and what forms these should take in practice.

By professional interests, I mean one's view of teachers (novice or experienced), teacher educators, and university researchers and, therefore, one's perceptions of the expertise, roles, work, and relationships of such persons in theory, practice, and research. For example, although suggested by few action research proponents, many people believe that university professionals generate new knowledge and research which should then be adopted and applied by teachers in their classrooms. Or, many teachers return for graduate study stating that they "want to catch up on the latest ideas and methods." Professional interests also include one's view of art and/or education as fields with codified interests, histories, expertise, and practices distinct from other professions. For example, one could argue that those who teach art should be certified art teachers because of their specialized interests, preparation, and expertise.

By sociopolitical interests, I refer not only to those dimensions mentioned above but to the larger institutional and social contexts in which research and its potential use and misuse are embedded, i.e., public schools, universities, reward structures for inquiry, professional publishing and mass media, government agencies, policy, or society at large. For example, given that American society is established on democratic principles, we must be concerned with the ethical dimensions of inquiry, its pedagogical good or worth, the conduct of inquiry and protection of human rights, who gets to conceptualize or participate in inquiry, who has a voice in the findings and can agree or disagree, and how findings of research are used, not used, or misused in social settings.

What Do Most Proponents of Action Research Believe?
Given the above interrelated interests in inquiry writ large, there are some common assumptions underlying action research or "teacher-as-researcher."

#1: Teachers Theorize
Teachers, like many other professionals (Schon, 1983), develop personal theories-in-practice, and these theories are constructed in action and constituted reflexively in their everyday practice. Teachers' theories may be tacit (Polyani, 1967) or difficult to articulate to themselves and others. These theories rest on practical arguments which differ from the kinds of elaborate arguments crafted by philosophers and theoreticians, whose arguments need not rest on empirical evidence (Buchmann, 1988; Schwab, 1969; Walker, 1990). Practical arguments are grounded in action, and, thus, judgments made in action are more dynamic and tentative than decision trees, flow charts, or prescribed steps.

Next, most proponents of action research acknowledge that teachers' personal theories-in-practice are also grounded in their histories or biographies, and not merely in their experience as teachers (Connelly & Clandinin, 1988; Pinar, 1988; van Manen, 1990b). Finally, theory and practice (or practice and research) are not viewed as separate entities or dichotomies in action research. They are two sides of the same thing, which is always in reflexive interplay, revision, and formation (van Manen, 1990a, 1990b).

#2: Action Research is Not Always Aimed at Problem Solving
Teachers can and often do develop a deeper understanding of their theories-in-action and improve their practice by engaging in action research. This may happen because action research is framed by the teachers' own questions of interest, and inquiry usually has a strong reflective component and methods to document and enhance teachers' search for meaning. However, teachers may or may not aim to solve specific problems or "improve" practice, even though such may happen. What one wishes to better understand may not be "improvable" or in need of improving.

Although it can be argued that technical interests are of practical concern to many teachers and such "problems" are legitimate to pursue at times, focusing only on such narrow problems can separate means from ends and increase attention to instrumental problems of practice rather than to meanings. For example, it may be quite misleading to view something like "classroom rules") or discipline as distinct from curricular goals, subject matter, or methods (Boostrom, 1991).

ACTION RESEARCH—Part 1: "Teachers-as-Researchers"

In one case study, Rachel first framed a "problem" in her art practice as a discipline problem, then decided a viable solution would be to post new rules and student job assignments (May, 1990). As chaos, student fighting, and disruption continued, it turned out that discipline wasn't the real problem, nor was posting new job assignments a solution. Rachel pursued several courses of action to solve this "discipline" problem by reframing the problem and her premises in a variety of ways, e.g., blaming the students, their classroom teacher, weekly school scheduling, short art periods.

Several weeks later and through many conversations, Rachel clarified her theory or image of art as "getting ideas." To her, this was what art was all about, and this was the challenge that all artists face. She then recognized what the real problem was. Essentially, Rachel could not answer two significant questions of her own practice: (a) "What art ideas (knowledge or experiences) are most worthwhile teaching and learning in this art class, and why?" (b) "What, then, is the best way to foster these ideas?"

Rachel realized that she wanted to honor students' "getting their own ideas," as one should honor an artist's need and capacity to do likewise. She was afraid of stifling students' creativity or promoting copying if she demonstrated techniques or showed examples of artwork created by her or other students. Although she engaged students in viewing prints and discussed these in terms of the elements of design, these presentations often were disconnected from the tasks at hand. Rachel's respect for students interpreted more so as a fear of stifling students' ideas or as an absence of her own ideas—also influenced her not having media and materials organized well in advance to make efficient use of limited class time. Frustrated because they didn't have a clear idea about what they might consider or do and because they then had to wait inordinately long for materials, Rachel's fifth graders created their own ideas and activities, or misbehaved. Despite her good intentions, Rachel wasn't giving students enough direction to help them create their art ideas and to act upon these in responsible, intelligent ways.

In clarifying one of the premises of her theory-in-action ("art is the stimulation and generation of ideas"), Rachel soon realized that she was unwittingly perpetuating the same frustration in her students that she had felt as a student teacher a few years previously and that she continued to feel as an artist. She said that as a student teacher, she needed "stimulation," to see concrete examples of art practice and how one crafts lessons but that she received little guidance and felt lost. Figuring out what to teach and how to teach it should be "her idea," she was told by her university teachers. In addition to "how-to" questions, "why" questions weren't attended to very well either.

In sum, action research need not always pursue narrowly defined, instrumental ends, e.g., improving time-on-task, classroom discipline, or documenting students' knowledge gains with pretest and posttest scores. Teachers may be more apt to uncover significant connections between their students' learning and their own experiences as learners in biographical and social contexts. In the case of Rachel, it helped her to have a colleague in the classroom to converse with informally, to share observations and "what-ifs," and to help her test out her emerging hypotheses and solutions in a variety of ways.

Finally, the topic and purposes of action research are defined by the teacher or action researcher, not by an outside expert or researcher. For example, in Rachel's case, I never said, "I believe you have a discipline problem, and you might try thus and so to solve it." Action research neither reveres nor promotes teachers' passive consumption and application of others' proposals, research findings, or methodological canons, although critical knowledge of such can inform teachers' questions, premises, and interpretations of their own professional stance and work.

#3: You Don't Have to Be an Art Teacher to Engage in Action Research

No matter the particular field or perceived level of expertise, action research can be conducted by any practitioner interested in his or her own practice. Artists, nurses, lawyers, doctors, administrators, teachers of all sorts of subjects, teacher educators, and researchers have engaged in action research. Although it is rare, university professors are beginning to examine their own teaching through action research (Ellsworth, 1989; Lampert, 1985; Lather, 1986, 1988; May, 1991).

Experienced art teachers and art teacher educators as well as preservice art teachers can engage in action research. Some undergraduate teacher education programs and their different specializations have been purposefully designed around inquiry using action research, journal writing, and ethnography (Clift, Houston, & Pugach, 1990; Schon, 1991). In general education, action research has been most widely introduced to experienced teachers enrolled in masters programs in curriculum and instruction or to participants associated with funded research projects along these lines. In the arts, action research has recently been conducted by secondary arts teachers across the nation affiliated with the National Arts Education Research Center at New York University, sponsored by the National Endowment for the Arts and the U.S. Department of Education (e.g., Fehrs-Rampolla, 1991; Manigo, 1991; Marcus, 1991; Packer & Newman, 1991). Although these studies represent examples of teachers' asking worthwhile questions in arts education, there are problems with these particular studies (to be discussed later).

#4: The Methods Matter

The genre of research methods most often used in action research is qualitative or interpretive in character, not quantitative or positivistic. There are at least two reasons for this. First, action research is always field-based, in situ, lending itself to ethnographic methods such as keeping fieldnotes or journals, participant observation, interviewing, engaging in dialogue, audiotaping, and collecting and analyzing documents and students' work. These methods provide more detailed, rich data bases than do simple tests or surveys.

Second, the primary interest of action researchers is to gain a better understanding of their beliefs/practice and how these came to be, and to enhance their practice if, when, and how they see fit. To do this, they try to attend to the nuances they often miss in the blur of routine practice, try to become more conscious of what they are thinking and feeling as they plan for and engage in practice, and pay closer attention to what students say and do in class in an effort to understand what sense students are making of their learning. Thus, journals, diaries, audiotaping or videotaping oneself, and much conversation and dialogue with students, colleagues, or other action researchers are important methodological vehicles.

#5: Action Research Can Be Collaborative

Action research need not be a solitary activity. In fact, there is an increasing interest in collaborative research whereby two or more practitioners pursue questions or problems of shared interest (Atkins, 1986; Carson, 1990). For example, two art teachers interested in better understanding what their students are thinking and learning in art might document their efforts by including portfolios, student writing, learning logs, and intermittent interviews with a small sample of students at one grade level. Meeting informally once a week in each others' homes and bringing examples of students' work and their own journals, these teachers could discuss their observations and experiences and explore what they believe their students are learning. New and revised questions are likely to emerge during the course of their study and conversations. Consider how Rachel (discussed earlier) reframed a perceived problem several times and was responsive to emergent questions and unanticipated insights.

University education programs and public schools are increasingly interested in collaborative research that diminishes hierarchical arrangements and fosters collegiality. Of particular interest may be site-based management and shared decision making, professional development, and institutional partnerships where practitioners in both university and public school settings slide back and forth across cultures and work as teachers and researchers in both settings. Collaboration based on locally shared questions and action research can produce more professionalism, thoughtful direction and planning, thick and descriptive data worthy of analysis, surprising evidence, and the need to explore and critique "new ideas" generated in a specific site or from reading professional literature (Lieberman, 1988).

If collaborative researchers have learned anything from such endeavors, it is that trust takes time, and members of a group never develop trust in synchrony. We know that collaboration is soul-searching, labor-intensive work for anyone participating, that shared understanding and significant change takes longer than expected, and that nothing is perfect (Bolin & Falk, 1987; Hall & Hord, 1987; Jackson,]988). Although these factors are sobering, such findings are better than feeling powerless and isolated in one's work setting.

Practitioners in collaborative inquiry may represent only teachers or teachers and university researchers working together. In the latter arrangement, the university member might assist a teacher in pursuing his or her own questions of interest as these emerge over time (May, 1990). For example, the researcher can help the teacher collect information he or she has expressed an interest in or demonstrate research strategies that are appropriate to the teacher's questions. The university partner might share published research syntheses or examples of other teachers' case studies on similar topics, upon request. She or he could conduct classroom observations with fieldnotes, audio or videotape lessons, periodically interview students using open-ended questions generated by the teacher, engage in numerous informal conversations with the teacher, and share all written records or transcripts for the teacher's personal reflection and analysis.

In the sort of collaboration discussed above, the university researcher's primary questions are likely to be: "What does it mean to help a teacher engage in action research?" and "What does my participation help me understand about my own theory-in-practice?" The questions would not be manipulative as in, "How can I get Mary to improve her practice or Bill to include more criticism in his art class?"

In summary, what best qualifies collaborative research as "action research" are questions of shared interest that are not coerced by an outsider and a self-reflexive, self-critical stance among all members in the project who are interested in studying their own practice. Individual assumptions, interpretations, relations, and negotiations are of as much interest to participants as the topic of the inquiry. A fine example of self-reflexive collaboration and disclosure is Miller's (1990) Creating Spaces and Finding Voices. Not only are participants' concerns, ruminations, and relationships explored with sensitivity and equity, but such work is conceived as ultimately empowering to all the participants involved, including Miller. This point leads to the next assumption about action research which not all proponents of action research share.

ACTION RESEARCH—Part 1: "Teachers-as-Researchers"

#6: Changes Toward Social Equip Are Possible and Desirable

With reference to neo-Marxist and feminist theories, several proponents of critical action research believe that through developed and enlightened understandings of those engaged in conversation, critical discourse, and inquiry that empowerment, social action, and reform are not only possible but desirable (Carr & Kemmis, 1986). Reform is aimed primarily at full, active democratic participation to change inequitable structures, policies, and practices that oppress groups in a particular context by gender, race, ethnicity, economic status or social class, and/or age.

For example, art teachers working together on their district or state art curriculum and on the development of supplemental resources make a concerted effort to include ideas and art forms from non-Western cultures, American ethnic groups, and women. This has great potential for influencing what kind of art gets taught in a larger context. Or, an art teacher, who recognizes that his or her best power base can be parents, begins working in a sustained way to educate parents about how and why art is important, demonstrates frequently what students are learning in art, and involves parents in the art program in a variety of ways. He or she hopes that, over the course of a year or so, this visibility will gradually put pressure back on the school to provide more support for the art program. Another example of critical action research is an art teacher who studies the images and subjects she or he presented to students over the previous term, noticing that she or he not only promoted more realistic representation than other legitimate art forms, styles, and subjects, but that she or he also seemed to foster stereotypical images by gender. ("The boys can draw cars, and the girls can draw butterflies.") She or he revises unit plans for the following term to emphasize diversity and possibility.

Where Did Action Research Come From and Why?

Interest in action research has received more theoretical attention and application in the United Kingdom (England, Canada, and Australia) than in the Ignited States, even though the term action research was coined by an American in 1946. Lewin's (1946) work focused on the dynamics of communication and social change in minority groups. Lewin's model for action research was a repeated cycle of "four basic moments: planning, acting, fact-finding, analysis. Because action research is an ongoing strategy, the cycle is repeated to form a spiral: reformulated plan, revised action, more fact-finding, re-analysis" (Tripp, 1990, p. 159). Conceived as such, action research should result in strategic action based on an "understanding resulting from an analysis of information gathered" (Tripp, p. 159), not as a result of habit, instinct, opinion, or mere whim. Although the language of Lewin's action research spiral is a bit disturbing in its military metaphors such as reconnaissance and strategic action, this is somewhat understandable given its historical context near the end of World War II.

Corey (1953) and Shumsky (1958) found Lewin's model of action research attractive for education and proposed ways that teachers could become researchers in their own classrooms. Taba and Noel (1957) also used a methodological sequence for teachers not much different from that of Lewin's (1946) original model: developing "action hypotheses," formulating action, and evaluating results of the action.

Although the form of action research is said to be a spiral, it is really quite linear, rationalistic, instrumental, and means-ends in its prescriptive methods and sequence. Its saving grace is its explicit inclusion of reflection, its attachment to practice, and its reflexive features. Otherwise, it would appear to be nothing more than the traditional "scientific method" used for designing experiments. Some scientists would argue, however, that their thinking and actual practice are far more like creating a painting or action research than the scientific method in its reflexivity. It's just that the documentation and published reports of their work require this arbitrary structure.

Later, in England, and in response to overly prescriptive curricula and the decentering of teachers in decision making, Stenhouse (1975) proposed that teachers become curriculum researchers and developers. His ideas informed the Ford Teaching Project during 1973-1976 wherein teachers engaged in collaborative action research in their classrooms (Elliott, 1977). Since this period and the emergence of scholarship derived from critical social theory, researchers in Australia have contributed greatly to this movement, as illustrated in the work by Carr and Kemmis (1986) and Kemmis and McTaggart (1988). Freire's (1970) earlier descriptions of emancipatory, critical pedagogy of poor, illiterate adults in Brazil and other researchers' more recent work framed by radical politics and feminist theories are promising additions.

Given the rigid, quasi-scientific tone of action research proposed in the United States in the 1950s and unrelenting tension between university and practitioner researchers in negotiating their expertise and relationships, action research seemed to disappear from the American scene for a while. It resurfaced in the 1980s and early 1990s, as demonstrated in a spate of proposals and research articles. Throughout history, action research seems to return in an ever-more invigorated form on the heels of and in reaction to top-down mandates, teacher-proof curricula, concern about teacher accountability and competency, social upheaval, public criticism of schools, and a subsequent flurry of reform proposals in education.

Today, action research is buoyed by kindred spirits in academe's colleges and schools of education and by major reform initiatives in teacher education and public schools. An interest in teaching as inquiry is revealed in researchers' growing interests over the past couple of decades in: (a) teacher thinking; (v) teachers' theories, practical arguments, metaphors, and images of practice; (c) professional development in terms of stages of teachers' concerns over their careers or during curriculum implementation efforts, novice-expert studies, collaboration, and mentoring; and (d) curriculum deliberation, redistribution of power relations in the workplace, and redefinition of teachers' roles so that more professional authority is appropriated to teachers (Wittrock, 1986).

Teaching as inquiry also is revealed by research interests in teachers' biographies and lived experience, in both personal and social contexts, which influence their pedagogical beliefs and practices. There is a visible strand of such work in the curriculum field (Butt, Raymond, & Yamagishi, 1988; Grumet, 1980; Kincheloe & Pinar, 1991). Finally, increased interest in action research is demonstrated in critiques which specifically address the socialization of teachers, structural constraints in schools and workplace conditions, and practices in university and teacher education programs that promote technocratic rationality and deskilling teachers rather than emphasizing professional inquiry and critique (Apple & Weis, 1983; Bullough, Goldstein, & Holt, 1984; May, 1989).

One major influence on the current interest in action research in teacher education is that over the past few decades the larger scholarly community has exhibited a growing tolerance for and use of interpretive forms of inquiry across diverse academic disciplines. As with quantitative research, qualitative inquiry represents a vast array of research designs and methods, from questionnaire surveys more akin to positivistic interests, to ethnography, autobiography, educational criticism or "connoisseurship" (Eisner, 1985), and critical pedagogy informed by critical and feminist theories.

Lingering Questions About Action Research

There are many questions not yet addressed which ought to be debated among art educators who are thinking about engaging in action research themselves or proposing it for others. Because of limited space, I will raise only a few that have not been addressed here nor to any great extent in the professional literature.

1. In action research, what is the role of professional literature or published "findings"? When, where, and how should these be used or useful to action researchers? What other forms of discourse might provoke or Clarify teachers questions, observations, theories-in-action, and conversations?

2. Should action research be presented or used differently with preservice teachers than with experienced teachers? If so, how, and on what grounds? If not, why not? How do we help both novice and experienced teachers

experience "the familiar" or "obvious" in more provocative and critical ways? How do we help them see subtlety and nuance in the blur of practice?

3. What is the best way to help novice action researchers learn about orientations to inquiry and multiple, but manageable, methods for pursuing their questions of interest? (An isolated research course, even with a mini-project, may not help teachers learn and practice these diverse skills with flexibility and confidence in their work settings.)

4. When and where can teachers learn to hone their skills in observation, analysis, interpretation, and critique of theoretical discourse, samples of students' work or verbal responses, observations of classroom practice, or in listening to or reading pedagogical discourse? How can we help teachers extend their depth of analysis and entertain multiple interpretations? Must teachers learn to craft and speak or write in an argumentative style? Must action research be reported or "publishable"? To whom, and for whom?

5. If engaged in action research projects, what are some meaningful, creative ways in which teachers can express, represent, and share what they have learned or are learning? Must they always write formal papers? Must they keep a diary or journal? For art educators and art teachers, are there more creative, provocative, and expressive ways to "record" and share with others what they are experiencing and learning?

6. Is all action research good or worthwhile just because the teachers involved believe they are pursuing worthwhile questions? As art teacher educators, should we ever intervene or suggest a different direction, particularly if a teacher's practice flies against our understanding of "best" practice and personal ethics or if it seriously diminishes the quality of youngsters' experiences art?

The Potential Misconduct and Promise of Action Research

Above, I have alluded to several potential problem areas in the conception, purpose, conduct, and use of action research. Three additional problems specifically concern art teacher educators and researchers: (a) the "do-as-I-say, not-as-I-do" principle, commonly practiced in university education programs; (b) questionable skills of university educators, researchers, or public school coordinators in processing the experiential learning of novice or experienced teachers; and (c) art teacher

ACTION RESEARCH—Part 1: "Teachers-as-Researchers"

educators or researchers who conceive of action research too narrowly, thus, imposing inappropriate structures, standards, and methods on teachers' thinking, projects, and practice. This can reinforce teachers' misconceptions and distrust of scholarly inquiry and perpetuate professional inequities.

With respect to the "do-as-I-say" principle, teacher educators and staff developers who do not themselves engage in thoughtful inquiry into their own practice and model such to novice or experienced practitioners are in little position to help others do likewise. It is rather arrogant to believe that we have teaching art nailed down, once and for all, and that our own pedagogy isn't quite interesting, complex, problematic, or worthy of inquiry.

With respect to the pedagogical thoughtfulness, tact (van Manen, 1991), and skill required in helping others process their experiential learning, there can be much ignorance on the part of those who promote action research. For example, it isn't pedagogically sound to require journal writing without sustained feedback or shared analysis, or to ask teachers to "be reflective" without giving them much guidance about what they should be reflective about and teaching them the many ways in which people act reflectively and responsively to their own beliefs, experiences, and practices.

Thoughtful teacher educators may be those who can help novice teachers (undergraduate students) make meaningful connections programmatically within and across courses, between university and field settings, and among multiple activities, assignments, and content areas with explicit, overarching goals. Unfortunately, the content, coursework "chunks," and vertical and horizontal articulation of teacher preparation programs have changed little over a century. Experiential connections may be more apt to occur for students if a program is conceived and presented in some deliberate, thematic, spiraling way by several committed faculty who engage in frequent dialogue about what it is they are trying to accomplish and toward what ends. Further, connections need to be made between novice and experienced teachers' lived experience or biographies and that which they encounter and learn in art teacher education or inservice programs. This requires multiple opportunities for teachers to develop their own voices along with the professional voices they encounter through journal writing, narrative, conversation, art, drama, poetry, and other forms of expression—and not just in argumentative papers where the narrative, "reflexive-I" often is disregarded (Willis & Schubert, 1991).

Next, many of us may be clumsy in helping teachers make sense of their feelings and experiences in responsive but re-constructive, educative ways. Those who propose critical reflection and action research walk a thin line. We are not trained therapists, but our commitment to teaching as inquiry requires more sensitivity, personal introspection, theoretical grounding, and ethical consideration from us than quoting others in the literature or skirting the moral dimensions of our work altogether.

With respect to misunderstanding or misrepresenting action research, if one peruses the action research projects of the teachers sponsored by the National Arts Education Research Center, one will understand why these are miseducative. The participating teachers' apparent efforts and commitment to the arts are commendable. But a reader of these reports cannot help but wonder: What did these teachers really experience? What did they really learn about their students and the contexts and communities in which they worked? And, most importantly, what did they learn about themselves as teachers and about their own practice? One only gets a tiny hint of their experience from the reports themselves.

The major problem in the above projects is that a positivistic, quantitative view of inquiry was imposed across all projects with the expectation for pretesting and posttesting, mostly of students' attitudes. The format of the reports is familiar: statement of the problem, methods, analysis of data (pretest, posttest), and conclusions. Most of these reports are quite short and the teachers' language strained and unnatural except for descriptions of their settings and limitations where we faintly hear the teachers' voices and lived experience. There are unexplained statistical tables clumsily inserted. The hesitant and limp interpretations and conclusions will leave most readers absolutely flat and cold—all form, little substance; wrong-feeling and against the grain of experience; a tight corset worn over a jogging suit; squeaky clean but unaesthetic in spirit.

This is because the above work is not authentic to teachers, despite the fact that teachers did the work. There is little energy or pedagogical reflection demonstrated in these reports. But I know that underneath the academic varnish and between the lines, these action researchers must be lively, reflective, passionate teachers, loved by their students. In sum, I believe that these teachers are much more than what they were constrained to be or to become in these action research projects and their reports. I only wish we could have learned more about these teachers and what it means to teach art from their work and reflections on such.

Hopefully, the assumptions undergirding teacher inquiry and examples of action research discussed here will help art educators be more thoughtful teachers of teachers and more discerning in what they ask themselves and others to do. On our collective behalf, I conclude with a quote from Madeleine Grumet (1988):

> I want to argue that we need to fortify the aesthetic boundaries that define teaching. We need to re-create safe places, even in schools, where teachers can concentrate, can attend to their experience of children and of the world, and we need to create community spaces where the forms that express that experience are shared.... And should we rely on the state or the

affluent, we will find ourselves, like the nineteenth-century artist, coopted by our patrons. (p. 90)

In art education, the subjects we teach and those who teach and learn have long been marginalized and decentered in our collective institutional press to "get the job done." Inquiry into our own practice centers us, grounds us viscerally in real place and time with real persons, begs our questions and possibilities, makes us responsible for what we believe and do. When done well, teaching as inquiry provokes our most aesthetic, pedagogical sensibilities. It helps us to envision and craft ourselves and our work.

References

Apple, M., & Weis, L. (Eds.). (1983). *Ideology and practice in schooling.* Philadelphia: Temple University Press.

Atkins, E. (1986). The deliberative process: An analysis from three perspectives. *Journal of Curriculum and Supervision, 1,* 265-293.

Bolin, F., & Falk, J. (Eds.). (1987). *Teacher renewal: Professional issues, personal choices.* New York: Teachers College Press.

Boostrom, R. (1991). The nature and functions of classroom rules. *Curriculum Inquiry, 21*(2), 193216.

Boud, D., Keogh, R., & Walker, D. (1985). *Reflection: Turning experience into learning.* New York: Nichols.

Buchmann, M. (1988). *Practical arguments are no accounts of teacher thinking: But then, what is?* (Occasional Paper No. 119). East Lansing: Michigan State University, Institute for Research on Teaching.

Bullough, R., Goldstein, S., & Holt, L. (1984). *Human interests in the curriculum: Teaching and learning in a technological society.* New York: Teachers College Press.

Butt, R., Raymond, D., & Yamagishi, L. (1988). Autobiographic praxis: The formation of teachers' knowledge (notes 1, 2). *Journal of Curriculum Theorizing 7*(4), 87-164.

Carr, W., & Kemmis, S. (1986). *Becoming critical: Education, knowledge and action research.* Philadelphia: Falmer.

Carson, T. (1990). What kind of knowing is critical action research? *Theory into Practice, 29*(3), 167173.

Clip, R., Houston, W. R., & Pugach, M. (Eds.). (1990). *Encouraging reflective practice in education: An analysis of issues and programs.* New York: Teachers College Press.

Connelly, M., & Clandinin, J. (1988). *Teachers as curriculum planners: Narratives of experience.* New York: Teachers College Press.

Corey, S. (1953). *Action research to improve school practices.* New York: Bureau of Publications, Teachers College, Columbia University.

Dewey, J. (1904). The relation of theory to practice in education. In C. McMurry (Ed.), *Third yearbook of the National Society for the Scientific Study of Education* (pp. 9-30). Chicago: University of Chicago Press.

Eisner, E. (1985). *The educational imagination: On the design and evaluation of school programs.* New York: Macmillan.

Elliott, J. (1977). Developing hypotheses about classrooms from teachers' practical constructs: An account of the Ford Teaching Project. *Interchange, 17*(2), 2-20.

Ellsworth, E. (1989). Why doesn't this feel empowering? Working through the repressive myths of critical pedagogy. *Harvard Educational Review, 59,* 297-324.

Fehrs-Rampolla, B. (1991).*Accepting diversity: A multicultural approach.* New York: National Arts Education Research Center, New York University.

Freire, P. (1970). *Pedagogy of the oppressed* (M. B. Ramos, Trans.). New York: Continuum.

Goswami, D., & Stillman, P. (1987). *Reclaiming the classroom: Teacher research as an agency for change.* Upper Montclair, NJ: Boynton/Cook.

Grumet, M. (1980). Autobiography and reconceptualization. Journal of Curriculum *Theorizing 2*(2), 155158.

Grumet, M. (1988). *Bitter milk: Women and teaching.* Amherst: University of Massachusetts Press.

Hall, G., & Hord, S. (1987). *Change in schools: Facilitating the process.* Albany, NY: State University of New York Press.

Hustler, D., Cassidy, A., & Cuff, E. C. (Eds.). (1986). *Action research in classrooms and schools.* London: Allen & Unwin.

Jackson, P. (Ed.). (1988). *Contributing to educational change: Perspectives on research and practice.* Berkeley, CA: McCutchan.

Kemmis, S., & McTaggart, R. (1988). *The action research planner.* Geelong, Victoria, Australia: Deakin University Press.

Kincheloe, J., & Pinar, W. (Eds.). (1991). *Curriculum as social psychoanalysis: The significance of place.* Albany, NY: State University of New York Press.

Lampert, M. (1985). How do teachers manage to teach? Perspectives on problems in practice. *Harvard Educational Review, 55*(2), 178-194.

Lather, P. (1986). Research as praxis. *Harvard Educational Review, 56,* 257-277.

Lather, P. (1988, April). *Educational research and practice in a postmodern era.* Paper presented at the annual meeting of the American Educational Research Association, New Orleans.

ACTION RESEARCH—Part 1: "Teachers-as-Researchers"

Lewin, K. (1946). Action research and minority problems. *Journal of Social Issues, 1*, 34-36.
Lieberman, A. (Ed.). (1988). *Building a professional culture in schools.* New York: Teachers College Press.
Manigo, K. (1991). *Teaching high school students to recognize African musical idioms in the music of South Carolina s Gullah people.* New York: National Arts Education Research Center, New York University.
Marcus, R. (1991). *Developing a methodology for stimulating and nurturing an appreciation of nonrepresentational art in an independent school setting.* New York: National Art Education Research Center, New York University.
May, W. (1989). Teachers, teaching, and the workplace: Omissions in curriculum reform. *Studies in Art Education, 30*(3), 142-156.
May, W. (1990). *Art/music teachers' curriculum deliberations.* (Elementary Subjects Center Series No. 22). East Lansing: Michigan State university, Institute for Research on teaching and Learning of Elementary Subjects.
May, W. (1991). Constructing history in a graduate curriculum class. *Curriculum Inquiry, 21*(2), 163-191.
Miller, J. (1990). *Creating spaces and finding voices: Teachers collaborating for empowerment.* Albany, NY: State University of New York Press.
Oberg, A., & McCutcheon, G. (Eds.). (1990). Teacher as researcher. *Theory into Practice, 29*,(3).
Packer, G., & Newman, D. (1991). *Developing an interdisciplinary middle school arts curriculum in an isolated, multicultural community.* New York: National Arts Education Research Center, New York University.
Pinar, W. (Ed.). (1988). *Contemporary curriculum discourses.* Scottdales, AZ: Gorsuch Scarisbrick.
Polyani, M. (1967). *The tacit dimension.* London: Routledge & Kegan Paul.
Schön, D. (Ed.). (1983). *The reflective practitioner: How professionals think in action.* New York: Basic.
Schön, D. (Ed.). (1991). *The reflective turn: Case studies in and on educational practice.* New York: teachers College Press.
Schwab, J. (1969). The practical: A language for curriculum. *School review, 77*, 1-23.
Shumsky, A. (1958). *The action research way of learning.* New York: Teachers College Press.
Sleeter, C. (Ed.). (1991). *Empowerment through multicultural education.* Albany, NY: State University of New York Press.

Stenhouse, L. (1975). *An introduction to curriculum research and development.* London: Heinemann.
Taba, H., & Noel, T. (1957). *Action research: A case study.* Washington, DC: Association for Supervision and Curriculum Development.
Tripp, D. (1990). Socially critical action research. *Theory into Practice, 29*(3), 158-166.
van Manen, M. (1990a). Beyond assumptions: Shifting the limits of action research. *Theory into Practice, 29*(3), 152-157.
van Manen, M. (1990b). *Researching lived experience: Human science for an action sensitive pedagogy.* Albany, NY: State University of New York Press.
van Manen, M. (1991). *The tact of teaching: The meaning of pedagogical thoughtfulness.* Albany, NY: State University of New York Press.
Walker, D. (1990). *Fundamentals of curriculum.* New York: Harcourt Brace Jovanovich.
Willis, G., & Schubert, W. (Eds.). (1991). *Reflections from the heart of educational inquiry: Understanding curriculum and teaching through the arts.* Albany, NY: State University of New York Press.
Wittrock, M. (Ed.). (1986). *Handbook of research on teaching: A project of the American Educational research Association.* New York: Macmillian.

ACTION RESEARCH

Part 2

Addendum: A Metaphor for Understanding Action-Oriented Study as Research

Read M. Diket
William Carey College

As early as the 1940s Kurt Lewin (1952) espoused action-oriented research procedures in the social sciences. Lewin defined action research in terms of a new goal for the field of social science; he sought the unification of programs of social action with experimental approaches in the social sciences (Oja & Smulyan, 1989). Art education action research has a congruent goal when its practitioners facilitate the integration and pedagogical/programmatic growth of individuals, institutions, and the field while using established or defining new quantitative and qualitative approaches. Sagor (1992) argues that teachers often implicitly support research and school-based informal norms which diminish rather than enhance "meaningful discourse with fellow professionals" (p. 2). Furthermore, Sagor states:

> As long as teaching remains a profession where isolation is the norm, where the knowledge that informs practice comes from outside the classroom, and where the quality control officers are removed from the classroom, teaching will be more like a blue-collar job than an intellectual professional pursuit. Eliminating these destructive features is essential to the health of our profession and the success of our schools. By changing the role of teachers, we can also profoundly change the teaching and learning process in our schools. (Sagor, 1992, p. 4).

Teachers as researchers and their collaborators can inform other research colleagues; they too can make contributions to the knowledge base. Action-oriented roles require action-oriented approaches.

Hodgkinson (1957) maintains that a call for action research is a logical result of the progressive education movement. In his explanation of action research, Hodgkinson suggests that teachers use the same collaborative methods they teach

Research Methods and Methodologies for Art Education

Figure 1
Conceptualized Within a Quantitative-Qualitative Continuum: Action Researchers Perform in Both Lablike and Natural Settings
(Original concept by R.M. Diket and graphics by L. Flanders)

to children. Collaboration with other educators or with students in their classes enables teachers to contribute research knowledge with considerable scope and conceptual depth.

When action research is defined by goal rather than methodology, the action researcher chooses both the equipment and the game (see Figure 1). Research types and methods in education can be conceptualized for action researchers much as one would cognitively map equipment and games associated with the sport of bow shooting. The conceptual schemas surrounding archery events lend convenient structure to understanding research events. Research classifications are institutionalized as are "official" archery equipment and games.

Research types can be likened to components of an arrow (refer to Figure 2), the point or *pile* of the arrow orients towards basic research, targeting general educational goals. Like the shaft of an arrow, **applied research** aligns the archer with immediate usefulness and solutions to educational problems while aiding the flight towards knowledge. Three feathers arranged on the *shaftment* contribute accuracy and stability in transit. Shaftment feathers function purposefully like the research counterparts of **evaluation research, research and development,** and **action research.** Extending from the shaftment of applied research, evaluation research involves systematic collection and analyses of data to decide the effectiveness of teaching and learning in various educational contexts. Evaluation issues

ACTION RESEARCH—Part 2: Action-Oriented Study as Research

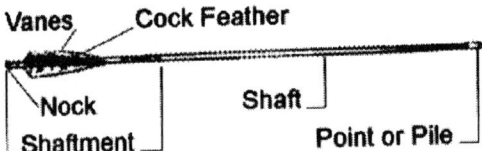

Figure 2
Parts of the Arrow
(Original concept by R.M. Diket and graphics by L. Flanders)

include questions of cost, comparisons of curricula, and decisions about placement. Research and development stresses the creation and improvement of products used in schools. Action research aids in local decision making processes relative to classroom problems, teacher training, school systems, collegiality, and specific applications of research to practice.

The feathers, each purposefully placed, lead to accuracy in flight. Action research, in this instance, assumes primacy as the *cock feather*. Situated at right angles to the *nock* which is placed on the string of the bow prior to releasing the arrow, action research stabilizes other forms of research. Elaborating the metaphor, action research positions to guide research arrows in art education.

The research orientations of art professionals follow, like bow choice, upon the needs of researchers/archers. The *straight bow* signifies methods typically used in **quantitative** research modeled after procedures in the physical sciences (see Bow Types, Figure 3). The *recurved bow*, a more ancient design, stands for **qualitative** methods gleaned from the social sciences which depend upon observation and reflection. The form of the research question determines the need for and then choice of quantitative or qualitative modes.

Action researchers estimate their targets and aim in three ways: by use of a *sight* fastened to the back of the bow (as do evaluation researchers), aiming over

Research Methods and Methodologies for Art Education

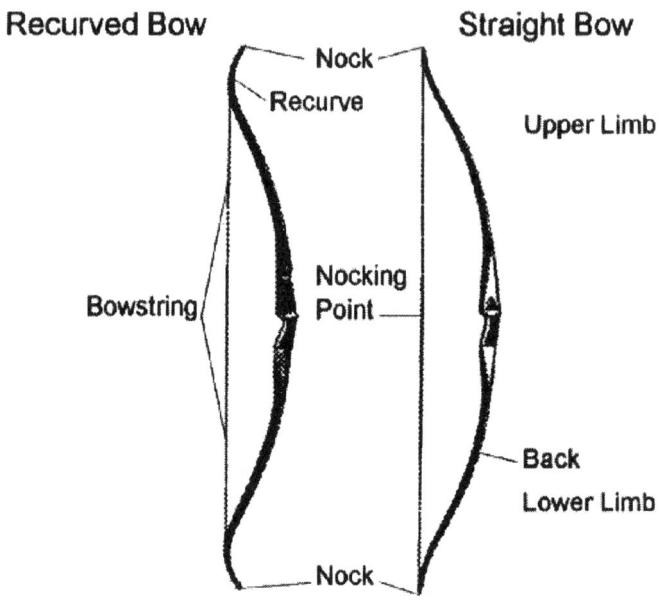

Figure 3
Bow Types
(Original concept by R.M. Diket and graphics by L. Flanders)

the point of the arrow at a point just below the spot they want to hit, called *point-of-aim* (as do research and development researchers), and *instinctively* by focusing eyes upon the target and shooting (as do classroom ethnographers). The distance an arrow flies is called its cast, similar in concept to the generalizability of a study. Instinct works best at close range; sighting best when the researcher remains distanced from the project.

Just as target shooting contests are held under *rules*, there are rules associated with quantitatively-oriented educational research. *Targets* (outcomes for subjects) must be described and/or accorded numeric weights (refer to Figure 1). The number of shots toward the target which make up a *round* depends upon the research design. The distance researchers assume relative to the target (relationship to subjects) also depends upon the design. Much like laboratory work in the sciences, educational research which is quantitative is like target shooting because it shows what a researcher might expect during future attempts with similar equipment and targets.

Qualitative research involves rules distinct from those associated with quantitative research. Rules for bow hunting in the natural environment differ from rules associated with target shoots which are more of a lablike setting. Like bow hunters, qualitative researchers seek a particular game (such as ethnic groups or creatively gifted individuals), use heavier bows (as in extensive narrative description), and employ retrieval lines like the archer who fishes in the stream (as with observer-participant roles). Rules are more open-ended for qualitative researchers than for quantitative researchers; thus ethnographers and reflective practitioners, like bow hunters operating in natural settings, answer ethical questions in context.

References

Hodgkinson, H. L. (1957). Action research—a critique. *Journal of Educational Sociology, 31*(4), 137-153.

Lewin, K. (1952). Group decision and social change. In T. M. Newcomb & E. L. Hartley (Eds.), *Readings in Social Psychology* (pp. 459-473). New York: Holt.

Oja, S. N., & Smulyan, L. (1989). *Collaborative action research: A developmental approach.* Philadelphia: Farmer Press.

Sagor, R. (1992). *How to conduct collaborative action research.* Alexandria, VA: Association for Supervision and Curriculum Development.